React Native By Example

Leverage the full potential of the React Native framework to build and deploy your own native mobile applications for iOS and Android

Richard Kho

BIRMINGHAM - MUMBAI

React Native By Example

First published: April 2017

Production reference: 2190517

Published by Packt Publishing Ltd.
Livery Place
35 Livery Street
Birmingham
B3 2PB, UK.
ISBN 978-1-78646-475-0

www.packtpub.com

Credits

Author
Richard Kho

Copy Editor
Shaila Kusanale

Reviewer
Brice Mason

Project Coordinator
Devanshi Doshi

Commissioning Editor
Ashwin Nair

Proofreader
Safis Editing

Acquisition Editor
Anurag Banerjee

Indexer
Francy Puthiry

Content Development Editor
Narendrakumar Tripathi

Graphics
Jason Monterio

Technical Editor
Huzefa Unwala

Production Coordinator
Melwyn Dsa

Foreword

React Native was introduced to the world in 2015, and it has since emerged as one of the most valuable skill sets a developer can acquire in order to enhance his or her career. Facebook continues to invest heavily in React Native, and with companies such as AirBNB, Tesla, Instagram, and Wal-Mart adopting React Native into their stacks, it will only continue to grow in demand. React Native by Example is one of the best resources you can use to get up and running with React Native as quickly as possible. Richard has continually proven himself to be a fantastic teacher and an extraordinary writer. Whether you're wanting to improve as a developer, learn how to build native mobile applications, or simply want to see what all the hype is about, this book will be a great worth.

Tyler McGinnis

- Partner at React Training

About the Author

Richard Kho is a software engineer living in San Francisco. He taught himself how to code in 2014 and has lived a past life as a photographer and cinematographer.

He currently works for Capital One and has taught software engineers at Hack Reactor in the past. Richard is also a technical advisor to Code Chrysalis, an advanced software engineering immersive in Tokyo.

I would like to immensely thank my girlfriend Ro for her support and encouragement in my life, and for her tremendous help overcoming a couple cases of writer's block while writing this book. I also want to thank my two cats, Mystique and Walter, for keeping me company during my writing sessions.

I also owe a deep amount of gratitude to my parents, Bakthong and Seuchyong, for encouraging this career change; without them I would not feel as empowered as I am today.

I'd like to thank Pavan Ravipati and Arian Faurtosh, who I worked closely with as we dove into a very beta release of React Native back in 2015 and helped spark my interest in this framework. Additionally, I owe a big thanks to Marlene Fong who has been a very generous and patient mentor during the times I struggled when first learning how to code.

About the Reviewer

Brice Mason is a husband, father, developer, writer, and speaker with over 15 years of software development experience. As a Senior Engineer at Modus Create, he's been fortunate to contribute to the delivery of several enterprise-level desktop and mobile applications using JavaScript. When not writing code or writing about code, Brice enjoys spending time with his wife and son. You can reach him via Twitter at @bricemason.

I would like to thank Richard Kho and the Packt Publishing team; it was a pleasure to chip in where I could. Special thanks to my wife Heather and son Chase for their constant love and support, my ultimate fuel.

www.PacktPub.com

For support files and downloads related to your book, please visit www.PacktPub.com.

Did you know that Packt offers eBook versions of every book published, with PDF and ePub files available? You can upgrade to the eBook version at www.PacktPub.com and as a print book customer, you are entitled to a discount on the eBook copy. Get in touch with us at service@packtpub.com for more details.

At www.PacktPub.com, you can also read a collection of free technical articles, sign up for a range of free newsletters and receive exclusive discounts and offers on Packt books and eBooks.

https://www.packtpub.com/mapt

Get the most in-demand software skills with Mapt. Mapt gives you full access to all Packt books and video courses, as well as industry-leading tools to help you plan your personal development and advance your career.

Why subscribe?

- Fully searchable across every book published by Packt
- Copy and paste, print, and bookmark content
- On demand and accessible via a web browser

Customer Feedback

Thanks for purchasing this Packt book. At Packt, quality is at the heart of our editorial process. To help us improve, please leave us an honest review on this book's Amazon page at https://www.amazon.com/dp/1786464756.

If you'd like to join our team of regular reviewers, you can e-mail us at customerreviews@packtpub.com. We award our regular reviewers with free eBooks and videos in exchange for their valuable feedback. Help us be relentless in improving our products!

Table of Contents

Preface

React Native is an incredibly powerful framework that makes development on multiple platforms more accessible for web-centric programmers. In this book, you are going to learn how to build mobile applications using React Native that are ready to be deployed to both the iOS App Store and Google Play.

What this book covers

Chapter 1, *First Project - Creating a Basic To-Do List App*, begins the process of writing a to-do list application with React Native. You will plan the app and gain an overview of StyleSheet, Flexbox, and ES6. You will also create the building blocks of the app with four different parts of the React Native SDK.

Chapter 2, *Advanced Functionality with the To-Do List App*, dives deeper into the app we started build in the first chapter. You will learn how to handle navigation, date and time selection, building buttons, and create a custom collapsible and animated component for use in the app. You will also take those lessons and translate them into an Android version of the app.

Chapter 3, *Second Project - The Budgeting App*, will begin the second project of the book. You will plan an expense-tracking application, install a third-party vector icon library for React Native, create utility files that can be used throughout the app, and create a Modal component.

Chapter 4, *Advanced Functionality with the Budgeting App*, is a continuation of the second project. You will learn how to create a dropdown-like component for users to select from a list of items and create tabbed navigation for the app.

Chapter 5, *Third Project - The Facebook Client*, will begin the third and final project of the book. You will plan an app that connects to the third-party Facebook SDK, install said SDK to your project, allow users to log in with their Facebook credentials, then make requests for information.

Chapter 6, *Advanced Functionality with the Facebook Client*, wraps up the project you began in the previous chapter. You will learn how to build a pull-to-refresh mechanism for the app, render images for your users, allow users to open links without having to leave the app, and then use those lessons to make an Android version of the app.

Chapter 7, *Adding Redux*, introduces the popular Redux architecture. You will learn how to convert the to-do list app in the second chapter to an app supported by the principles of Redux.

Chapter 8, *Deploying Your Applications*, shows you how to package, upload and make your apps available for download on the Apple iOS App Store and Google Play Store. You will also gain some tips on creating app logos and screenshots, as well as how to launch beta tests for your apps.

Chapter 9, *Additional React Native Components*, dives into parts of the React Native SDK that we were not able to fit into the rest of the book. In it, you will build a playground style app learning different parts of the SDK. You will grab data from any third-party endpoints, control the user's vibration motor, open other installed apps with links in your app, and much more. You will also learn how to convert the budgeting app in the fourth chapter to Android, since space in that chapter was limited.

What you need for this book

Hardware-wise, you will need a Mac for this book. The content in this book is iOS-first, and to develop iOS apps you must have an Apple computer. Optionally, both an iOS and Android device would be helpful for testing apps on-device, but not mandatory. There is one API in the final chapter of the book that requires a physical device to test (Vibration), and another where testing would be easier on a physical device (Linking).

You will need to install the React Native SDK for your Mac. Instructions can be found at `https://facebook.github.io/react-native/docs/getting-started.html`. Prerequisites for installing the React Native SDK are available on that page.

Instructions to install Xcode and Android Studio are also available on that same page for installing the React Native SDK to your machine.

Who this book is for

If you are keen on learning to use the revolutionary mobile development tool React Native to build native mobile applications, then this book is for you. Prior experience with JavaScript would be useful.

Conventions

In this book, you will find a number of text styles that distinguish between different kinds of information. Here are some examples of these styles and an explanation of their meaning.

Code words in text, database table names, folder names, filenames, file extensions, pathnames, dummy URLs, user input, and Twitter handles are shown as follows: "Based on this layout, we see that the entry point for the iOS version of our app is index.ios.js and that a specific iOS folder (and Android for that matter) is generated."

A block of code is set as follows:

```
class Tasks extends Component {
  render () {
    return (
      <View style = {{ flex: 1, justifyContent: 'center',
        alignItems: 'center', backgroundColor: '#F5FCFF'
      }}>
        <Text style = {{ fontSize: 20, textAlign:
          'center', margin: 10 }}>
          Welcome to React Native!
        </Text>
      </View>
    )
  }
}
```

Any command-line input or output is written as follows:

```
react-native init Tasks
```

New terms and **important words** are shown in bold. Words that you see on the screen, for example, in menus or dialog boxes, appear in the text like this: "When you open the **Developer** menu, you'll see the following options."

Warnings or important notes appear in a box like this.

Tips and tricks appear like this.

Reader feedback

Feedback from our readers is always welcome. Let us know what you think about this book-what you liked or disliked. Reader feedback is important for us as it helps us develop titles that you will really get the most out of.

To send us general feedback, simply e-mail `feedback@packtpub.com`, and mention the book's title in the subject of your message.

If there is a topic that you have expertise in and you are interested in either writing or contributing to a book, see our author guide at `www.packtpub.com/authors`.

Customer support

Now that you are the proud owner of a Packt book, we have a number of things to help you to get the most from your purchase.

Downloading the example code

You can download the example code files for this book from your account at `http://www.packtpub.com`. If you purchased this book elsewhere, you can visit `http://www.packtpub.com/support` and register to have the files e-mailed directly to you.

You can download the code files by following these steps:

1. Log in or register to our website using your e-mail address and password.
2. Hover the mouse pointer on the **SUPPORT** tab at the top.
3. Click on **Code Downloads & Errata**.
4. Enter the name of the book in the **Search** box.
5. Select the book for which you're looking to download the code files.
6. Choose from the drop-down menu where you purchased this book from.
7. Click on **Code Download**.

Once the file is downloaded, please make sure that you unzip or extract the folder using the latest version of:

* WinRAR / 7-Zip for Windows
* Zipeg / iZip / UnRarX for Mac
* 7-Zip / PeaZip for Linux

The code bundle for the book is also hosted on GitHub at `https://github.com/PacktPubl ishing/React-Native-By-Example`. We also have other code bundles from our rich catalog of books and videos available at `https://github.com/PacktPublishing/`. Check them out!

Downloading the color images of this book

We also provide you with a PDF file that has color images of the screenshots/diagrams used in this book. The color images will help you better understand the changes in the output. You can download this file from `https://www.packtpub.com/sites/default/files/down loads/ReactNativeByExample_ColorImages.pdf`.

Errata

Although we have taken every care to ensure the accuracy of our content, mistakes do happen. If you find a mistake in one of our books-maybe a mistake in the text or the code-we would be grateful if you could report this to us. By doing so, you can save other readers from frustration and help us improve subsequent versions of this book. If you find any errata, please report them by visiting `http://www.packtpub.com/submit-errata`, selecting your book, clicking on the **Errata Submission Form** link, and entering the details of your errata. Once your errata are verified, your submission will be accepted and the errata will be uploaded to our website or added to any list of existing errata under the Errata section of that title.

To view the previously submitted errata, go to `https://www.packtpub.com/books/conten t/support` and enter the name of the book in the search field. The required information will appear under the **Errata** section.

Piracy

Piracy of copyrighted material on the Internet is an ongoing problem across all media. At Packt, we take the protection of our copyright and licenses very seriously. If you come across any illegal copies of our works in any form on the Internet, please provide us with the location address or website name immediately so that we can pursue a remedy.

Please contact us at `copyright@packtpub.com` with a link to the suspected pirated material.

We appreciate your help in protecting our authors and our ability to bring you valuable content.

Questions

If you have a problem with any aspect of this book, you can contact us at questions@packtpub.com, and we will do our best to address the problem.

1
First Project - Creating a Basic To-Do List App

Having set up our environment for React Native development in the preface, let's start developing the application. Throughout this book, I'll refer to this application by the project name I began with--`Tasks`. In this chapter, we will cover the following topics:

- Planning the features that a to-do list app should have
- Basic project architecture
- Introducing `StyleSheet`, the React Native component for working with styles
- An overview of Flexbox, a layout mode inspired by CSS for styling in React Native
- Become acquainted with ES6, the new JavaScript syntax we will be writing our code in
- Creating the building blocks of `Tasks` with `TextInput`, `ListView`, `AsyncStorage`, `Input`, state, and props
- Learning about the iOS Simulator's **Developer** menu, which can help us during the writing of our app

Initializing a new project

With the React Native SDK already installed, initializing a new React Native project is as simple as using the following command line:

```
react-native init Tasks
```

Let the React Native command line interface do its work for a few moments, then open the directory titled `Tasks` once it is completed.

From there, running your app in iOS Simulator is as easy as typing the following command:

```
react-native run-ios
```

This will start a process to build and compile your React Native app, launch the iOS Simulator, import your app to the Simulator, and start it. Whenever you make a change to the app, you will be able to reload and see those changes immediately.

Feature planning

Before writing any code, I'd like to take the time to plan out what I want to accomplish in my project and scope out a **minimum viable product** (**MVP**) to aim for prior to building out any advanced functionalities. This helps with the prioritization of what key components of our app are necessary to have a functioning prototype so that we can have something up and running.

For me, the MVP is a fantastic way to quantify my ideas into something I can interact with and use to validate any assumptions I have, or catch any edge cases, while spending the minimum amount of time necessary on coming to those conclusions. Here's how I approach feature planning:

- What does the product I'm building do?
- Ideally, what are some of the highlighting features that make this application stand out?
- Which of the features on the preceding list are necessary to have a working product? Once you know the necessary features, cut out everything that doesn't give you the bare-bones functionality.
- Give some thought to its design, but don't stress on every single detail just yet.

With these intentions in mind, here's what I've come up with:

- This is an application that will let me create and track a list of tasks that I have. These can be as small as a shopping list or as big as long-term goals.
- I'd like to set a reminder for each unique task so that I can get to each one in an orderly fashion. Ideally, the items on the list can be grouped into categories. Category grouping could perhaps be simplified by something like icons. This way, I can also sort and filter my list by icons.

- The only things that are necessary from the beginning are that I can use a text input field to type a task, have it rendered onto a list of items, and mark them off as they are completed; everything else is secondary.

Now that we've got a clearer picture of our app, let's break down some actionable steps we can take to make it a reality:

1. Let's *generate a list of default items*. These don't have to be manually entered as we just want to see our list populated in the app itself.
2. After that, your users should be able to *input their own tasks* using a text field and the native keyboard.
3. Next, I'd like to *make that list scrollable* in case my list of tasks spans past an entire vertical screen's height.
4. Then, we should *let items be marked as complete* with some sort of visual indicator.

That's it! These are the four goals we currently have. As I previously mentioned, everything else is secondary for the time being. For now, we just want to get an MVP up and running, and then we will tweak it to our hearts' content later.

Let's move ahead and start thinking about architecture.

Project architecture

The next important thing I'd like to tackle is architecture; this is about how our React Native app will be laid out. While the projects we build for this book are meant to be done individually, I firmly believe that it is important to always write and architect code in a manner that expects the next person to look at it to be an axe-murderer with a short temper. The idea here is to make it simple for anyone to look at your application's structure and be able to follow along.

First, let's take a look at how the React Native CLI scaffolds our project; comments on each relevant file are noted to the right-hand side of the double slashes (//):

```
|Tasks // root folder
|__Android*
|__ios*
|__node_modules
|__.buckconfig
|__.flowconfig
|__.gitignore
|__.watchmanconfig
|__index.android.js // Android entry point
```

```
|__index.ios.js // iOS entry point
|__package.json // npm package list
```

The `Android` and `iOS` folders will go several layers deep, but this is all part of its scaffolding and something we will not need to concern ourselves with at this point.

Based on this layout, we see that the entry point for the iOS version of our app is `index.ios.js` and that a specific `iOS` folder (and `Android` for that matter) is generated.

Rather than using these platform-specific folders to store components that are only applicable to one platform, I'd like to propose a folder named `app` alongside these which will encapsulate all the logic that we write.

Within this `app` folder, we'll have subfolders that contain our components and assets. With components, I'd like to keep its style sheet coupled alongside the JS logic within its own folder.

Additionally, component folders should never be nested--it ends up being way too confusing to follow and search for something. Instead, I prefer to use a naming convention that makes it immediately obvious what one component's relation to its parent/child/sibling happens to be.

Here's how my proposed structure will look:

```
|Tasks
|__app
|____components
|_____TasksList
|_____index.js
|_____styles.js
|_____TasksListCell
|_____index.js
|_____styles.js
|_____TasksListInput
|_____index.js
|_____styles.js
|____images
|__Android
|__ios
|__node_modules
|__.buckconfig
|__.flowconfig
|__.gitignore
|__.watchmanconfig
|__index.android.js
|__index.ios.js
```

```
|__package.json
```

From just a quick observation, you might be able to infer that `TasksList` is the component that deals with our list of tasks shown on the screen. `TasksListCell` will be each individual row of that list, and `TasksListInput` will deal with the keyboard input field.

This is very bare-bones and there are optimizations that we can make. For example, we can think about things such as platform-specific extensions for iOS and Android, as well as building in further architecture for Redux; but for the purpose of this specific app, we will just start with the basics.

StyleSheet

React Native's core visual components accept a prop called `style` and the names and values more or less match up with CSS's naming conventions, with one major exception-- kebab-case is swapped out for camelCase, similar to how things are named in JavaScript. For example, a CSS property of `background-color` will translate to `backgroundColor` in React Native.

For readability and reuse, it's beneficial to break off inline styling into its own `styles` object by defining all of our styles into a `styles` object using React Native's `StyleSheet` component to create a style object and reference it within our component's `render` method.

Taking it a step further, with larger applications, it's best to separate the style sheet into its own JavaScript file for readability's sake. Let's take a look at how each of these compare, using a very annotated version of the Hello World sample that's generated for us. These samples will contain only the code necessary to make my point.

Inline styles

An inline style is one that is defined within the markup of your code. Check this sample out:

```
class Tasks extends Component {
  render () {
    return (
      <View style = {{ flex: 1, justifyContent: 'center',
        alignItems: 'center', backgroundColor: '#F5FCFF'
      }}>
        <Text style = {{ fontSize: 20, textAlign:
          'center', margin: 10 }}>
```

```
          Welcome to React Native!
        </Text>
      </View>
    )
  }
}
```

In the preceding code, you can see how inline style can create a very convoluted and confusing mess, especially when there are several style properties that we want to apply to each component. It's not practical for us to write our styles like this in a large-scale application, so let's break apart the styles into a StyleSheet object.

With StyleSheet, within the same file

This is how a component accesses a StyleSheet created in the same file:

```
class Tasks extends Component {
  render () {
    return (
      <View style = { styles.container }>
        <Text style = { styles.welcome }>
          Welcome to React Native!
        </Text>
      </View>
    )
  }
}

const styles = StyleSheet.create({
  container: {
    flex: 1,
    justifyContent: 'center',
    alignItems: 'center',
    backgroundColor: '#F5FCFF'
  },
  welcome: {
    fontSize: 20,
    textAlign: 'center',
    margin: 10
  }
)};
```

This is much better. We're moving our styles into an object we can reference without having to rewrite the same inline styles over and over. However, the problem we face is an extraordinarily long file with a lot of application logic, where a future maintainer might have to scroll through lines and lines of code to get to the styles. We can take it one step further and separate the styles into their own module.

StyleSheet as an imported module

In your component, you can import your styles, as shown:

```
import styles from './styles.js';

class Tasks extends Component {
  render(){
    return (
      <View style = { styles.container }>
        <Text style = { styles.welcome }>
          Welcome to React Native!
        </Text>
      </View>
    )
  }
}
```

Then, you can define them in a separate file:

```
const styles = StyleSheet.create({
  container: {
    flex: 1,
    justifyContent: 'center',
    alignItems: 'center',
    backgroundColor: '#F5FCFF'
  },
  welcome: {
    fontSize: 20,
    textAlign: 'center',
    margin: 10
  }
)};

export default styles;
```

This is much better. By encapsulating our style logic into its own file, we are separating our concerns and making it easier for everyone to read it.

Flexbox

One thing you might have noted in our `StyleSheet` is a property called `flex`. This pertains to Flexbox, a CSS layout system that provides consistency in your layout across different screen sizes. Flexbox in React Native works similar to its CSS specification, with only a couple of differences. The most important differences to be noted are that the default `flex` direction has been flipped to `column` on React Native, as opposed to `row` on the Web, aligning items, by default, to the `stretch` property for React Native instead of `flex-start` in the browser, and the `flex` parameter only supports a single number as its value in React Native.

We will pick up a lot on Flexbox as we go through these projects; we'll start by taking a look at just the basics.

flex

The `flex` property of your layout works a bit differently from how it operates in CSS. In React Native, it accepts a single digit number. If its number is a positive number (meaning greater than 0), the component that has this property will become flexible.

flexDirection

Your layout also accepts a property called `flexDirection`. There are four options for this: `row`, `row-reverse`, `column`, and `column-reverse`. These options dictate the direction that the children of your flex container will be laid out in.

Writing in ES6

ECMAScript version 6 (ES6) is the latest specification of the JavaScript language. It is also referred to as ES2016. It brings new features and syntax to JavaScript, and they are the ones you should be familiar with to be successful in this book.

Firstly, `require` statements are now `import` statements. They are used to `import` functions, object, and so on from an external module or script. In the past, to include React in a file, we would write something like this:

```
var React = require('react');
var Component = React.Component;
```

Using ES6 `import` statements, we can rewrite it to this:

```
import React, { Component } from 'react';
```

The importing of `Component` around a curly brace is called destructuring assignment. It's an assignment syntax that lets us extract specific data from an array or object into a variable. With `Component` imported through destructuring assignment, we can simply call `Component` in our code; it's automatically declared as a variable with the exact same name.

Next up, we're replacing `var` with two different statements: `let` and `const`. The first statement, `let`, declares a block-scoped variable whose value can be mutated. The second statement, `const`, declares another block-scoped variable whose value cannot change through reassignment nor redeclaration.

In the prior syntax, exporting modules used to be done using `module.exports`. In ES6, this is done using the `export default` statement.

Building the app

Going back to our list from a few pages back, this is the first thing I'd like to do with the app:

- Let's generate a list of default items. These don't have to be manually entered; we just want to see our list populated in the app itself.

ListView

While looking at the documentation for React Native's components, you may note a component named `ListView`. This is a core component that is meant to display vertically scrolling lists of data.

Here's how `ListView` works. We will create a data source, fill it up with an array of data blobs, create a `ListView` component with that array as its data source, and pass it some JSX in its `renderRow` callback, which will take the data and render a row for each blob within the data source.

On a high level, here is how it looks:

```
class TasksList extends Component {
  constructor (props) {

    super (props);

    const ds = new ListView.DataSource({
      rowHasChanged: (r1, r2) => r1 !== r2 });

    this.state = {
      dataSource: ds.cloneWithRows(['row 1', 'row 2'])
    };
  }

  render () {
    return (
      <ListView
        dataSource = { this.state.dataSource }
        renderRow = { (rowData) => <Text>
          { rowData } </Text> }
      />
    );
  }
}
```

Let's look at what's going on. In the `constructor` of our component, we create an instance of `ListViewDataSource`. The constructor for a new `ListViewDataSource` accepts, as a parameter, an argument that can contain any of these four:

- `getRowData(dataBlob, sectionID, rowID)`
- `getSectionHeaderData(dataBlob, sectionID)`
- `rowHasChanged(previousRowData, nextRowData)`
- `sectionHeaderHasChanged(previousSectionData, nextSectionData)`

The `getRowData` is a function that gets the data required to render the row. You can customize the function however you like as you pass it in to the constructor of `ListViewDataSource`, but `ListViewDataSource` will provide a default if you don't specify.

The `getSectionHeaderData` is a function that accepts a blob of data and a section ID and returns just the data needed to render a section header. Like `getRowData`, it provides a default if not specified.

The `rowHasChanged` is a function that serves as a performance optimization designed to only re-render any rows that have their source data changed. Unlike `getRowData` and `getSectionHeaderData`, you will need to pass your own version of `rowHasChanged`. The preceding example, which takes in the current and previous values of the row and returns a Boolean to show if it has changed, is the most common implementation.

The `sectionHeaderHasChanged` is an optional function that compares the section headers' contents to determine whether they need to be re-rendered.

Then, in our `TasksView` constructor, our state receives a property of `dataSource` whose value is equal to calling `cloneWithRows` on the `ListViewDataSource` instance we created earlier. `cloneWithRows` takes in two parameters: a `dataBlob` and `rowIdentities`. The `dataBlob` is any arbitrary blob of data passed to it, and `rowIdentities` represents a two-dimensional array of row identifiers. The `rowIdentities` is an optional parameter--it isn't included in the preceding sample code. Our sample code passes a hardcoded blob of data--two strings: `'row 1'` and `'row 2'`.

It's also important to mention right now that the data within our `dataSource` is immutable. If we want to change it later, we'll have to extract the information out of the `dataSource`, mutate it, and then replace the data within the `dataSource`.

The `ListView` component itself, which is rendered in our `TasksList`, can accept a number of different properties. The most important one, which we're using in our example, is `renderRow`.

The `renderRow` function takes data from the `dataSource` of your `ListView` and returns a component to render for each row of data in your `dataSource`. In our preceding example, `renderRow` takes each string inside our `dataSource` and renders it in a `Text` component.

With the preceding code, here is how `TasksList` will render. Because we have not yet styled it, you will see that the iOS Status Bar overlaps the first row:

Great! There's not much to see, but we accomplished something: we created a `ListView` component, passed it some data, and got that data to be rendered on our screen. Let's take a step back and create this component in our application properly.

Creating the TasksList component

Going back to the proposed file structure from earlier, your project should look like this:

Let's start by writing our first component--the `TasksList` module.

The first thing we will need to do is import our dependency on React:

```
import React, { Component } from 'react';
```

Then, we'll import just the building blocks we need from the React Native (`react-native`) library:

```
import {
  ListView,
  Text
} from 'react-native';
```

Now, let's write the component. The syntax for creating a new component in ES6 is as follows:

```
export default class TasksList extends Component {
  ...
}
```

From here, let's give it a constructor function to fire during its creation:

```
export default class TasksList extends Component {
  constructor (props) {
    super (props);
    const ds = new ListView.DataSource({
     rowHasChanged: (r1, r2) => r1 !== r2
    });

    this.state = {
     dataSource: ds.cloneWithRows([
        'Buy milk',
        'Walk the dog',
        'Do laundry',
        'Write the first chapter of my book'
      ])
    };
  }
}
```

Our constructor sets up a dataSource property in the TasksList state as equal to an array of hardcoded strings. Again, our first goal is to simply render a list on the screen.

Next up, we'll utilize the render method of the TasksList component to do just that:

```
render () {
  return (
    <ListView
      dataSource={ this.state.dataSource }
      renderRow={ (rowData) =>
        <Text> { rowData } </Text> }
    />
  );
}
```

Consolidated, the code should look like this:

```
// Tasks/app/components/TasksList/index.js

import React, { Component } from 'react';
```

```
import {
  ListView,
  Text
} from 'react-native';

export default class TasksList extends Component {
  constructor (props) {
    super (props);

    const ds = new ListView.DataSource({
      rowHasChanged: (r1, r2) => r1 !== r2
    });

    this.state = {
      dataSource: ds.cloneWithRows([
        'Buy milk',
        'Walk the dog',
        'Do laundry',
        'Write the first chapter of my book'
      ])
    };
  }

  render () {
    return (
      <ListView
        dataSource={ this.state.dataSource }
        renderRow={ (rowData) =>
          <Text>{ rowData }</Text> }
      />
    );
  }
}
```

Great! That should do it. However, we need to link this component over to our application's entry point. Let's hop over to index.ios.js and make some changes.

Linking TasksList to index

Our iOS app's entry point is index.ios.js and everything that it renders starts from here. Right now, if you launch iOS Simulator using the react-native run-ios command, you will see the same Hello World sample application that we were acquainted with in the preface.

What we need to do right now is link the `TasksList` component we just built to the `index` and remove all the unnecessary JSX automatically generated for us. Let's go ahead and clear nearly everything in the `render` method of our `Tasks` component, except the top layer `View` container. When you're done, it should look like this:

```
class Tasks extends Component {
  render () {
    return (
      <View style={styles.container}>
      </View>
    );
  }
}
```

We'll want to insert `TasksList` within that `View` container. However, before we do that, we have to give the `index` file access to that component. Let's do so using an `import` statement:

```
import TasksList from './app/components/TasksList';
```

While this `import` statement just points to the folder that our `TasksList` component is in, React Native intelligently looks for a file named `index` and assigns it what we want.

Now that `TasksList` is readily available for us to use, let's include it in the `render` method for `Tasks`:

```
export default class Tasks extends Component {
  render () {
    return (
      <View style={styles.container}>
        <TasksList />
      </View>
    );
  }
}
```

If you don't have an iOS Simulator running anymore, let's get it back up and running using the `react-native run-ios` command from before. Once things are loaded, this is what you should see:

This is awesome! Once it's loaded, let's open up the iOS Simulator **Developer** menu by pressing *Command + D* on your keyboard and search for an option that will help us save some time during the creation of our app.

At the end of this section, your `index.ios.js` file should look like this:

```
// Tasks/index.ios.js

import React, { Component } from 'react';
import {
  AppRegistry,
  StyleSheet,
  View
} from 'react-native';

import TasksList from './app/TasksList';

export default class Tasks extends Component {
  render() {
    return (
      <View style={styles.container}>
        <TasksList />
      </View>
    );
  }
}
```

The following code renders the `TasksList` component:

```
const styles = StyleSheet.create({
  container: {
    flex: 1,
    justifyContent: 'center',
    alignItems: 'center',
    backgroundColor: '#F5FCFF',
  }
});

AppRegistry.registerComponent('Tasks', () => Tasks);
```

The iOS Simulator Developer menu

When you open the **Developer** menu, you'll see the following options:

I would like to go through some of the options available in this menu, which will help you make the development of your applications a lot smoother. Some of the options are not covered here, but are available for you to read about in the React Native documentation.

First, we will cover the options for reloading:

- **Reload**: This reloads your application code. Similar to using *Command + R* on the keyboard, the **Reload** option takes you to the beginning of your application flow.
- **Enable Live Reload**: Turning Live Reload on will result in your application automatically performing a reload action whenever your code has changed while you save a file in your project. Live Reload is great because you can enable it once and have your app show you its latest changes whenever you save your file. It's important to know that both **Reload** and **Enable Live Reload** perform a *full* reload of your application, including resetting your application state.

- **Enable Hot Reloading**: Hot Reloading is a new feature introduced in React Native in March 2016. If you've worked with React on the Web, this term might be familiar to you. The idea of a Hot Reload is to keep your app running and to inject new code at runtime, which prevents you from losing your application state like with a **Reload** (or, by extension, **Enable Live Reload**).
  - One of the bottlenecks of building a feature with Live Reload turned on is when you work on a feature several layers deep and rely on your application's state to properly note changes to it. This adds several seconds to the feedback loop of writing and reloading your application. A Hot Reload solves this issue, letting your feedback loop be reduced to less than a second or two.
  - Something to be aware of with Hot Reloading is that, in its current iteration, it's not perfect. The React Native documentation notes that, in some instances, you will need to use a regular **Reload** to reset your app when Hot Reloading fails.

It's equally important to know that if you ever add new assets to your application or modify native Objective-C/Swift or Java/C++ code, your application will need to be fully rebuilt before the changes will take effect.

The next set of options have to do with debugging:

- **Debug JS Remotely**: Enabling this will open up Chrome on your machine and take you to a Chrome tab that will allow you to use Chrome Developer Tools to debug your application.
- **Show Inspector**: Similar to inspecting an element on the Web, you can use the **Inspector** in React Native development to inspect any element of your application and have it open up parts of your code and the source code that affect that element. You can also view the performance of each specific element this way.

Using the **Developer** menu, we will enable Hot Reloading. It will give us the quickest feedback loop on the code we're writing, allowing us to move efficiently.

Now that we've got Hot Reloading enabled and a basic list of tasks rendering to the screen, it's time to think about an input--we'll come back to styling later.

TextInput

The second goal for building out an MVP was as follows:

- Our users should be able to input their own tasks using a text field and the native keyboard

To successfully create this input, we have to break down the problem into some necessary requirements:

- We need to have an input field that will spring up our keyboard to type with
- The keyboard should hide itself when we tap outside of it
- When we successfully add a task, it needs to be added to `dataSource` in `TasksList`, which is stored in its state
- The list of tasks needs to be stored locally in the application so that a state reset doesn't delete the entire list of tasks we've created
- There're also a couple of forks in the road we should address:
    - What happens when the user hits return on the keyboard? Does that automatically create a task? Alternatively, do we implement and support a line break?
    - Is there a dedicated *Add this task* button?
    - Does the successful act of adding a task cause the keyboard to go away, requiring the user to tap on the input field again? Alternatively, do we allow the user to keep adding tasks until they tap outside the keyboard?
    - How many characters do we support? How long is too long for a task? What kind of feedback is presented to the user of our software if they exceed that limit?

This is a lot to take in, so let's take it one step at a time! I will propose that we ignore the big decisions for now and have the simple act of having an input on the screen, and then having that input be added to our list of tasks.

Since input should be saved to state and then rendered in the `ListView`, it makes sense for the input component to be a sibling of the `ListView`, allowing them to share the same state.

Architecturally, this is how the `TasksList` component will look:

```
|TasksList
|__TextInput
|__ListView
|_____RowData
|_____RowData
|_____...
|_____RowData
```

React Native has a `TextInput` component in its API that fulfills our need for a keyboard input. Its code is customizable and will allow us to take input and add it to our list of tasks.

This `TextInput` component can accept a multitude of props. I have listed the ones we will use here, but the documentation for React Native will provide much more depth:

- `autoCorrect`: This is a Boolean that turns autocorrection on and off. It is set to `true` by default
- `onChangeText`: This is a callback that is fired when the input field's text changes. The value of the component is passed as an argument to the callback
- `onSubmitEditing`: This is a callback that is fired when a single-line input's submit button is pressed
- `returnKeyType`: This sets the title of the return key to one of many different strings; `done`, `go`, `next`, `search`, and `send` are the five that work across both the platforms

We can break down the task at hand into a couple of bite-sized steps:

- Update container styling in `index.ios.js` so that its contents take up the entire screen and not just the center
- Add a `TextInput` component to our `TasksList` component's `render` method
- Create a submit handler for the `TextInput` component that will take the value of the text field and add it to `ListView`
- Clear the contents of the `TextInput` once submitted, leaving a blank field for the next task to be added

Take some time to try and add this first feature into our app! In the next section, I will share some screenshots of my results and break down the code I wrote for it.

Here's a screen to show how my input looks at this stage:

It meets the four basic requirements listed in the preceding section: the contents aren't centered on the screen, a TextInput component is rendered at the top, the submit handler takes the value of the TextInput component and adds it to the ListView, and the contents of the TextInput are emptied once that happens.

Let's look at the code to see how I tackled it--yours may be different!:

```
// Tasks/index.ios.js

import React, { Component } from 'react';
import {
  AppRegistry,
  View
} from 'react-native';

import TasksList from './app/components/TasksList';

export default class Tasks extends Component {
  render() {
    return (
      <View>
        <TasksList />
      </View>
    );
  }
}

AppRegistry.registerComponent('Tasks', () => Tasks);
```

This is the updated styling for `TasksList`:

```
// Tasks/app/components/TasksList/styles.js

import { StyleSheet } from 'react-native';
const styles = StyleSheet.create({
  container: {
    flex: 1
  }
});

export default styles;
```

What I did here was remove the `justifyContent` and `alignItems` properties of the container so that items weren't constrained to just the center of the display.

Moving on to the `TasksList` component, I made a couple of major changes:

```
// Tasks/app/components/TasksList/index.js

import React, { Component } from 'react';

import {
```

```
    ListView,
    Text,
    TextInput,
    View
} from 'react-native';

import styles from './styles';

export default class TasksList extends Component {
  constructor (props) {
    super (props);

    const ds = new ListView.DataSource({
      rowHasChanged: (r1, r2) => r1 !== r2
    });

    this.state = {
      ds: new ListView.DataSource({
        rowHasChanged: (r1, r2) => r1 !== r2
      }),
      listOfTasks: [],
      text: ''
    };
  }
```

The constructor now saves three things to state: our local instance of
`ListView.DataSource`, an empty string to keep track of the value of `TextInput`, and an
array to store the list of tasks.

The `render` function creates a reference to a `dataSource` that we will use for our
`ListView` component, cloning the `listOfTasks` array stored in state. Once again, the
`ListView` just presents plain text:

```
  render () {
    const dataSource =
    this.state.ds.cloneWithRows(this.state.listOfTasks);
```

The `TextInput` component has a couple of options. It binds the `value` of its input field to
the `text` value of our state, changing it repeatedly as the field is edited. On submitting it by
pressing the *done* key on the keyboard, it fires a callback called `_addTask`:

```
    return (
      <View style={ styles.container }>
        <TextInput
          autoCorrect={ false }
          onChangeText={ (text) => this._changeTextInputValue(text) }
          onSubmitEditing={ () => this._addTask() }
```

```
            returnKeyType={ 'done' }
            style={ styles.textInput }
            value={ this.state.text }
        />
```

It renders a `ListView` component with the `_renderRowData` method being responsible for returning each individual row of the component:

```
        <ListView
            dataSource={ dataSource }
            enableEmptySections={ true }
            renderRow={ (rowData) => this._renderRowData(rowData) }
        />
      </View>
    );
  }
```

I like to start the name of methods that I personally create in a React component with an underscore so that I can visually distinguish them from the default life cycle methods.

The `_addTask` method uses the array spread operator introduced in ES6 to create a new array and copy over an existing array's values, adding the newest task to the list at the end. Then, we assign it to the `listOfTasks` property in state. Remember that we have to treat our component state as an immutable object and simply pushing to it will be an anti-pattern:

```
_addTask () {
    const listOfTasks = [...this.state.listOfTasks, this.state.text];

    this.setState({
      listOfTasks
    });

    this._changeTextInputValue (''
  }
```

Finally, we call `_changeTextInputValue` so that the `TextInput` box is emptied:

```
_changeTextInputValue (text) {
    this.setState({
      text
    });
  }

_renderRowData (rowData) {
    return (
      <Text>{ rowData }</Text>
```

```
    )
  }
}
```

For now, just returning the name of the to-do list item is fine.

When setting the `listOfTasks` property in the `_addTask` method and the `text` property in `_changeTextInputValue`, I'm using a new notation feature of ES6, called shorthand property names, to assign a value to a key with the same name as the value. This is the same as if I were to write as follows:

```
this.setState({
  listOfTasks: listOfTasks,
  text: text
})
```

Moving on, you might note that, as you refresh the application, you lose your state! This is impractical for a to-do list app, since we should never expect the user to re-enter the same list whenever they re-open the app. What we want is to store this list of tasks locally in the device so that we can access it whenever needed. This is where `AsyncStorage` comes into play.

AsyncStorage

The `AsyncStorage` component is a simple key-value store that is globally available to your React Native application. It's persistent, meaning that data within `AsyncStorage` will continue to exist through quitting or restarting the application or your phone. If you've worked with HTML `LocalStorage` and `SessionStorage`, `AsyncStorage` will seem familiar. It's powerful for light usage, but Facebook recommends that you use an abstraction layer on top of `AsyncStorage` for anything more than that.

As the name implies, `AsyncStorage` is asynchronous. If you haven't yet been introduced to asynchronous JavaScript, this means the methods of this storage system can run concurrently with the rest of your code. The methods of `AsyncStorage` return a `Promise`-- an object that represents an operation that hasn't yet completed, but is expected to in the future.

Each of the methods in `AsyncStorage` can accept a callback function as an argument, and will fire that callback once the `Promise` is fulfilled. This means that we can write our `TasksList` component to work around these promises, saving and retrieving our array of tasks when needed.

One final thing about `AsyncStorage` though--it's a simple key-value store. It expects a string for both its key and value, which means that we'll need to transform the data we send using `JSON.stringify` to turn the array into a string when sending it into storage and `JSON.parse` to transform it back into an array when retrieving it.

Play with `AsyncStorage` and update your `TasksList` component to support it. Here are some goals you'll want to have with `AsyncStorage`:

- Once `TasksList` is loaded, we want to see whether any tasks exist locally in storage. If they do, present this list to the user. If they don't, start off with an empty array for storage. Data should always persist through a restart.
- When a task is entered, we should update the list of tasks, save the updated list into `AsyncStorage`, and then update the `ListView` component.

Here's the code I ended up writing:

```
// TasksList/app/components/TasksList/index.js

...
import {
  AsyncStorage,
  ...
} from 'react-native';
...
```

Import the `AsyncStorage` API from the React Native SDK.

```
export default class TasksList extends Component {
  ...
  componentDidMount () {
    this._updateList();
  }
}
```

Call the `_updateList` method during the `componentDidMount` life cycle.

```
  ...
  async _addTask () {
    const listOfTasks = [...this.state.listOfTasks, this.state.text];

    await AsyncStorage.setItem('listOfTasks',
    JSON.stringify(listOfTasks));

    this._updateList();
  }
```

Update _addTask to use the `async` and `await` keywords as well as `AsyncStorage`. Refer to the following for details on using `async` and `await`:

```
...
async _updateList () {
  let response = await AsyncStorage.getItem('listOfTasks');
  let listOfTasks = await JSON.parse(response) || [];

  this.setState({
    listOfTasks
  });

  this._changeTextInputValue('');
  }
}
```

What we are doing with `AsyncStorage` in _updateTask is grabbing the value locally stored using the `listOfTasks` key. From here, we parse the result, transforming the string back into an array. Then, we check to see whether the array exists and set it to an empty array if it returns `null`. Finally, we set the state of our component by updating `listOfTasks` and firing _changeTextInputValue to reset `TextInput` value.

The preceding example also uses the new `async` and `await` keywords that are part of the ES7 specification proposal and readily available to use with React Native.

Using the Async and Await keywords

Normally, to deal with an asynchronous function, we would chain some promises to it in order to grab our data. We can write _updateList, like this:

```
_updateList () {
  AsyncStorage.getItem('listOfTasks');
    .then((response) => {fto
      return JSON.parse(response);
    })
    .then((parsedResponse) => {
      this.setState({
        listOfTasks: parsedResponse
      });
    });
}
```

However, this can become quite complicated. Instead, we will use the `async` and `await` keywords to create a simpler solution:

```
async _updateList () {
  let response = await AsyncStorage.getItem('listOfTasks');
  let listOfTasks = await JSON.parse(response) || [];

  this.setState({
    listOfTasks
  });

  this._changeTextInputValue('');
}
```

The `async` keyword in front of _updateList declares it as an asynchronous function. It automatically returns promises for us and can take advantage of the `await` keyword to tell the JS interpreter to temporarily exit the asynchronous function and resume running when the asynchronous call is completed. This is great for us because we can express our intent in a sequential order in a single function and still receive the exact same results that we would enjoy with a promise.

Custom RenderRow component

The final thing on our list to have a usable minimum viable product is to allow each task to be marked as complete. This is where we'll create the `TasksListCell` component and render that in our `renderRow` function of `ListView` instead of just the text.

Our goals for this component should be as follows:

- Accept text from the parent component as a prop, rendering it in `TasksListCell`
- Update `listOfTasks` to take in an array of objects rather than an array of strings, allowing each object to track the name of the task and whether or not it's completed
- Provide some sort of visual indicator when a task is tapped, marking it as complete both visually and within the task's `data` object, so this persists through application reloads

Custom RenderRow example

Let's look at how I created this component:

```
// Tasks/app/components/TasksList/index.js

...
import TasksListCell from '../TasksListCell';
...
export default class TasksList extends Component {
  ...
  async _addTask () {
    const singleTask = {
      completed: false,
      text: this.state.text
    }
```

Firstly, tasks are now represented as objects within the array. This allows us to add properties to each task, such as its completed state, and leaves room for future additions.

```
    const listOfTasks = [...this.state.listOfTasks, singleTask];
    await AsyncStorage.setItem('listOfTasks',
    JSON.stringify(listOfTasks));
    this._updateList();
  }
  ...
  _renderRowData (rowData, rowID) {
    return (
      <TasksListCell
        completed={ rowData.completed }
        id={ rowID }
        onPress={ (rowID) => this._completeTask(rowID) }
        text={ rowData.text }
      />
    )
  }
  ...
}
```

The _renderRowData method is also updated to render a new TasksListCell component. Four props are shared to TasksListCell: the task's completed state, its row identifier (provided by renderRow), a callback to alter the task's completed state, and the details of that task itself.

Here's how that `TasksListCell` component was written:

```
// Tasks/app/components/TasksListCell/index.js

import React, { Component, PropTypes } from 'react';

import {
  Text,
  TouchableHighlight,
  View
} from 'react-native';

export default class TasksListCell extends Component {
  static propTypes = {
    completed: PropTypes.bool.isRequired,
    id: PropTypes.string.isRequired,
    onLongPress: PropTypes.func.isRequired,
    onPress: PropTypes.func.isRequired,
    text: PropTypes.string.isRequired
  }
```

Use `PropTypes` to explicitly declare the data this component expects to be given. Read on for an explanation on prop validation in React.

```
  constructor (props) {
    super (props);
  }

  render () {
    const isCompleted = this.props.completed ? 'line-through' : 'none';
    const textStyle = {
      fontSize: 20,
      textDecorationLine: isCompleted
    };
```

Use a ternary operator to calculate styling for a task if it is completed.

```
    return (
      <View>
        <TouchableHighlight
          onPress={ () => this.props.onPress(this.props.id) }
          underlayColor={ '#D5DBDE' } >
          <Text style={ textStyle }>{ this.props.text }</Text>
        </TouchableHighlight>
      </View>
    )
  }
}
```

The preceding component provides a `TouchableHighlight` for each task on the list, giving us visual opacity feedback when an item is tapped on. It also fires the `_completeTask` method of `TasksListCell`, which subsequently calls the `onPress` prop that was passed to it and makes a visual change to the style of the cell, marking it *completed* with a *line through* the horizontal center of the task.

Prop validation in React

By declaring a propTypes object for a component, I can specify the expected props and their types for a given component. This is helpful for future maintainers of our code and provides helpful warnings when props are incorrectly entered or missing.

To take advantage of prop validation, first import the `PropTypes` module from React:

```
import { PropTypes } from 'react';
```

Then, in our component, we give it a static property of `propTypes`:

```
class Example extends Component {
  static propTypes = {
    foo: PropTypes.string.isRequired,
    bar: PropTypes.func,
    baz: PropTypes.number.isRequired
  }
}
```

In the preceding example, `foo` and `baz` are the required props for the `Example` component. `foo` is expected to be a string, while `baz` is expected to be a number. `bar`, on the other hand, is expected to be a function but is not a required prop.

Moving beyond MVP

Now that we have a very bare-bones MVP completed, the next goal is to add some features to the application so that it's fully-fledged.

Here's what I wrote earlier regarding some nice-to-have features:

 I'd like to set a reminder for each unique task so that I can get to each one in an orderly fashion. Ideally, the items on the list can be grouped into categories. Category grouping could perhaps be simplified by something like icons. This way, I can also sort and filter my list by icons.

In addition to the features, we should tweak the styling of the application so that it looks better. In my sample code, the app's components conflict with the iOS's status bar and the rows aren't formatted at all. We should give the app its own identity.

The next chapter will dive deeper into our MVP and transform it into a fully-featured and styled application. We'll also look at things we would do differently if the app were written for Android instead.

Summary

In this chapter, you started out strong by planning a minimum viable product version of a to-do list app, complete with adding tasks to the list and marking them as completed. Then, you learned about basic styling in React Native with Flexbox and became acquainted with new syntax and functionalities of the ES6 specification. You also discovered the iOS simulator debugging menu, which is a helpful tool for writing apps.

Afterward, you created a `ListView` component to render an array of items, and then implemented a `TextInput` component to save user input and render that into the `Listview`. Then, you used `AsyncStorage` to persist the data added to the app by the user, utilizing the new `async` and `await` keywords to write clean asynchronous functions. Finally, you implemented a `TouchableHighlight` cell that marks tasks as completed.

2
Advanced Functionality and Styling the To-Do List App

Having built an MVP for `Tasks`, our to-do list app, it's time to delve into building out advanced functionality, and styling the application to make it look nice. This chapter will explore the following topics:

- Utilizing the `NavigatorIOS` component to build an edit screen to add details to a task
- Taking in a date and time for tasks to be due with `DatePickerIOS`
- Creating a custom collapsible component for our app and utilizing `LayoutAnimation` to give us fluid transitions
- Building a `Button` component for our UI to clear a to-do item's due date
- Saving the data of an edited task and rendering a due date, if applicable
- Porting the application over to Android, swapping out `DatePickerIOS` for `DatePickerAndroid` and `TimePickerAndroid` and `NavigatorIOS` for `Navigator`, and exploring the control flow in deciding which component is used

Navigator and NavigatorIOS

Implementing navigation in a mobile application helps us control how our users interact with and experience our apps. It lets us assign context to situations that would otherwise not have any--for example, in `Tasks`, it will not make sense to show a user an edit view for a task that they haven't selected; only showing this to the user when they select a task to edit builds situational context and awareness.

React Native's `Navigator` component handles the transitions between different views in your application. Glancing at the documentation, you may note that there's both a `Navigator` and `NavigatorIOS` component. `Navigator` is available on iOS and Android and implemented with JavaScript. On the other hand, `NavigatorIOS` is specifically available for iOS and is a wrapper around iOS's native `UINavigationController`, animating it and behaving the way you would expect from any iOS application.

Later in this chapter, we will take a closer look at the Navigator.

An important note about NavigatorIOS

While `NavigatorIOS` supports UIKit animations and is a great choice for building the iOS version of `Tasks`, one thing to keep in mind is that `NavigatorIOS` happens to be a community-driven component of the React Native SDK. Facebook has openly stated from the beginning that it utilizes `Navigator` heavily in its own applications, but all support for future improvements and additions to the `NavigatorIOS` component will come directly from open source contributions.

Looking at NavigatorIOS

The `NavigatorIOS` component is set up at the top level of your React Native app. We'll provide at least one object, identified as `routes`, in order to identify each view in our app. Additionally, `NavigatorIOS` looks for a `renderScene` method, which is responsible for rendering each scene in our app. Here's an example of how you can render a basic scene with `NavigatorIOS`:

```
import React, { Component } from 'react';
import {
  NavigatorIOS,
  Text
} from 'react-native';

export default class ExampleNavigation extends Component {
  render () {
    return (
      <NavigatorIOS
        initialRoute={{
          component: TasksList,
          title: 'Tasks'
        }}
        style={ styles.container }
      />
    );
```

```
    }
  }
```

This is just a rudimentary example. All we're doing is initializing the `NavigatorIOS` component and rendering it as a basic route with a simple `text` component. What we're really interested in doing is switching between `routes` to edit a task. Let's break down this goal into a number of subtasks that are easier to tackle:

- Create a new `EditTask` component. It can start off as a simple screen with some filler info on it.
- Set up `NavigatorIOS` to route to `EditTask` when a task is long-pressed.
- Build logic for `EditTask` to accept the exact task as a prop in the component to render task-specific data. Add appropriate input fields to allow this component to be marked as complete from the edit screen as well as for it to have the ability to set a due date and tag.
- When edits are saved, add logic to save the edited data to `AsyncStorage`.

We'll take some time to complete each step and go over them when necessary. Take a few minutes to build a simple `EditTask` component, and then refer to how I built mine.

A simple EditTasks component

In my application folder structure, my `EditTasks` component is nested as such:

```
|Tasks
|__android
|__app
|____components
|_____EditTask
|_____TasksList
|_____TasksListCell
|__ios
|__node_modules
|__...
```

Here is a basic component just to have something appear on the screen:

```
// Tasks/app/components/EditTask/index.js

import React, { Component } from 'react';

import {
  Text,
```

```
      View
    } from 'react-native';

    import styles from './styles';

    export default class EditTask extends Component {
      render () {
        return (
          <View style={ styles.editTaskContainer }>
            <Text style={ styles.editTaskText }>Editing Task</Text>
          </View>
        );
      }
    }
```

The preceding code returns text to render to the screen for now.

Now comes the fun part. Let's set up `NavigatorIOS` to play nicely with `TasksList`:

```
    // Tasks/app/components/EditTask/styles.js

    import { Navigator, StyleSheet } from 'react-native';

    const styles = StyleSheet.create({
      editTaskContainer: {
        flex: 1,
        paddingTop: Navigator.NavigationBar.Styles.General.TotalNavHeight
      },
      editTaskText: {
        fontSize: 36
      }
    })

    export default styles;
```

First, we should modify `TasksList` so that it:

- Adds a function, called `_editTask`, to push the `EditTask` component to the Navigator
- Passes the `_editTask` function into `TasksListCell` as a prop, titled `onLongPress`

Then, we should modify `EditTask` so that the `TouchableHighlight` component in its `render` method calls this prop during its own `onLongPress` callback:

```
// Tasks/app/components/TasksList/index.js

...
import EditTask from '../EditTask';
...
export default class TasksList extends Component {
  ...
  render () {
    ...
    return (
      <View style={ styles.container }>
        ...
        <ListView
          ...
          automaticallyAdjustContentInsets={ false }
          style={ styles.listView }
        />
      </View>
    );
  }
```

We added a Boolean set to disable the automatic adjustment of content insets. With this defaulting to `true`, we saw an inset of ~55px between our `Input` and `ListView` components. In our styling for both this component and `EditTask`, we started importing the `Navigator` component.

This is so that we can set the `paddingTop` property of our container to take into consideration the height of the navigation bar so that content is not left tucked behind the navigation bar. The reason this happens is because the navigation bar is rendered over our components after they are done loading.

Call the `push` method of `NavigatorIOS`, rendering the `EditTask` component that we just imported:

```
...
_editTask (rowData) {
  this.props.navigator.push({
    component: EditTask,
    title: 'Edit'
  });
}
```

Assign `TasksListCell` a callback, titled `onLongPress`, that executes the `_editTask` method we just defined:

```
_renderRowData (rowData, rowID) {
  return (
```

```
        <TasksListCell
          ...
          onLongPress={ () => this._editTask() }
        />
      )
    }
    ...
}
```

Setting the `paddingTop` property to the height of the Navigator solves the issue of our navigation bar hiding the content of our app behind it:

```
// Tasks/app/components/TasksList/styles.js

import { Navigator, StyleSheet } from 'react-native';

const styles = StyleSheet.create({
  container: {
    ...
    paddingTop: Navigator.NavigationBar.Styles.General.TotalNavHeight
  ...
});

export default styles;
```

Using DatePickerIOS

A key feature in `Tasks` is the ability to set a reminder for when a task is due. Ideally, our users can set a day as well as a time for when a task should be completed so that they can be reminded of the due date. To accomplish this, we'll use an iOS component named `DatePickerIOS`. This is a component that renders a date and time selector that we can utilize in our application.

Listed here are the two props that we will be using with our `DatePickerIOS` component. Other props exist in the React Native documentation in case you are interested:

- `date`: This is one of the two required props that track the current selected date. Ideally, this information is stored within the state of the component that renders `DatePickerIOS`. The `date` should be an instance of the `Date` object in JavaScript.
- `onDateChange`: This is the other required prop and is fired when a user changes the `date` or `time` in the component. It accepts one argument, which is the `Date` object representing the new date and time.

Here's how a simple `DatePicker` component looks:

```
// Tasks/app/components/EditTask/index.js

...
import {
  DatePickerIOS,
  ...
} from 'react-native';
...
export default class EditTask extends Component {
  constructor (props) {
    super (props);

    this.state = {
      date: new Date()
    }
  }
```

It creates a new instance of the JavaScript `Date` object and saves it to state.

```
  render () {
    return (
      <View style={ styles.editTaskContainer }>
        <DatePickerIOS
          date={ this.state.date }
          onDateChange={ (date) => this._onDateChange(date) }
          style={ styles.datePicker }
        />
      </View>
    );
  }
```

This results in rendering a `DatePickerIOS` component using the `date` value in the component state as its prop of the same name.

The callback to change the `date` in the component state when the user interacts with the `DatePickerIOS` component:

```
  _onDateChange (date) {
    this.setState({
      date
    });
  }
}
```

This is how the `DatePicker`, when rendered, will look:

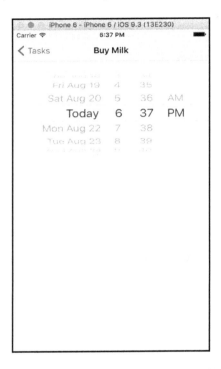

This leaves a lot to be desired. For one, the `DatePickerIOS` component is always visible! Normally, when we interact with this type of selector in iOS applications, it is collapsed and only expands when tapped on. What we want is to replicate that exact experience, that is, render a touchable row that either displays the current set due date or something along the lines of *No Due Date Set*, animating the expansion of `DatePickerIOS` when the row is tapped on.

Writing a collapsible component

Our collapsible component should accomplish the following goals:

- It should show and hide other components passed to it when tapped on
- An animation will accompany this component, adding to the user experience of our app

- The component should not make any assumptions about the type of data it is showing and hiding; it should not be strictly specific to `DatePickerIOS` in case we want to reuse the component for other purposes in the future

We'll need to take advantage of React Native's fantastic `LayoutAnimation` API, which is designed to let us create fluid and meaningful animations.

To begin, I've created an `ExpandableCell` component within the `components` folder of our project, like this:

```
|Tasks
|__android
|__app
|____EditTask
|____ExpandableCell
|____TasksList
|____TasksListCell
|__ios
|__...
```

The LayoutAnimation API

Our goal is to tap on the `date/time` component in `EditTask` and then have it expand downward to reveal the hidden `DatePickerIOS` component. React Native has an API, called `LayoutAnimation`, that allows us to create automatically animating layouts.

`LayoutAnimation` comes with three methods representing default animation curves: `easeInEaseOut`, `linear`, and `spring`. These dictate how the animation behaves throughout its transition. You can simply call one of the three methods under the `componentWillUpdate` life cycle method and, should a change in your component's state trigger a rerender, `LayoutAnimation` will add its animation to your changes.

To hide and show the children components passed to `ExpandableCell`, I can manipulate its `maxHeight` style based on whether or not the component should be shown or hidden. Additionally, I can hide the component when not needed by setting its `overflow` property to `hidden`.

Take some time to hide the children components passed into `ExpandableCell` and set up some logic to show and hide this content as needed. When you're ready, look at my implementation.

Basic ExpandableCell implementation

This is how we can start building `ExpandableCell`:

```
// Tasks/app/components/ExpandableCell/index.js

import React, { Component, PropTypes } from 'react';

import {
  LayoutAnimation,
  Text,
  TouchableHighlight,
  View
} from 'react-native';

import styles from './styles';

export default class ExpandableCell extends Component {
```

This sets the `title` as an expected string `PropTypes` for the component:

```
static propTypes = {
  title: PropTypes.string.isRequired
}
```

Now we track a Boolean named `expanded` in the component `state`. By default, our child components should not be visible:

```
constructor (props) {
  super (props);

  this.state = {
    expanded: false
  }
}
```

Set the `LayoutAnimation` style for whenever this component changes:

```
componentWillUpdate () {
  LayoutAnimation.linear();
}
```

Wrap a `TouchableHighlight` component around the `Text` of the `ExpandableCell`. It calls `_onExpand` when pressed:

```
render () {
  return (
    <View style={ styles.expandableCellContainer }>
      <View>
        <TouchableHighlight
          onPress={ () => this._expandCell() }
          underlayColor={ '#D3D3D3' }
        >
```

Add a ternary operator to add a `maxHeight` property to the styling of this `View` in the event that the component is not expanded:

```
        <Text style={ styles.visibleContent }>
        { this.props.title}</Text>
      </TouchableHighlight>
    </View>
    <View style={ [styles.hiddenContent,
    this.state.expanded ? {} : {maxHeight: 0}]}>
```

This renders any children nested within the component itself:

```
      { this.props.children }
    </View>
  </View>
  )
}
```

The following is a callback to toggle the `expanded` Boolean in the component state:

```
  _expandCell () {
    this.setState({
      expanded: !this.state.expanded
    });
  }
}
```

This is the styling for `ExpandableCell`:

```
// Tasks/app/components/ExpandableCell/styles.js

import { StyleSheet } from 'react-native';

const styles = StyleSheet.create({
  expandableCellContainer: {
    flex: 1,
```

```
    padding: 10,
    paddingTop: 0
  },
  hiddenContent: {
    overflow: 'hidden'
  },
  visibleContent: {
    fontSize: 24
  }
})
```

A basic implementation of this in `EditTask` will look like this:

```
// Tasks/app/components/EditTask/index.js

...
import ExpandableCell from '../ExpandableCell';

export default class EditTask extends Component {
  ...
```

Render an ExpandableCell component with a title:

```
render () {
    return (
      <View style={ styles.editTaskContainer }>
        <ExpandableCell title={ 'Due On' }>
```

Nest `DatePickerIOS` within `ExpandableCell` so that it initially stays hidden:

```
        <DatePickerIOS
          ...
        />

        </ExpandableCell>
      </View>
    );
  }
  ...
}
```

Ideally, this component will show one of the following:

- The due date of the selected task, if it exists
- A blank placeholder to select a date if a due date does not exist

We'll worry about things such as clearing the due date later but, for now, we should modify `EditTask` so that the `title` prop it passes to `ExpandableCell` is dependent on whether the task has a due date assigned to it or not. This is how the component should currently look:

Here is how I solved the problem. The only file changed since the last example is the `EditTask` component:

```
// Tasks/app/components/EditTask/index.js

...
import moment from 'moment';
...
export default class EditTask extends Component {
  ...
  render () {
 const noDueDateTitle = 'Set Reminder';
    const dueDateSetTitle = 'Due On ' + this.state.formattedDate;
```

Set two strings to show the `title` prop for `ExpandableCell`.

```
return (
      <View style={ styles.editTaskContainer }>
        <ExpandableCell
          title={ this.state.dateSelected ?
          dueDateSetTitle : noDueDateTitle }>
```

Use a ternary operator to decide which string to pass in to `ExpandableCell`.

```
        . . .
        </ExpandableCell>
      </View>
    );
  }

  _formatDate (date) {
    return moment(date).format('lll');
  }
```

I also imported `moment` from `npm` to use its powerful date formatting capabilities. Moment is a very popular, widely-used library that allows us to manipulate dates with JavaScript. Installing it was as simple as opening the Terminal to the project's root folder and typing as follows:

npm install --save moment

The MomentJS library is well documented and its main page, found at `https:// momentjs .com`, will show you all the ways you can utilize it. For this file, I used Moment's the format method and set the formatting to show an abbreviated month name, followed by the day and year in numbers and the time.

A sample Moment date formatted with the `'lll'` flag will appear like this:

```
Dec 25, 2016 12:01 AM
```

There are different ways to format your dates with Moment, and I would encourage you to play around with the library to find a date format that works best for you.

Set `dateSelected` to `true` and add the Moment-formatted version of the date to state, which in turn fires the `render` method of this component again to update the `title` string passed into `ExpandableCell`:

```
  _onDateChange (date) {
    this.setState({
      . . .
      dateSelected: true,
      formattedDate: this._formatDate(date)
    });
  }
}
```

By the end of this section, your app should look something like the following screenshot:

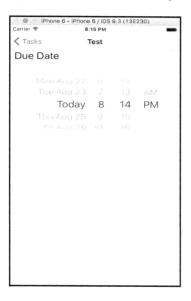

Using onLayout

In our preceding example, we don't need to specify the height of the DatePickerIOS component when expanded. However, there may be scenarios in which you may need to manually get the dimensions of a component.

To calculate a component's height, we can utilize its onLayout property to fire a callback and then use that callback to save properties passed to the callback. The onLayout property is an event that is invoked on mount and layout changes, giving the event object a nativeEvent object that nests the component's layout properties. Using DatePickerIOS as an example, you can pass a callback to its onLayout prop like this:

```
<DatePickerIOS
  date={ this.state.date }
  onDateChange={ (date) => this._onDateChange(date) }
  onLayout={ (event) => this._getComponentDimensions(event) }
  style={ styles.datePicker }
/>
```

The `event` from `onLayout` gives access to the following property:

```
event: {
  nativeEvent: {
    layout: {
      x: //some number
      y: //some number
      width: //some number
      height: //some number
    }
  }
}
```

Button

Let's build a *clear due date* button for the `EditTask` component and only selectively enable it if a due date has been selected for the to-do item. The `Button` component in React Native should help us render one quickly.

The `Button` component accepts a couple of props; the following four will be used in our application:

- `color`: This is a string (or stringified hex) that sets either the text color on iOS or the background color on Android
- `disabled`: This is a Boolean that disables the button if set to `true`; it defaults to `false`
- `onPress`: This is a callback that is fired when a button is pressed
- `title`: This is the text to display within the button

A sample `Button` component can be rendered like this:

```
<Button
  color={ 'blue' }
  disabled={ this.state.buttonDisabled }
  onPress={ () => alert('Submit button pressed') }
  title={ 'Submit' }
/>
```

Modify `EditTask` so that it has the following features:

- It contains a Boolean, titled `expanded`, in its state to control the open/closed status of the `ExpandableCell`.

- It modifies the rendering of `ExpandableCell` to accept the `expanded` and `onPress` props. The `expanded` prop should point to the `expanded` Boolean in `EditTask`'s state and the `onPress` prop should fire a method that flips the `expanded` Boolean.
- Add an `onLayout` callback to `DatePickerIOS` to calculate its height, saving it to state.
- Include a `Button` component with a `title` prop that prompts the user to clear the due date. Give it an `onPress` prop that will clear the `dateSelected` Boolean in state. Also, selectively disable it if the `dateSelected` Boolean is set to `false`.

Clearing due date example

Here's what I did to get the button to clear a selected date and expand/collapse our cells to play nicely:

```
// Tasks/app/components/EditTask/index.js

...
import {
  Button,
  ...
} from 'react-native';
...
export default class EditTask extends Component {
  constructor (props) {
    ...
    this.state = {
      ...
      expanded: false
    }
  }

  render () {
    ...
    return (
      <View style={ styles.editTaskContainer }>
        <View style={ [styles.expandableCellContainer,
        { maxHeight: this.state.expanded ?
        this.state.datePickerHeight : 40 }]}>
```

I wrapped a new `View` around `ExpandableCell`. Its styling is modified based on the expanded `Boolean` in the state of `EditTask`. If the component is expanded, then its `maxHeight` property is set to the height of its child component. Otherwise, it is set to 40 pixels.

Then, pass in the `expanded` and `onPress` props to this component:

```
<ExpandableCell
  ...
  expanded={ this.state.expanded }
  onPress={ () => this._onExpand() }
>
```

Call `_getDatePickerHeight` during the `onLayout` event:

```
<DatePickerIOS
  ...
  onLayout={ (event) => this._getDatePickerHeight(event) }
/>
</ExpandableCell>
</View>
```

The `Button` component is also encapsulated in its own `View`. This is so that the `Button` and `ExpandableCell` stack on top of each other:

```
<View style={ styles.clearDateButtonContainer }>
  <Button
    color={ '#B44743' }
    disabled={ this.state.dateSelected ? false : true }
    onPress={ () => this._clearDate() }
    title={ 'Clear Date' }
  />
</View>
</View>
);
}
```

Set the `dateSelected` Boolean in state to `false`, changing the `title` that `ExpandableCell` is passed:

```
_clearDate () {
  this.setState({
    dateSelected: false
  });
}
```

This saves the width of the `DatePickerIOS` component to state:

```
_getDatePickerHeight (event) {
  this.setState({
    datePickerHeight: event.nativeEvent.layout.width
  });
}

_onExpand () {
  this.setState({
    expanded: !this.state.expanded
  });
}
}
```

I added a `clearDateButtonContainer` style to this component's `StyleSheet`:

```
// Tasks/app/components/EditTask/styles.js

import { Navigator, StyleSheet } from 'react-native';

const styles = StyleSheet.create({
  ...
  clearDateButtonContainer: {
    flex: 1
  }
})

export default styles;
```

Let's continue working on this and build a couple more features into this screen. Next up, we should have a field to edit the name of the task at the very top followed by a `Switch` component to toggle a complete or an incomplete state for the task.

Switch

Switch is a component that renders a Boolean input and allows the user to toggle back and forth.

With `Switch`, these are the props that we will use:

- `onValueChange`: This is a callback that is invoked with the new value of the switch when the value changes

- `value`: This is a Boolean that determines whether the switch is set to its 'on' position or not; it defaults to `false`

A simple `Switch` component can look like this:

```
<Switch
  onValueChange={ (value) =? this.setState({ toggled: value })}
  value={ this.state.toggled }
/>
```

As stated earlier, `Switch` has two props that are required: its `value` and a callback to change its value when toggled.

Using this knowledge, let's make changes to the `TasksList` component so that it passes the `completed`, `due`, `formattedDate`, and `text` properties of each row to the `EditTask` component for use.

Then, make additions to the `EditTask` component so that it:

- Expects the `completed`, `due`, `formattedDate`, and `text` props as part of its `propTypes` declaration.
- Contains a `TextInput` field that is preloaded with the name of the to-do list item and allows the user to edit the name.
- Adds a `Switch` component that is preloaded with the completion status of the to-do list item. When toggled, its completion status should change.

This is the solution that I came up with:

```
// Tasks/app/components/TasksList/index.js

...
export default class TasksList extends Component {
  ...
  _editTask (rowData) {
    this.props.navigator.push({
      ...
      passProps: {
        completed: rowData.completed,
        due: rowData.due,
        formattedDate: rowData.formattedDate,
        text: rowData.text
      },
      ...
    });
  }
```

```
    . . .
}
```

Pass in the four required fields for EditTask so that the view has access to rendering a to-do list item's existing details. If the row does not contain one or more of these fields, it will pass in undefined.

Declare the four propTypes that this component expects. Since completed and text are the only two that are set when a to-do list item is created by the app, they are marked as the required props.

```
// Tasks/app/components/EditTask/index.js

import React, { Component, PropTypes } from 'react';
...
import {
  ...
  Switch,
  TextInput,
  ...
} from 'react-native';
...
export default class EditTask extends Component {
  static propTypes = {
    completed: PropTypes.bool.isRequired,
    due: PropTypes.string,
    formattedDate: PropTypes.string,
    text: PropTypes.string.isRequired
  }

  constructor (props) {
    super (props);

    this.state = {
      completed: this.props.completed,
      date: new Date(this.props.due),
      expanded: false,
      text: this.props.text
    }
  }
}
```

Using props in state is considered an anti-pattern, but we have them here for good reason since we will be modifying these as part of the component.

In the next section, we will also create a Save button that lets us save the to-do item's updated details, and so we need a locally available copy of that data in state to reflect the EditTask component's changes.

Render a `TextInput` component to handle changing a to-do list item's name:

```
render () {
  ...
  return (
    <View style={ styles.editTaskContainer }>
      <View>
        <TextInput
          autoCorrect={ false }
          onChangeText={ (text) => this._changeTextInputValue(text) }
          returnKeyType={ 'done' }
          style={ styles.textInput }
          value={ this.state.text }
        />
      </View>
```

Render the `Switch` below `ExpandableCell` but above the clear due date `Button`:

```
      ...
      <View style={ styles.switchContainer } >
        <Text style={ styles.switchText } >
          Completed
        </Text>
        <Switch
          onValueChange={ (value) => this._onSwitchToggle(value) }
          value={ this.state.completed }
        />
      </View>
      ...
    </View>
  );
}
```

The following callback methods change the values of `TextInput` and `Switch`:

```
_changeTextInputValue (text) {
  this.setState({
    text
  });
}
...
_onSwitchToggle (completed) {
  this.setState({
    completed
  });
}
}
```

A few styling additions for the new components:

```
// Tasks/app/components/EditTask/styles.js

import { Navigator, StyleSheet } from 'react-native';

const styles = StyleSheet.create({
  ...
  switchContainer: {
    flex: 1,
    flexDirection: 'row',
    justifyContent: 'space-between',
    maxHeight: 50,
    padding: 10
  },
  switchText: {
    fontSize: 16
  },
  textInput: {
    borderColor: 'gray',
    borderWidth: 1,
    height: 40,
    margin: 10,
    padding: 10
  }
})

export default styles;
```

Save button

In this section, we will create a button in the upper-right corner of the navigation bar that is labeled as `Save`. When it is tapped on, the following two things must happen:

- The changes the user made to the to-do item (such as its name, completion status, and due date) must be saved to `AsyncStorage`, overwriting its previous details
- The `TasksList` must be updated so that the user visually sees the changes they made right away

Rendering the `Save` button is easy with React Native. The object that gets pushed to `NavigatorIOS` needs to receive the following two key/value pairs:

- `rightButtonTitle`: This is a string that renders the text shown in that area
- `onRightButtonPress`: This is a callback that is fired when that button is pressed

At face value, this looks simple. However, we can't pass any information to the `onRightButtonPress` method of `NavigatorIOS` from a rendered child. Instead, we have to keep a copy of the changes we make inside our `TasksList` component as well, and update them as the `DatePickerIOS`, `TextInput`, and `Switch` components within `EditTask` are updated.

```
// Tasks/app/components/TasksList/index.js

...
export default class TasksList extends Component {
  constructor (props) {
    ...
    this.state = {
      currentEditedTaskObject: undefined,
      ...
    };
  }
  ...
  _completeTask (rowID) {
    const singleUpdatedTask = {
      ...this.state.listOfTasks[rowID],
      completed: !this.state.listOfTasks[rowID].completed
    };

    this._saveAndUpdateSelectedTask(singleUpdatedTask, rowID);
  }
```

This is no longer an asynchronous function. The part of the function that took advantage of `async`/`await` is broken off into `_saveAndUpdateSelectedTask`.

Set the currently edited task object to state:

```
_editTask (rowData, rowID) {
  this.setState({
    currentEditedTaskObject: rowData
  });
```

Add an `onRightButtonPress` callback and string for the right button's title:

```
this.props.navigator.push({
  ...
  onRightButtonPress: () => this._saveCurrentEditedTask(rowID),
  rightButtonTitle: 'Save',
```

Pass in four new functions to EditTask that deal with the item's details:

```
passProps: {
  changeTaskCompletionStatus: (status) =>
  this._updateCurrentEditedTaskObject('completed', status),
  changeTaskDueDate: (date, formattedDate) =>
  this._updateCurrentEditedTaskDueDate
  (date, formattedDate),
  changeTaskName: (name) =>
  this._updateCurrentEditedTaskObject('text', name),
  clearTaskDueDate: () =>
  this._updateCurrentEditedTaskDueDate(undefined, undefined),
  }
});
}
```

Add arguments for _editTask to accept:

```
_renderRowData (rowData, rowID) {
  return (
    <TasksListCell
      ...
      onLongPress={ () => this._editTask(rowData, rowID) }
      ...
    />
  )
}
```

This is the logic previously found in componentDidMount. It was broken into its own function since _saveCurrentEditedTask needs to call it:

```
async _saveAndUpdateSelectedTask (newTaskObject, rowID) {
  const listOfTasks = this.state.listOfTasks.slice();
  listOfTasks[rowID] = newTaskObject;

  await AsyncStorage.setItem('listOfTasks',
  JSON.stringify(listOfTasks));

  this._updateList();
}
```

To save the current edited task, we pass the object and `rowID` to `_saveAndUpdateSelectedtask`, and then call `pop` on the navigator:

```
_saveCurrentEditedTask (rowID) {
this._saveAndUpdateSelectedTask(this.state.currentEditedTaskObject,
rowID);
  this.props.navigator.pop();
}
```

This function updates the `date` and `formattedDate` of the current edited task object:

```
_updateCurrentEditedTaskDueDate (date, formattedDate) {
  this._updateCurrentEditedTaskObject ('due', date);
  this._updateCurrentEditedTaskObject ('formattedDate',
  formattedDate);
}
```

The following function accepts a key and value, creates a clone of `currentEditedTaskObject` with the new value, and sets it in state:

```
_updateCurrentEditedTaskObject (key, value) {
  let newTaskObject = Object.assign({},
  this.state.currentEditedTaskObject);

  newTaskObject[key] = value;

  this.setState({
    currentEditedTaskObject: newTaskObject
  });
}
 ...
}
```

The last two functions' purpose is to update the `TasksList` local state copy of the object being edited. This is done for two reasons:

- Any updates we make to `EditTask`, such as changing the name, completion status, and due date, currently do not propagate up to its parent
- Additionally, we can't just point the values in `EditTask` to what gets passed in as props since the `EditTask` component does not rerender whenever the props being passed to it change

EditTask gets a couple of changes including new propTypes for the component to expect:

```
// Tasks/app/components/EditTask/index.js

...
export default class EditTask extends Component {
  static propTypes = {
    changeTaskCompletionStatus: PropTypes.func.isRequired,
    changeTaskDueDate: PropTypes.func.isRequired,
    changeTaskName: PropTypes.func.isRequired,
    clearTaskDueDate: PropTypes.func.isRequired,
    ...
  }
```

The changes that EditTask receives involve calling the functions that are passed to it as props to update the parent component's data for saving:

```
  ...
  render () {
    ...
      const dueDateSetTitle = 'Due On ' +
      this.state.formattedDate || this.props.formattedDate;
    ...
  }

  _changeTextInputValue (text) {
    ...
    this.props.changeTaskName(text);
  }

  _clearDate () {
    ...
    this.props.clearTaskDueDate();
  }
  ...
  _onDateChange (date) {
    ...
    this.props.changeTaskDueDate(date, formattedDate);
  }
  ...
  _onSwitchToggle (completed) {
    ...
    this.props.changeTaskCompletionStatus(completed);
  }
}
```

TasksListCell modifications

Finally, we want to edit each row rendered by our `ListView` to display the due date, if one exists.

To do this, we will have to write some conditional logic to show the formatted date, if one is assigned to the to-do item we are rendering. This is also a good time to create a custom `styles` folder for this component as we will be needing it.

Spend some time creating your version of this feature. My solution is as follows:

```
// Tasks/app/components/TasksListCell/index.js

...
import styles from './styles';
```

You might notice from the above import statement that `TasksListCell` now imports its `StyleSheet`.

Add `formattedDate` to `propTypes` as an optional string:

```
export default class TasksListCell extends Component {
  static propTypes = {
    ...
    formattedDate: PropTypes.string,
  }

...
  render () {
    ...
    return (
      <View style={ styles.tasksListCellContainer }>
        <TouchableHighlight
          ...
        >
          <View style={ styles.tasksListCellTextRow }>
            <Text style={ [styles.taskNameText,
            { textDecorationLine: isCompleted }] }>
              { this.props.text }
            </Text>
```

Call `_getDueDate` to render a string for the due date, if it exists:

```
            <Text style={ styles.dueDateText }>
              { this._getDueDate() }
            </Text>
          </View>
```

```
        </TouchableHighlight>
      </View>
    )
  }

  _getDueDate () {
    if (this.props.formattedDate && !this.props.completed) {
      return 'Due ' + this.props.formattedDate;
    }

    return '';
  }
}
```

This component has been modified to support a second line of text to show a due date, but only if it exists.

The logic is set to only display the due date should the task not be marked as completed, so that a user won't be confused if they see a due date on a task they've already checked off.

Additionally, styling's been added to make the two lines appear on the same row:

```
// Tasks/app/components/TasksListCell/styles.js

import { StyleSheet } from 'react-native';

const styles = StyleSheet.create({
  dueDateText: {
    color: 'red',
    flex: 1,
    fontSize: 12,
    paddingTop: 0,
    textAlign: 'right'
  },
  taskNameText: {
    fontSize: 20
  },
  tasksListCellContainer: {
    flex: 1
  },
  tasksListCellTextRow: {
    flex: 1
  }
});

export default styles;
```

Here's a screenshot of how this looks:

This is a pretty neat application at this point, and you will be able to make more enhancements to it with the skills you'll pick up in our next project. As we wind down this project, I want to turn your attention to a question I often receive:

How would we do it on Android?

It's a great question and one that we will explore at the end of each project in this book. I will assume that you have already set up your development environment to work on Android apps in React Native. If not, go do that before proceeding further. If developing for Android is not of any interest to you, feel free to skip this portion and move on to the next chapter!

Modifying tasks for Android

First, we need to point to the Android SDK directory in our app's Android folder under a new local.properties file that you will create. Add the following line, where USERNAME is your machine's username:

```
// Tasks/android/local.properties

sdk.dir = /Users/USERNAME/Library/Android/sdk
```

If your Android SDK is installed in a different location from the preceding example, you will need to modify this file to point to the right place.

Then, launch an **Android Virtual Device** (**AVD**) and execute the `react-native run-android` command in your project's root folder. You will see the following screen, which looks just like the default template when we first built `Tasks` for iOS:

 When working in Android, press RR to reload the app and *Command + M* to enter the Developer menu.

You may find that, with remote JS debugging turned on, animations from simple things, such as `TouchableHighlight` shadows and navigation, can be painfully slow. At the time of writing, some technical solutions are being proposed to address this issue but, for the time being, it's strongly recommended that you enable and disable remote JS debugging as necessary.

Navigator

The `Navigator` component works a bit differently from its native iOS component, but it's still very powerful to work with. One of the changes with using `Navigator` is that your routes should be explicitly defined. We can do this by setting up an array of routes and rendering a specific scene based on which route we're accessing. Here's a sample:

```
export default class Tasks extends Component {
  render () {
    const routes = [
      { title: 'First Component', index: 0 },
      { title: 'Second Component', index: 1 }
    ];
```

Create a `routes` array, as shown in the preceding code.

You might notice that we are explicitly defining our routes from the beginning, setting up an initial route and then passing in props to each route's component here:

```
    return (
      <Navigator
        initialRoute={{ index: 0 }}
        renderScene={ (routes, navigator) =>
        this._renderScene(routes, navigator) } />
    )
  }
```

The route object passed in to _renderScene contains a `passProps` object, which we can set when pushing the navigator.

Instead of passing our component when pushing into the `Navigator`, we pass it an `index`; this is where the _renderScene method of `Navigator` identifies which scene to show the user. Here is how pushing to the `Navigator` looks:

```
    _renderScene (route, navigator) {
      if (route.index === 0) {
        return (
          <FirstComponent
            title={ route.title }
            navigator={ navigator } />
        )
      }

      if (route.index === 1) {
        return (
          <SecondComponent
```

```
        navigator={ navigator }
        details={ route.passProps.details } />
      )
    }
  }
}
```

This is how we would use the Navigator component to push different routes. Notice that instead of passing a component like in in `NavigatorIOS`, we are passing the index of the route:

```
_renderAndroidNavigatorView () {
  this.props.navigator.push({
    index: 1,
    passProps: {
      greeting: 'Hello World'
    }
  });
}
```

If you're comparing this to how we rendered `EditTask` in iOS, you'll note that we're not setting up our navigation bar at all. Android apps typically handle navigation through a combination of `Drawer` and `ToolbarAndroid` components that we will address in a later project. This will help our app by making it look and feel the way any Android app should.

Navigator example

The following code is an example for Navigator:

```
// index.android.js

import React, { Component } from 'react';
import {
  AppRegistry,
  Navigator,
} from 'react-native';

import TasksList from './app/components/TasksList';
import EditTask from './app/components/EditTask';

class Tasks extends Component {

  render () {
    const routes = [
      { title: 'Tasks', index: 0 },
```

```
    { title: 'Edit Task', index: 1 }
  ];
```

Again, establish routes for our app.

```
  return (
    <Navigator
      initialRoute={{ index: 0}}
      renderScene={ (routes, navigator) =>
      this._renderScene(routes, navigator) }/>
  );
}
```

Import the `Navigator` component and render it for the user. It starts at `index:0`, which returns the `TasksList` component.

It returns `TasksList` if the index is 0. This is the default `route`:

```
_renderScene (route, navigator) {
  if (route.index === 0) {
    return (
      <TasksList
        title={ route.title }
        navigator={ navigator } />
    )
  }
```

If the route index is 1, return `EditTask`. It will receive the aforementioned props via the `passProps` method:

```
    if (route.index === 1) {
      return (
        <EditTask
          navigator={ navigator }
          route={ route }
          changeTaskCompletionStatus={
          route.passProps.changeTaskCompletionStatus }
          changeTaskDueDate={ route.passProps.changeTaskDueDate }
          changeTaskName={ route.passProps.changeTaskName }
          completed={ route.passProps.completed }
          due={ route.passProps.due }
          formattedDate={ route.passProps.formattedDate }
          text={ route.passProps.text }
        />
      )
    }
  }
}
```

```
AppRegistry.registerComponent('Tasks', () => Tasks);
```

At this stage, without making further modifications, we can create new to-do items and mark them as completed. However, because the `Navigator` component's push method accepts different arguments than the push method of iOS, we will need to create some conditional logic in the `TasksList` file to accommodate it.

Platform

When your files have such little variance in the differences between their iOS and Android functionalities, it's okay to use the same file. Utilizing the `Platform` API, we can identify the type of mobile device the user is on and conditionally send them down a specific path.

Import the `Platform` API along with the rest of your React Native components:

```
import { Platform } from 'react-native';
```

Then call its `OS` property within a component:

```
_platformConditional () {
  if (Platform.OS === 'ios') {
    doSomething();
  }

  if (Platform.OS === 'android') {
    doSomethingElse();
  }
}
```

This lets us control the path our app takes and allows for a little bit of code reuse.

Android-specific files

If we need to create a file that is supposed to only run on Android devices, simply name it `<FILENAME>.android.js`, just like the two index files. React Native will know exactly which file to build with, and this lets us create components that are platform-specific when we need to add a lot of logic that one universal `index.js` file shouldn't handle. Name files `<FILENAME>.ios.js` to set iOS-specific files too.

Using the `Platform` API, we can create conditional logic to decide how the `Navigator` should push the next component depending on the user's platform. Import the `Platform` API:

```
// Tasks/app/components/TasksList/index.js

...
import {
  ...
  Platform,
  ...
} from 'react-native';
```

Modify the styling of `TextInput` based on the user's platform so that it has a design language that resonates with its platform. On Android, it is usually displayed as a single underline without any border; so, we eliminate the border in the Android-specific styling of this component:

```
...
export default class TasksList extends Component {
  ...
  render () {
  ...
    return (
      <View style={ styles.container }>
        <TextInput
          ...
          style={ Platform.os === 'IOS' ? styles.textInput :
          styles.androidTextInput }
          ...
        />
        ...
      </View>
    );
  }
```

I changed the `_editTask` function to run conditional logic. If our platform is iOS, we call `_renderIOSEditTaskComponent`; otherwise, our platform must be Android and we call `_renderAndroidEditTaskComponent` instead:

```
_editTask (rowData, rowID) {
  ...
  if (Platform.OS === 'ios') {
    return this._renderIOSEditTaskComponent(rowID);
  }

  return this._renderAndroidEditTaskComponent(rowID);
```

```
    }

  _renderAndroidEditTaskComponent (rowID) {
    this.props.navigator.push({
      index: 1,
      passProps: {
        changeTaskCompletionStatus: (status) =>
        this._updateCurrentEditedTaskObject('completed', status),
        changeTaskDueDate: (date, formattedDate) =>
        this._updateCurrentEditedTaskDueDate(date, formattedDate),
        changeTaskName: (name) =>
        this._updateCurrentEditedTaskObject('text', name),
        clearTaskDueDate: () =>
        this._updateCurrentEditedTaskDueDate(undefined, undefined),
        completed: this.state.currentEditedTaskObject.completed,
        due: this.state.currentEditedTaskObject.due,
        formattedDate:
        this.state.currentEditedTaskObject.formattedDate,
        text: this.state.currentEditedTaskObject.text
      }
    })
  }
```

The preceding code pushes the `index` of `EditTask` to the Navigator. It passes the same props that the iOS version of the app previously passed.

The contents of `_renderIOSEditTaskComponent` are the same as those that `_editTask` previously contained:

```
  _renderIOSEditTaskComponent (rowID) {
    this.props.navigator.push({
      ...
    });
  }
  ...
}
```

In the following code we added a custom Android style for `TextInput`, omitting the border:

```
// Tasks/app/components/EditTask/styles.js

...
const styles = StyleSheet.create({
  androidTextInput: {
    height: 40,
    margin: 10,
    padding: 10
```

```
  },
  ...
});
```

DatePickerAndroid and TimePickerAndroid

Setting a time and date on Android is much different from iOS. With iOS, you have a `DatePickerIOS` component that includes both the date and time. On Android, this is split into two native modals, `DatePickerAndroid` for the date and `TimePickerAndroid` for the time. It's not a component to render either, it's an asynchronous function that opens the modal and waits for a natural conclusion before applying logic to it.

To open one of these, wrap an asynchronous function around it:

```
async renderDatePicker () {
  const { action, year, month, day } = await DatePickerAndroid.open({
    date: new Date()
  });

  if (action === DatePickerAndroid.dismissedAction) {
    return;
  }

  // do something with the year, month, and day here
}
```

Both the `DatePickerAndroid` and `TimePickerAndroid` components return an object, and we can grab the properties of each object by using ES6 destructuring assignment, as shown in the preceding snippet.

As these components will render as modals by default, we also don't have any use for the `ExpandableCell` component that we built for the iOS version of the app. To implement Android-specific date and time pickers, we should create an Android-specific `EditTask` component to handle it.

Rather than an expanding cell, we should create another `Button` component to open and close the dialog boxes.

In the example given in the following section, I cloned the iOS `index.js` file for `EditTask` and renamed it `index.android.js` before making changes to it. Any code that has not changed from the iOS version has been omitted. Anything that has been deleted has also been noted.

DatePickerAndroid and TimePickerAndroid example

Remove DatePickerIOS and ExpandableCell from the import statements:

```
// Tasks/app/components/EditTask/index.android.js

...
import {
  ...
  DatePickerAndroid,
  TimePickerAndroid,
} from 'react-native';
...
```

I removed the expanded Boolean from state in this component's constructor function:

```
export default class EditTask extends Component {
  ...
```

This new Button for DatePicker calls _showAndroidDatePicker when pressed. It is placed right below TextInput and replaces ExpandableCell:

```
render () {
  ...
  return (
    <View style={ styles.editTaskContainer }>
      ...
      <View style={ styles.androidButtonContainer }>
        <Button
          color={ '#80B546' }
          title={ this.state.dateSelected ? dueDateSetTitle :
          noDueDateTitle }
          onPress={ () => this._showAndroidDatePicker() }
        />
      </View>
```

There have been no changes to the clear due date Button, but its styling has changed:

```
      <View style={ styles.androidButtonContainer }>
```

```
        </View>
      </View>
    );
  }
```

An asynchronous function that calls `open` on `DatePickerAndroid` extracts the `action`, `year`, `month`, and `day`, sets them to state, and then calls `_showAndroidTimePicker`:

```
async _showAndroidDatePicker () {
  const options = {
    date: this.state.date
  };

  const { action, year, month, day } = await
  DatePickerAndroid.open(options);

  if (action === DatePickerAndroid.dismissedAction) {
    return;
  }

  this.setState({
    day,
    month,
    year
  });

  this._showAndroidTimePicker();
}
```

The following is the same strategy we used with `_showAndroidDatePicker` before, but calls `_onDateChange` at the end:

```
async _showAndroidTimePicker () {
  const { action, minute, hour } = await TimePickerAndroid.open();

  if (action === TimePickerAndroid.dismissedAction) {
    return;
  }

  this.setState({
    hour,
    minute
  });

  this._onDateChange();
}
```

Create a new instance of the Date object using the five combined values that
DatePickerAndroid and TimePickerAndroid return:

```
...
_onDateChange () {
  const date = new Date(this.state.year, this.state.month,
  this.state.day, this.state.hour, this.state.minute);
  ...
}
...
}
```

I removed _getDatePickerHeight and _onExpand since they pertain to parts of
EditTask that are not available in the Android version of the app. I added some styling
changes to this component as well:

```
// Tasks/app/components/EditTask/styles.js

...
const styles = StyleSheet.create({
  androidButtonContainer: {
    flex: 1,
    maxHeight: 60,
    margin: 10
  },
  ...
  textInput: {
    height: 40,
    margin: 10,
    padding: 10
  }
});
```

Saving updates

As we aren't using a navigation bar with the Android version of the app, we should create a
Save button that handles the same save logic.

First, we should modify index.android.js to pass a saveCurrentEditedTask prop to
EditTask from the TasksList component:

```
// index.android.js

...
class Tasks extends Component {
```

```
...
_renderScene (route, navigator) {
  ...
  if (route.index === 1) {
    return (
      <EditTask
        ...
        saveCurrentEditedTask={ route.passProps
        .saveCurrentEditedTask }
        ...
      />
    )
  }
}
}
```

Then, modify `TasksList` to pass the `_saveCurrentEditedTask` method to `EditTask` in `_renderAndroidEditTaskComponent`:

```
// Tasks/app/components/TasksList/index.js

...
export default class TasksList extends Component {
  ...
  _renderAndroidEditTaskComponent (rowID) {
    this.props.navigator.push({
      ...
      passProps: {
        ...
        saveCurrentEditedTask: () =>
        this._saveCurrentEditedTask(rowID),
        ...
      }
    })
  }
  ...
}
```

After this, modify the Android version of `EditTask` to contain a new `Button` that calls its `saveCurrentEditedTask` when pressed:

```
// Tasks/app/components/EditTask/index.android.js

...
export default class EditTask extends Component {
  static propTypes = {
    ...
    saveCurrentEditedTask: PropTypes.func.isRequired,
```

```
    ...
  }

  render () {
    ...
    return (
      <View style={ styles.editTaskContainer }>
        ...
        <View style={ styles.saveButton }>
          <Button
            color={ '#4E92B5' }
            onPress={ () => this.props.saveCurrentEditedTask() }
            title={ 'Save Task' }
          />
        </View>
      </View>
    );
  }
  ...
}
```

Finally, add some styling with a new saveButton property:

```
// Tasks/app/components/EditTask/styles.js

import { Navigator, StyleSheet } from 'react-native';

const styles = StyleSheet.create({
  ...
  saveButton: {
    flex: 1,
    marginTop: 20,
    maxHeight: 70,
  },
  ...
});
```

BackAndroid

The last thing we need to handle is the back button. A universal back button, either a hardware or software implementation, is found on each Android device. We will need to use the BackAndroid API to detect back button presses and set our own custom functionality. If we don't do this, the back button will automatically close the app each time it is pressed.

To use it, we can add an event listener during the `componentWillMount` life cycle event that will pop the navigator when a back button press is detected. We can also remove the listener when the component is unmounted.

During `componentWillMount`, add an event listener to the `BackAndroid` API for a `hardwareButtonPress` event, firing `_backButtonPress` when triggered:

```
// Tasks/app/components/EditTask/index.android.js

...
import {
  BackAndroid,
  ...
} from 'react-native';
...
export default class EditTask extends Component {
  ...
  componentWillMount () {
    BackAndroid.addEventListener('hardwareButtonPress', () =>
    this._backButtonPress());
  }
```

Remove the same listener if the component is unmounted:

```
  componentWillUnmount () {
    BackAndroid.removeEventListener('hardwareButtonPress', () =>
    this._backButtonPress())
  }
```

Call `pop` on the navigator with `_backButtonPress`:

```
  ...
  _backButtonPress () {
    this.props.navigator.pop();
    return true;
  }
  ...
}
```

Summary

This was a long chapter! We accomplished a lot of things. First, we used `NavigatorIOS` to establish custom routes and created a component to edit a to-do item's details, including marking it as completed and adding a due date.

Then, we built a custom, reusable component with fluid animations to expand and collapse a child component, allowing `DatePickerIOS` to expand and collapse as needed. Afterward, we implemented logic to save the changes we make to a task using the navigation bar.

We also ported our app to support the Android operating system! We started by swapping out `NavigatorIOS` for `Navigator`, using the `Platform` API to trigger conditional logic depending on the type of mobile device our user is on, and creating iOS-and Android-specific components by appending `.android` and `.ios` to each index file.

We finished up the port to Android by rendering date and time pickers on Android, which are two separate popups, and creating a save button within our Android-specific `EditTask` component so that our users can save the changes they made. Finally, listening for back button presses with the `BackAndroid` API allowed our users to go back from editing a to-do item to the to-do list screen instead of leaving the app entirely.

3
Our Second Project - The Budgeting App

Staying within a monthly budget is something that I've found difficult to do in the past. For our second project, we will build an app that keeps track of our budget by letting us set a goal for how much we'd like to spend in a month, and then lets us enter expenses into the application and categorize them under simple labels. At any point, we can go and look at how we're doing for the month and look at our previous months' results.

In this chapter, we will cover the following topics:

- Planning our second app, `Expenses`
- Installing a popular vector icon library for React Native
- Building a series of helper methods that will be used throughout our app
- Creating a modal that lets us enter our expenses
- Rendering a list for the current month, showing the month's progress

Getting started

Like always, let's begin by initializing a new React Native project using the following statement in our command line:

```
react-native init Expenses
```

While the React Native CLI is doing its work in scaffolding our project, we should plan out the functionality of the app.

App planning

Once this app is complete, we would like for it to function in the following ways:

- Upon launching the app, if a budget for the month has not yet been set, it should ask the user to input their monthly goal and save it in `AsyncStorage`.
- Once a budget for the month has been set, the user should be shown a screen that contains a button to add their expenses for the month.
- Upon tapping on that button, the user should be shown a modal that allows them to input details for their expenses: the name, amount, date the purchase was made on, and an icon to categorize the item. The modal should allow the user to either cancel or save the entry that they make.
- If the expense is saved, it should then be rendered in a list on the main screen that contains the button to add further expenses.
- This list should also prominently display the user's set budget for the month along a progress indicator showing how close they are to hitting their budget.
- The app should also contain a second tab, where the user can view their previous months' histories.
- Users should be able to add expenses to any month and delete any expenses as well.

For the first part of this project, we'll tackle the top half of the list.

Let's start by installing the vector icon library as we'll be using it in this app.

Installing vector icons

One of the most popular vector icon packs for React Native is `react-native-vector-icons`. It includes a plethora of icons from different sources, including FontAwesome and Google's Material icons pack.

Installing this vector icons pack takes a couple of steps, but we'll start by pulling it down:

```
npm install react-native-vector-icons --save
```

This is now installed as a module, but we still need to link it to our project so that this app knows where to look for the files. This is because not every app we build will utilize all the native capabilities of the iOS and Android platforms. Including all the binaries to support every imaginable native capability will increase the size of our applications; instead, any components that rely on native iOS and Android code will have to be manually linked to our application, thus giving our application access to those pieces of code.

The simple way to link this vector icon library is with the following command line:

```
react-native link
```

The preceding command will automatically link libraries with native dependencies to your project.

Folder structure

The following structure includes components that we will wind up building in this very chapter:

```
|Expenses
|__app
|_____components
|_____AddExpenses
|_____AddExpensesModal
|_____CurrentMonthExpenses
|_____EnterBudget
|_____ExpandableCell
|_____ExpenseRow
|_____utils
|_____dateMethods.js
|_____storageMethods.js
|_____App.js
|_____styles.js
|__ios
|__index.ios.js
```

Utilities

The `utils` folder stores helper methods that we will be using in our application. The `dateMethods` deals with the different methods that we will use to get different parts of the date, while `storageMethods` handles access to `AsyncStorage`.

Our first bullet point from app planning says that upon launching the app, if a budget for this month has not yet been set, it should ask the user to input their monthly goal and save it into `AsyncStorage`.

Based on the preceding intent, we want to do the following things:

- Grab the current month and year
- Retrieve the object storing our expenses in `AsyncStorage` and check the month and year to check whether a budget has been set
- If it hasn't, then prompt the user to enter a budget for the month and save it into `AsyncStorage`

Let's create some helper methods that deal with the dates.

Date methods

These are the things that the `dateMethods.js` file should contain:

- An object that maps the number of the month to its name
- Four methods get different parts of the date. Each should accept an optional date object or create a new instance of the `Date` object if one is not passed in the following ones:
    - `getYear`: This grabs the year number and returns a stringified form of it
    - `getMonth`: This grabs the month number and returns a stringified form of it
    - `getDay`: This grabs the day number and returns a stringified form of it
    - `getMonthString`: This returns the name of the month using the object created previously

This is how my `dateMethods` file looks after completing the preceding bullet points. This is an object mapping month numbers to the stringified name of the month:

```
// Expenses/app/utils/dateMethods.js

const monthNames = {
    1: 'January',
    2: 'February',
    3: 'March',
    4: 'April',
    5: 'May',
    6: 'June',
    7: 'July',
    8: 'August',
```

```
  9: 'September',
 10: 'October',
 11: 'November',
 12: 'December'
}
```

The next one grabs the current year and returns it as a string:

```
export const getYear = (date) => {
  date = date || new Date();
  return date.getFullYear().toString();
}
```

This one gets the current month which is zero-indexed and returns which number it is:

```
export const getMonth = (date) => {
  date = date || new Date();
  const zeroIndexedMonth = date.getMonth();
  return (zeroIndexedMonth + 1).toString();
}
```

The following one gets the day and returns it as a string:

```
export const getDay = (date) => {
  date = date || new Date();
  return date.getDate().toString();
}
```

This one returns the name of the month, given its number:

```
export const getMonthString = (monthInt) => {
  if (typeof monthInt === 'string') {
    monthInt = parseInt(monthInt);
  }

  return monthNames[monthInt];
}
```

Now, it is time to create some methods to access AsyncStorage.

Storage methods

The `listOfExpenses` we will store in our application will be a multi-layered object.

Visually, we will build it to look like this:

```
listOfExpenses = {
  2017: {
    01: {
      budget: 500,
      expenses: [
        {
          amount: '4',
          category: 'Coffee',
          date: 'Jan 12, 2017'
          description: 'Latte @ Coffeeshop'
        },
        {
          amount: '1.50',
          category: 'Books',
          date: 'Jan 17, 2017'
          description: 'Sunday Newspaper'
        }
      ]
    }
  }
}
```

The methods we want to create for storage involve the following things:

- `getAsyncStorage`: This retrieves the list of expenses in `AsyncStorage`
- `setAsyncStorage`: This accepts an object and saves it into `AsyncStorage` as the list of expenses
- `checkCurrentMonth`: This lets us accept a month and year as stringified numbers and finds out whether a budget has been set for that given month and year, returning `false` if it has not, and the budget, if it has been set
- `saveMonthlyBudget`: This accepts a month and year as stringified numbers and a budget as a number, then creates that `month` object and stores it in the right year in our list of expenses, saving it to `AsyncStorage` at the end
- `saveExpenseToMonth`: This accepts a month and year as stringified numbers and a single `expense` object, then saves that to the budget for that month and year
- `resetAsyncStorage`: This is a development-specific method that will erase the data in `AsyncStorage` so that we can clear our list whenever we need to

- `logAsyncStorage`: This is another development-specific method to log the object currently stored in `AsyncStorage` so that we can view it whenever needed

Import the `AsyncStorage` API from React Native and the `dateMethods` utility file:

```
// Expenses/app/utils/storageMethods.js

import { AsyncStorage } from 'react-native';

import * as dateMethods from './dateMethods';
```

Grab the object in storage under the key `expenses` and return it:

```
export const getAsyncStorage = async () => {
  let response = await AsyncStorage.getItem('expenses');
  let parsedData = JSON.parse(response) || {};

  return parsedData;
}
```

Override the `expenses` object in storage with the object passed in as an argument:

```
export const setAsyncStorage = (expenses) => {
  return AsyncStorage.setItem('expenses', JSON.stringify(expenses));
}
```

Grab the `month` and `year` from `dateMethods`, then grab the `expenses` object in storage. If that object does not exist or does not have any data for the given `year` and/or `month`, return `false`, otherwise return the `budget`:

```
export const checkCurrentMonthBudget = async () => {
  let year = dateMethods.getYear();
  let month = dateMethods.getMonth();

  let response = await getAsyncStorage();

  if (response === null || !response.hasOwnProperty(year) ||
  !response[year].hasOwnProperty(month)) {
    return false;
  }

  return response[year][month].budget;
}
```

In `saveMonthlyBudget`, we grab the `expenses` object, then we check to see whether the result exists; this is so that we can seed `AsyncStorage` with a default empty object if we need to, which is important for a new user who hasn't entered data into the app before:

```
export const saveMonthlyBudget = async (month, year, budget) => {
  let response = await getAsyncStorage();

  if (!response.hasOwnProperty(year)) {
    response[year] = {};
  }

  if (!response[year].hasOwnProperty(month)) {
    response[year][month] = {
      budget: undefined,
      expenses: [],
      spent: 0
    }
  }

  response[year][month].budget = budget;

  await setAsyncStorage(response);

  return;
}
```

We also make checks along the way to see whether our `expenses` object has an object pertaining to the specific year passed to it, and then whether that `year` object has an object pointing to the specific `month` we're pointing to; if not, we create it. After setting up the `month` object with an entered `budget`, `expenses` array, and amount already `spent` (number defaulting to zero), we save it right back to `AsyncStorage`.

The following code calls `setAsyncStorage` and passes it an empty object, erasing the `expenses` object:

```
export const resetAsyncStorage = () => {
  return setAsyncStorage({});
}
```

Grab the `expenses` object in storage and log it to the console:

```
export const logAsyncStorage = async () => {
  let response = await getAsyncStorage();

  console.log('Logging Async Storage');
  console.table(response);
}
```

App.js and index.ios.js

App.js will serve as the initial route for our app's navigation. It will handle the logic that decides whether to show the current month's expenses or a prompt to enter a budget for the month.

The root index.ios.js file will be modified in the same way as we structured it in the first project of this book, Tasks:

```
// Expenses/index.ios.js

import React, { Component } from 'react';
import {
  AppRegistry,
  NavigatorIOS,
  StyleSheet
} from 'react-native';

import App from './app/App';

export default class Expenses extends Component {
  render() {
    return (
      <NavigatorIOS
        initialRoute={{
          component: App,
          title: 'Expenses'
        }}
        style={ styles.container }
      />
    );
  }
}

const styles = StyleSheet.create({
  container: {
    flex: 1,
  }
});

AppRegistry.registerComponent('Expenses', () => Expenses);
```

Now, let's create the `App.js` file and have it do the following things during its `componentDidMount` lifecycle:

- On load, we should use our `storageMethods` file to find out whether a budget has been set for the current month:
    - If the budget for the current month has been set, we should render it on the screen using a `Text` component for the user to see
    - If it has not been set, let's throw a basic alert stating the same for the user to see

This is how i built the `App` component:

```
// Expenses/app/App.js

import React, { Component } from 'react';

import styles from './styles';

import {
  Text,
  View
} from 'react-native';

import * as storageMethods from './utils/storageMethods';

export default class App extends Component {
  constructor (props) {
    super ();

    this.state = {
      budget: undefined
    }
  }
```

Check the current month's budget and set it in state. If there is no budget, alert the user:

```
async componentWillMount () {
    let response = await storageMethods.checkCurrentMonthBudget();

    if (response !== false) {
      this.setState({
        budget: response
      });

      return;
    }

    alert('You have not set a budget for this month!');
  }
```

Render a `Text` element that states the current month's budget, if set:

```
  render () {
    return (
      <View style={ styles.appContainer }>
        <Text>
          Your budget is { this.state.budget || 'not set' }!
        </Text>
      </View>
    )
  }
}
```

The `marginTop` property offsets the height of the navigation bar:

```
// Expenses/app/styles.js

import { Navigator, StyleSheet } from 'react-native';

const styles = StyleSheet.create({
  appContainer: {
    flex: 1,
    marginTop: Navigator.NavigationBar.Styles.General.TotalNavHeight
  }
});

export default styles;
```

Next, let's create a component that will let the user know their budget for the month.

The EnterBudget component

The component to enter a budget should do the following things:

- Prompt the user to enter their budget for the month with a numerical input
- Include a button that lets them save the budget. When saved, we will do the following things:
    - Have the parent App.js component use saveMonthlyBudget, created in our storageMethods file, to save the entered budget
    - Update the parent App.js component to reflect the entered budget
    - Pop out of the EnterBudget component and go back to the App.js component

We should also modify the App.js component so that it does the following things:

- Pushes the EnterBudget component to the navigator in the event that a budget has not been set. This should replace the current call to alert the user that they have not yet set a budget. This component should not contain a back button so that the user is required to enter a budget for the month.
- Passes the name of the current month in string form to the EnterBudget component.
- Stores the current month and year in numerical form in its local state so that it can refer to them when required
- Contains a method that updates itself with the new budget once the user saves a number in the EnterBudget component. This should be in the form of a prop passed into it.

Like always, spend some time building out this component yourself. When you're finished, keep reading and check out the solution I came up with.

EnterBudget component example

Building and linking this component involved changing the App.js file. Let's take a look at that one first since it passes props down to the EnterBudget component:

```
// Expenses/app/App.js

...
import EnterBudget from './components/EnterBudget';
```

```
export default class App extends Component {
  . . .
```

Set the `month` and `year` in state, then call `_updateBudget`:

```
componentWillMount () {
  this.setState({
    month: dateMethods.getMonth(),
    year: dateMethods.getYear()
  });

  this._updateBudget();
}
```

Push `EnterBudget` to the navigator and pass it two props. Hide the navigation bar so that the user cannot leave without entering a budget for the month:

```
  . . .
_renderEnterBudgetComponent () {
  this.props.navigator.push({
    component: EnterBudget,
    navigationBarHidden: true,
    passProps: {
      monthString: dateMethods.getMonthString( this.state.month),
      saveAndUpdateBudget: (budget) =>
      this._saveAndUpdateBudget(budget)
    }
  });
}
```

Save the budget into storage. The argument is passed from the `EnterBudget` component:

```
async _saveAndUpdateBudget (budget) {
  await storageMethods.saveMonthlyBudget(this.state.month,
  this.state.year, budget);

  this._updateBudget();
}
```

Previously found in `componentWillMount`, set the `budget` in state if it exists and render `EnterBudget` if it does not:

```
async _updateBudget () {
  let response = await storageMethods.checkCurrentMonthBudget();

  if (response !== false) {
    this.setState({
      budget: response
```

```
    });

    return;
  }

  this._renderEnterBudgetComponent();
  }
}
```

Next, let's take a look at the new `EnterBudget` component.

```
// Expenses/app/components/EnterBudget/index.js

import React, { Component, PropTypes } from 'react';

import {
  Text,
  TextInput,
  Button,
  View
} from 'react-native';

import styles from './styles';

import * as dateMethods from '../../utils/dateMethods';

export default class EnterBudget extends Component {
```

Explicitly define the `props` this component expects:

```
static propTypes = {
  monthString: PropTypes.string.isRequired,
  saveAndUpdateBudget: PropTypes.func.isRequired
}

 constructor (props) {
  super(props);

  this.state = {
    budget: undefined
  }
}
```

Store the value of the `TextInput` field in state. Prompt the user to enter their budget for the month with a numeric `TextInput`:

```
render () {
  let month = dateMethods.getMonthString(dateMethods.getMonth());

  return (
    <View style={ styles.enterBudgetContainer }>
      <Text style={ styles.enterBudgetHeader }>
        Enter Your { this.props.monthString } Budget
      </Text>
      <Text style={ styles.enterBudgetText }>
        What's your spending goal?
      </Text>
      <TextInput
        style={ styles.textInput }
        onChangeText={ (budget) => this._setBudgetValue(budget) }
        value={ this.state.budget }
        placeholder={ '0' }
        keyboardType={ 'numeric' }
      />
```

The `Button` calls `_saveAndUpdateBudget` on press and is disabled if `TextInput` is empty:

```
      <View>
        <Button
          color={ '#3D4A53' }
          disabled={ !this.state.budget }
          onPress={ () => this._saveAndUpdateBudget() }
          title={ 'Save Budget' }
        />
      </View>
    </View>
  )
}
```

The following code calls `saveAndUpdateBudget` from the `App` component and `pop` on the navigator:

```
_saveAndUpdateBudget () {
  this.props.saveAndUpdateBudget(this.state.budget);
  this.props.navigator.pop();
}
```

Finally, `_setBudgetValue` sets the value of the `TextInput`:

```
_setBudgetValue (budget) {
  this.setState({
    budget
  });
}
}
```

This component also received some styling shown as follows:

```
// Expenses/app/components/EnterBudget/styles.js

import { Navigator, StyleSheet } from 'react-native';

const styles = StyleSheet.create({
```

Like in the previous containers, we import `Navigator` so that we can offset the top margin by its `height`:

```
enterBudgetContainer: {
    flex: 1,
    marginTop: Navigator.NavigationBar.Styles.General.TotalNavHeight
},
```

Styling for the header, text, and input field in `EnterBudget` are as follows:

```
enterBudgetHeader: {
  color: '#3D4A53',
  fontSize: 24,
  margin: 10,
  textAlign: 'center'
},
enterBudgetText: {
  color: '#3D4A53',
  fontSize: 16,
  margin: 10,
  textAlign: 'center'
},
textInput: {
  height: 40,
  borderColor: '#86B2CA',
  borderWidth: 1,
  color: '#3D4A53',
  margin: 10,
  padding: 10,
  textAlign: 'center'
}
```

```
});

export default styles;
```

By the end of this section, you should have an `EnterBudget` component that looks like this:

Great job! In the next section, let's style `App.js` and add a button to open a modal.

The AddExpenses container and modal

When planning this app, I wrote that once a budget for the month has been set, the user should be shown a screen that contains a button to add their expenses for the month.

The button's behavior was also detailed, and we said that upon tapping on that button, the user should be shown a modal that allows them to input details for their expenses--the name, amount, date the purchase was made on, and an icon to categorize the item. The modal should allow the user to either cancel or save the entry they make.

We can create one component to add expenses that will contain both the `Button` and `Modal`, with the `Modal` defaulting to a hidden state unless activated by the `Button`.

Let's start by creating a component, titled `AddExpenses`, which will start off by doing the following things:

- Accepting the `month` and `year` as props
- Rendering a `Button` that, when pressed, will alert the user for now

Additionally, we should render the `AddExpenses` component within `App.js`:

```
// Expenses/app/components/AddExpenses/index.js

import React, { Component, PropTypes } from 'react';

import {
  Button,
  View
} from 'react-native';

export default class AddExpenses extends Component {
  static propTypes = {
    month: PropTypes.string.isRequired,
    year: PropTypes.string.isRequired
  }
```

The `Modal` we render will take advantage of these props. I also rendered a `Button` that will eventually launch this modal:

```
  constructor (props) {
    super (props);
  }

  render () {
    return (
      <View>
        <Button
          color={ '#86B2CA' }
          onPress={ () => alert('Add Expenses Button pressed!') }
          title={ 'Add Expense' }
        />
      </View>
    )
  }
}
```

These are the changes to the `App` component:

```
// Expenses/app/App.js

...
import AddExpenses from './components/AddExpenses';
...
export default class App extends Component {
  ...
  render () {
    return (
      <View style={ styles.appContainer }>
```

Pass in the `month` and `year` to `AddExpenses`:

```
        <AddExpenses
          month={ this.state.month }
          year={ this.state.year }
        />
      </View>
    )
  }
  ...
}
```

At this point, you should have a button rendered on the screen:

Great work! Next, we will create a modal that opens when the button is pressed.

Looking at modals

Modals let us present content over another view. In React Native, we can render one using the `Modal` tag. Any child elements within a `Modal` tag are rendered within it.

Modals have a couple of props that we can take advantage of. The ones listed as follows will be used in this project, though there are more available in the React Native documentation:

- `animationType`: This controls how a modal animates when it appears for the user. The three options are slide (from bottom), fade, and none.
- `onRequestClose`: This is a callback that is fired when a modal is dismissed.
- `transparent`: This is a Boolean that determines modal transparency.
- `visible`: This is a Boolean to determine whether a modal is visible.

Since this modal will encapsulate a large amount of logic, let's create a new `AddExpensesModal` component that will return this modal. It should do the following things:

- Contains a hidden `Modal` component that starts off hidden
- Accept the `month` and `year` props from the `AddExpenses` component
- Accept a `modalVisible` Boolean as a prop from `AddExpenses`
- Render a string with the current month and year

We should also update the existing `AddExpenses` component to do the following things:

- Render the `AddExpensesModal` component when the `AddExpenses` button is pressed, passing the `month`, `year`, and `modalVisible` props
- Modify the existing button to toggle the modal's visibility

Let's start by looking at `AddExpenses`:

```
// Expenses/app/components/AddExpenses/index.js

...
import AddExpensesModal from '../AddExpensesModal';

export default class AddExpenses extends Component {
  ...
```

```
constructor (props) {
  super (props);
```

Track the `modalVisible` Boolean in state:

```
this.state = {
  modalVisible: false
}
}
```

Render `AddExpensesModal`, passing it a Boolean for visibility, the `month`, and `year`:

```
render () {
  return (
    <View>
      <AddExpensesModal
        modalVisible={ this.state.modalVisible }
        month={ this.props.month }
        year={ this.props.year }
      />
```

Modify the `Button` to call `_toggleModal` instead of `alert`:

```
      <Button
        color={ '#86B2CA' }
        onPress={ () => this._toggleModal() }
        title={ 'Add Expense' }
      />
    </View>
  )
}
```

Flip the `modalVisible` Boolean in state:

```
_toggleModal () {
  this.setState({
    modalVisible: !this.state.modalVisible
  });
}
}
```

Here is how I built the `AddExpensesModal`:

```
// Expenses/app/components/AddExpensesModal/index.js

import React, { Component, PropTypes } from 'react';

import {
  Modal,
```

```
    Text,
    View
} from 'react-native';

import styles from './styles';

export default class AddExpensesModal extends Component {
```

Explicitly declare the expected `props` and their datatypes:

```
static propTypes = {
  modalVisible: PropTypes.bool.isRequired,
  month: PropTypes.string.isRequired,
  year: PropTypes.string.isRequired
}

constructor (props) {
  super (props);
}
```

Render a modal with a `slide` animation. Visibility is controlled by the `modalVisible` Boolean:

```
render () {
  return (
    <Modal
      animationType={ 'slide' }
      transparent={ false }
      visible={ this.props.modalVisible }
    >
```

Render a `View` with `Text` within the `Modal`:

```
      <View style={ styles.modalContainer }>
        <Text>
          This is a modal to enter your { this.props.month + ' ' +
          this.props.year } budget.
        </Text>
      </View>
    </Modal>
  )
}
}
```

This is the styling for `AddExpensesModal`:

```
// Expenses/app/components/AddExpensesModal/styles.js

import { Navigator, StyleSheet } from 'react-native';

const styles = StyleSheet.create({
  modalContainer: {
    flex: 1,
    marginTop: Navigator.NavigationBar.Styles.General.TotalNavHeight
  }
});

export default styles;
```

Header and TextInput fields

You may note that we currently don't have a way to close this modal or add any data to create new expenses for our list. Let's change that by adding the following things:

- A header that prompts the user to add an expense
- A normal `TextInput` field that prompts the user for the name of the expense
- A numeric `TextInput` field, set to a numeric keyboard, that prompts the user for the cost of the expense

Here are the changes I made to `AddExpensesModal`:

```
// Expenses/app/components/AddExpensesModal/index.js

...
import {
  ...
  TextInput,
  ...
} from 'react-native';
...
export default class AddExpensesModal extends Component {
...
```

Store the `amount` and `description` values for the two `TextInput` fields:

```
constructor (props) {
  super (props);

  this.state = {
```

```
        amount: '',
        description: '',
    }
}
```

The `render` method of `AddExpensesModal` wraps any components that the Modal displays as its children:

```
render () {
  return (
    <Modal
      animationType={ 'slide' }
      transparent={ false }
      visible={ this.props.modalVisible }
    >
      <View style={ styles.modalContainer }>
        <Text style={ styles.headerText }>
          Add an Expense
        </Text>
        <View style={ styles.amountRow }>
          <Text style={ styles.amountText }>
            Amount
          </Text>
```

Create the `TextInput` field specifically for numeric `amount` input:

```
          <TextInput
            keyboardType={ 'numeric' }
            onChangeText={ (value) => this._changeAmount(value) }
            placeholder={ '0' }
            style={ styles.amountInput }
            value={ this.state.amount }
          />
        </View>
```

Create the `TextInput` field specifically for the description:

```
        <Text style={ styles.descriptionText }>
          Description
        </Text>
        <TextInput
          onChangeText={ (value) => this._changeDescription(value) }
          placeholder={ 'Book on React Native development' }
          style={ styles.descriptionInput }
          value={ this.state.description }
        />
      </View>
    </Modal>
```

```
    )
  }
```

These two methods set the `amount` and `description` values in state:

```
  _changeAmount(amount) {
    this.setState({
      amount
    });
  }

  _changeDescription(description) {
    this.setState({
      description
    });
  }
}
```

New styling has also been added to this component:

```
// Expenses/app/components/AddExpensesModal/styles.js

...
const styles = StyleSheet.create({
```

The three amount-related styles are for the row where the `expense` amount is entered.

```
  amountInput: {
    borderColor: '#86B2CA',
    borderRadius: 10,
    borderWidth: 1,
    color: '#3D4A53',
    height: 40,
    margin: 10,
    padding: 10,
    width: 200
  },
```

The `amountRow` has a `justifyContent` property of `space-between` to evenly space the `Text` and `TextInput` components:

```
  amountRow: {
    flexDirection: 'row',
    justifyContent: 'space-between'
  },
  amountText: {
    color: '#3D4A53',
    margin: 10,
```

```
        marginLeft: 20,
        paddingTop: 10
    },
```

These styles deal with the `description` and `header` elements:

```
    descriptionInput: {
      borderColor: '#86B2CA',
      borderRadius: 10,
      borderWidth: 1,
      color: '#3D4A53',
      height: 40,
      margin: 10,
      padding: 10
    },
    descriptionText: {
      color: '#3D4A53',
      marginBottom: 5,
      marginLeft: 20,
      marginRight: 10,
      marginTop: 10
    },
    headerText: {
      color: '#7D878D',
      fontSize: 18,
      fontWeight: 'bold',
      marginBottom: 15,
      textAlign: 'center'
    },
    ...
});
```

Your `AddExpensesModal` should resemble something like this now:

DatePickerIOS plus ExpandableCell

In the next step, you should modify the AddExpensesModal component to contain the following things:

- A DatePickerIOS component that sets only the date--without time--the expense was made on. It should default to today's date if not specified:
  - You should import and wrap DatePickerIOS around the ExpandableCell component we built for Tasks.
- A line of text that explains the date on which the expense was made.

This is how I added ExpandableCell to AddExpensesModal:

```
// Expenses/app/components/AddExpensesModal/index.js

...
import {
  DatePickerIOS,
  ...
} from 'react-native';
```

```
import moment from 'moment';
import ExpandableCell from '../ExpandableCell';
...
export default class AddExpensesModal extends Component {
  ...
  constructor (props) {
    super (props);
```

Two new properties are now saved in state: the current `date` and the `expanded` Boolean:

```
this.state = {
  ...
  date: new Date(),
  expanded: false
}
}
```

There is no new code in the `ExpandableCell` module from Chapter 2, *Advanced Functionality and Styling the To-Do List App.*

```
render () {
  const expandableCellTitle = 'Date: ' + moment(this.state.date).
  format('ll') + ' (tap to change)';

  return (
    <Modal
      animationType={ 'slide' }
      transparent={ false }
      visible={ this.props.modalVisible }
    >
      ...
        <View style={ [styles.expandableCellContainer,
        { maxHeight: this.state.expanded ?
        this.state.datePickerHeight : 40 }]}>
```

Placement of the `ExpandableCell` component comes right after the `TextInput` for the expense's description:

```
<ExpandableCell
  expanded={ this.state.expanded }
  onPress={ () => this._onExpand() }
  title={ expandableCellTitle }>
```

The `DatePickerIOS` component's `mode` is set to `date` so that time cannot be selected:

```
<DatePickerIOS
  date={ this.state.date }
  mode={ 'date' }
```

```
          onDateChange={ (date) => this._onDateChange(date) }
          onLayout={ (event) => this._getDatePickerHeight(event)
          }
        />
      </ExpandableCell>
    </View>
  </View>
  </Modal>
)
}
```

The logic to get the height of DatePickerIOS is unchanged from, Chapter 2: *Advanced Functionality and Styling the To-Do List App*:

```
...
_getDatePickerHeight (event) {
  this.setState({
    datePickerHeight: event.nativeEvent.layout.width
  });
}
```

Three new methods can be found in this component, all of which are reused from our earlier project, Tasks, handled by the ExpandableCell and its DatePickerIOS child.

```
_onDateChange (date) {
  this.setState({
    date
  });
}

_onExpand () {
  this.setState({
    expanded: !this.state.expanded
  });
}
}
```

Styling for this component involves just one new property:

```
// Expenses/app/components/AddExpensesModal/styles.js

expandableCellContainer: {
    flex: 1
},
```

By this point, your app will look like the following screenshot:

Great job with the updates! The AddExpensesModal will end up with a lot of fields for the user to interact with.

You may have noted that the keyboard does not dismiss itself when ExpandableCell is interacted with, which can lead to information that the user is unable to access.

It's time to look at the ScrollView component to learn how to dismiss the keyboard.

ScrollView

By default, the *return* key on the software keyboard handles a dismiss action for our apps. However, a *return* key does not exist on a numeric keyboard. Instead, we can replace our top-level View with the ScrollView component.

The ScrollView component wraps around the rest of your component, providing scrolling capabilities.

An important thing to know is that ScrollView requires all its children to have a height property in its styling. If it does not have one, then the child element will not render.

Let's quickly replace the View that AddExpensesModal encapsulates around its Modal component with a ScrollView.

ScrollView example

This is how I updated AddExpensesModal to include a ScrollView:

```
// Expenses/app/components/AddExpensesModal/index.js

...
import {
  ...
  ScrollView,
  ...
} from 'react-native';
...
export default class AddExpensesModal extends Component {
  ...
```

Replace the modal's View with ScrollView. The maxHeight of the View inside is now height:

```
render () {
  ...
  return (
    <Modal
      animationType={ 'slide' }
      transparent={ false }
      visible={ this.props.modalVisible }
    >
      <ScrollView style={ styles.modalContainer }>
        ...
        <View style={ [styles.expandableCellContainer,
          { height: this.state.expanded ?
          this.state.datePickerHeight : 40 }]}>
          ...
        </View>
      </ScrollView>
    </Modal>
  )
}
```

The outer `View` container that was the direct child of the `Modal` component has been swapped out with a `ScrollView`.

The `maxHeight` property in the `View` that encapsulates `ExpandableCell` has been changed into a `height` property so that it renders in the `ScrollView`.

Saving expenses

The next step is to allow entries to be saved to the app. Let's modify `AddExpensesModal` again and add the following features; you will also need to add some methods into `storageMethods` as well as the `AddExpenses` component:

- A button to save the expense, with the following conditions:
    - It should only be enabled if all the fields of the modal are filled out.
    - When pressed, the expense name, amount, and date should be saved into `AsyncStorage`.
    - The date should be formatted with Moment the same way we formatted it for the `ExpandableCell` title.
    - When this logic finishes, the modal should be closed and the information entered should be cleared. The closing of the modal should be passed in as a prop from the parent `AddExpenses` component since it already has a method to toggle the modal:
        - A new helper method in `storageMethods` should be created to handle the logic of saving an expense into `AsyncStorage`.
        - Another helper method in `storageMethods` should be written to tally each expense for the month and set it to the `spent` property of that specific month. It should be fired when a new expense is added to the month's `expenses` array, and then modify that month's `spent` property with the tally before the expense is saved into `AsyncStorage`.
        - Another button to cancel the expense, closing the `AddExpensesModal` and clearing any information previously entered. It should also have access to the same method from `AddExpenses` to toggle the modal.

As a reminder, earlier in the chapter, we visualized a single object in our list of expenses to be structured in the following way:

```
{
  amount: '4',
  category: 'Coffee',
  date: 'Jan 12, 2017'
  description: 'Latte @ Coffeeshop'
},
```

Do not worry about the `category` key for now; that will come in the next chapter.

The first thing I did was go to `storageMethods` and create two new methods: `getTotalSpentForMonth` and `saveItemToBudget`. The first function, `getTotalSpentForMonth`, takes in an array and iterates through it. It returns the total amount spent by converting the strings to numbers with `parseInt`:

```
// Expenses/app/utils/storageMethods.js

...
const getTotalSpentForMonth = (array) => {
  let total = 0;

  array.forEach((elem) => {
    total += parseInt(elem.amount)
  });

  return total;
}
```

The second function, `saveItemToBudget`, is an asynchronous one and starts by taking in the `month`, `year`, and `expenseObject` as arguments:

```
export const saveItemToBudget = async (month, year, expenseObject)
=> {
  let response = await getAsyncStorage();

  let newExpensesArray = [
    ...response[year][month].expenses,
    expenseObject
  ];

  let newTotal = getTotalSpentForMonth(newExpensesArray);
```

```
      response[year][month].expenses = newExpensesArray;
      response[year][month].spent = newTotal;

      await setAsyncStorage(response);

      return true;
   }
   ...
```

It grabs the `expenses` object stored in `AsyncStorage`, creates a new array with the array spread operator (`...`) to add the new `expenseObject` argument to it, and then calls `getTotalSpentForMonth` with the new array.

Afterwards, it assigns the new array to the `expenses` property for the month and the total is calculated as the new total amount spent. Finally, it saves it to `AsyncStorage`.

The next file I modified was `AddExpenses`:

```
// Expenses/app/components/AddExpenses/index.js

...
export default class AddExpenses extends Component {
  ...
  render () {
    return (
      <View>
        <AddExpensesModal
          modalVisible={ this.state.modalVisible }
          month={ this.props.month }
          toggleModal={ () => this._toggleModal() }
          year={ this.props.year }
        />
        ...
      </View>
    )
  }
  ...
}
```

In the preceding code, I'm passing `_toggleModal` into the `AddExpensesModal` component so that it can toggle the modal between its visible and invisible states.

```
// Expenses/app/components/AddExpensesModal/index.js

...
import {
  Button,
```

```
  ...
} from 'react-native';

...

export default class AddExpensesModal extends Component {
  static propTypes = {
    ...
    toggleModal: PropTypes.func.isRequired,
  }
  ...
  render () {
    ...
    return (
      <Modal
        ...
      >
```

The two `Buttons` are rendered after the `View` that encapsulates `ExpandableCell`. The **Save** button is disabled unless each field contains a value:

```
        <ScrollView style={ styles.modalContainer }>
          ...
          <Button
            color={ '#86B2CA' }
            disabled={ !(this.state.amount && this.state.description) }
            onPress={ () => this._saveItemToBudget() }
            title={ 'Save Expense' }
          />
          <Button
            color={ '#E85C58' }
            onPress={ () => this._clearFieldsAndCloseModal() }
            title={ 'Cancel' }
          />
        </ScrollView>
      </Modal>
    )
  }
  ...
```

The following code sets the `amount` and `description` values to empty strings, clearing them:

```
_clearFieldsAndCloseModal () {
  this.setState({
    amount: '',
    description: ''
  });
```

The following code creates an `expense` object and calls `saveItemToBudget` from `storageMethods`, passing it in. Then, it clears the `amount` and `description`:

```
...
async _saveItemToBudget () {
  const expenseObject = {
    amount: this.state.amount,
    date: moment(this.state.date).format('ll'),
    description: this.state.description
  };
  let month = this.state.date.getMonth() + 1;
  let year = this.state.date.getFullYear();
  await storageMethods.saveItemToBudget(month, year,
  expenseObject);

  this._clearFieldsAndCloseModal();
  }
}
```

By this point, your `AddExpensesModal` should be nearly complete:

Good job on your progress! Let's switch gears and begin to address the rendering of our month's expenses. We will revisit this component in the next chapter so that we can add the functionality of categorizing expenses by icons.

Displaying the current month's expenses

The next feature we wrote about earlier in this chapter was that if the expense is saved, it should then be rendered in a list on the main screen that contains the button to add further expenses.

In this section, we will create that list. We should create a component called CurrentMonthExpenses and make modifications to the existing files to support it.

You should add a new function to storageMethods that accepts a month and year, returning the budget, list of expenses, and the amount spent for that month and year.

The CurrentMonthExpenses component should do the following things:

- Render a header that shows the current month's name and budget.
- Display a ListView of the month's expenses, retrieved from AsyncStorage, with some styling and formatting. At the very least, it should include the description of the expense as well as the dollar amount.
    - The ListView being rendered should be its own component so that we can reuse it in the next chapter for the prior months.
    - The rows being rendered in the ListView should be written as its component as well.

Then, your App.js file should do the following things:

- Render CurrentMonthExpenses right before the AddExpenses component.
- Load this list when the component is mounted.
- Update ListView in CurrentMonthExpenses when a new expense has been added by AddExpenses.

As a result, you may need to modify AddExpenses to do as follows:

- Accept a callback as a prop that will propagate up to App.js when the modal is toggled.

When you have finished the preceding procedure, come back and check out the code I wrote.

CurrentMonthExpenses example

The first thing I did was add and export a function called `getMonthObject` into `storageMethods.js`:

```
// Expenses/app/utils/storageMethods.js

...
export const getMonthObject = async (month, year) => {
  let response = await getAsyncStorage();

  if (response[year] && response[year][month]) {
    return response[year][month];
  }
}
...
```

The `getMonthObject` method grabs the `expenses` object from `AsyncStorage`, checks for the existence of the `year` and `month` object, then returns it if possible. Here is how I used that method within the new `currentMonthExpenses` component:

```
// Expenses/app/components/CurrentMonthExpenses/index.js

import React, { Component, PropTypes } from 'react';

import {
  ListView,
  Text,
  View
} from 'react-native';

import styles from './styles';
import * as dateMethods from '../../utils/dateMethods';
import * as storageMethods from '../../utils/storageMethods';

import ExpenseRow from '../ExpenseRow';

export default class CurrentMonthExpenses extends Component {
  static propTypes = {
    budget: PropTypes.string.isRequired,
    expenses: PropTypes.array.isRequired,
    month: PropTypes.string.isRequired,
    spent: PropTypes.number.isRequired,
```

```
    year: PropTypes.string.isRequired,
  }
```

I start by setting up a `ListView.DataSource` instance in anticipation of the `ListView` being rendered:

```
constructor (props) {
  super (props);

  this.state = {
    ds: new ListView.DataSource({
      rowHasChanged: (r1, r2) => r1 !== r2
    }),
  }
}
```

The `render` method of `CurrentMonthExpenses` creates a header for our `month` and `budget`, then creates a `ListView`. This `ListView` is also using the `renderSeparator` prop, which renders a horizontal line to separate the items on the list.

```
render () {
  const dataSource = this.state.ds.cloneWithRows
  (this.props.expenses || []);
```

Data pertaining to the `expenses` array and `budget` are obtained as props passed down to this component from its parent, `App.js`:

```
return (
  <View style={ styles.currentMonthExpensesContainer }>
    <View style={ styles.currentMonthExpensesHeader }>
      <Text style={ styles.headerText }>
        Your { dateMethods.getMonthString(this.props.month)
        + ' ' + this.props.year } budget:
      </Text>
      <Text style={ styles.subText }>
        { this.props.budget }
      </Text>
    </View>
    <ListView
      automaticallyAdjustContentInsets={ false }
      dataSource={ dataSource }
      enableEmptySections={ true }
      renderRow={ (rowData, sectionID, rowID) =>
        this._renderRowData(rowData, rowID) }
      renderSeparator={ (sectionID, rowID) =>
        this._renderRowSeparator(sectionID, rowID) }
    />
  </View>
```

```
    )
  }
```

The `_renderRowData` function renders a single expense row using the `ExpenseRow` component, which we will look at in the following section. Then, `_renderRowSeparator` returns a simple view that contains a style for the separator. Check this out here:

```
  _renderRowData (rowData, rowID) {
    if (rowData) {
      return (
        <ExpenseRow
          amount={ rowData.amount }
          description={ rowData.description }
        />
      )
    }
  }

  _renderRowSeparator (sectionID, rowID) {
    return (
      <View
        key={ rowID }
        style={ styles.rowSeparator }
      />
    )
  }
};
```

This is the styling for `CurrentMonthExpenses`:

```
// Expenses/app/components/CurrentMonthExpenses/styles.js

import { StyleSheet } from 'react-native';

const styles = StyleSheet.create({
  currentMonthExpensesContainer: {
    flex: 1,
  },
  currentMonthExpensesHeader: {
    height: 80,
  },
  headerText: {
    color: '#7D878D',
    fontSize: 24,
    marginBottom: 10,
    marginTop: 10,
    textAlign: 'center'
  },
```

```
    rowSeparator: {
      backgroundColor: '#7D878D',
      flex: 1,
      height: StyleSheet.hairlineWidth,
      marginLeft: 15,
      marginRight: 15
    },
    subText: {
      color: '#3D4A53',
      fontSize: 18,
      fontWeight: 'bold',
      textAlign: 'center'
    },
});

export default styles;
```

Styling is standard for our component, though `rowSeparator` is a new one. The `height` for this component is set to the `hairlineWidth` property of the `StyleSheet`. This is how we render the thin line that separates each individual row in a `ListView`.

```
// Expenses/app/components/ExpenseRow/index.js

import React from 'react';

import {
  Text,
  View
} from 'react-native';

import styles from './styles';

export default (props) => {
  return (
    <View style={ styles.expenseRowContainer }>
      <Text style={ styles.descriptionText }>
        { props.description }
      </Text>
      <Text style={ styles.amountText }>
        { props.amount }
      </Text>
    </View>
  )
}
```

This syntax might look new to you, and it's worth taking a moment to cover it. What you are seeing here is a **stateless functional component**. It is a function that takes in any number of props passed into it, and returns a component that can be used in React applications.

The reason `ExpenseRow` is being written as a stateless functional component is because we don't intend on adding any heavy logic to it or using any React life cycle events.

There are two big changes to the `render` method of `App.js`: First, we are rendering `CurrentMonthExpenses` prior to `AddExpenses` and, second, we are passing a callback to `AddExpenses`, titled `updateCurrentMonthExpenses`, pointing to the similarly named `_updateCurrentMonthExpenses` method in this component. We will look at that one shortly:

```
// Expenses/app/App.js

...
import CurrentMonthExpenses from './components/CurrentMonthExpenses';
...
export default class App extends Component {
  ...
  render () {
    return (
      <View style={ styles.appContainer }>
        <CurrentMonthExpenses
          budget={ this.state.budget || '0' }
          expenses={ this.state.expenses }
          month={ this.state.month }
          spent={ this.state.spent || 0 }
          year={ this.state.year }
        />
        <AddExpenses
          month={ this.state.month }
          updateCurrentMonthExpenses={ () =>
          this._updateCurrentMonthExpenses() }
          year={ this.state.year }
        />
      </View>
    )
  }
}
```

The main change to `_updateBudget` is that we are firing `_updateCurrentMonthExpenses` so that when the app is opened by the user, we can populate the list of expenses:

```
...
async _updateBudget () {
  let response = await storageMethods.checkCurrentMonthBudget();

  if (response !== false) {
    this.setState({
      budget: response
    });

    this._updateCurrentMonthExpenses();
    return;
  }

  this._renderEnterBudgetComponent();
}
```

The following is the function that does the bulk of the legwork. As an asynchronous function, it starts using the getMonthObject function from storageMethods that we built earlier in this section and then checks to see whether it exists. If it does, then it will set the budget, expenses array, and amount spent to state. This in turn triggers a re-render, passing any changed values down to the CurrentMonthExpenses component.

```
async _updateCurrentMonthExpenses () {
  let responseObject = await
  storageMethods.getMonthObject(this.state.month, this.state.year);

  if (responseObject) {
    this.setState({
      budget: responseObject.budget,
      expenses: responseObject.expenses,
      spent: responseObject.spent
    });
  }
}
}
```

In the AddExpense component, the _toggleModal method now fires the updateCurrentMonthExpenses callback so that when the modal is toggled, the most up-to-date list of expenses is passed to the CurrentMonthExpenses component:

```
// Expenses/app/components/AddExpense/index.js

...
export default class AddExpenses extends Component {
  static propTypes = {
    ...
    updateCurrentMonthExpenses: PropTypes.func.isRequired
```

```
    }
    ...
    _toggleModal (boolean) {
       this.setState({
          modalVisible: !this.state.modalVisible
       });
       this.props.updateCurrentMonthExpenses();
    }
 }
```

Here is how the `CurrentExpenses` modal should now look:

Great job on your progress so far! This is just the beginning of how we will build this app, and we will do even more in the next chapter.

Summary

In this chapter, we started building our budgeting app. We installed a popular vector icon library, discovered how to link that library to our project in Xcode, and then wrote a basic version of our app.

This included a basic helper library that managed date methods and another to manage storage.

In the app, we created a prompt for the user to enter their budget for the month and ensured that it collected this data before letting them proceed to add in expenses. Then, we used a modal to show and hide the fields for a user to add a new expense into the app and updated the `ListView` component to reflect the newly added expense.

The next chapter will get more advanced. We will finally put that vector icon library to good use by letting the user categorize their expenses by icon, and then let them look at the past months' data by creating a second section of our app, which is controlled by a tab bar. Additionally, we will create a progress view to track the total amount already spent by the user for the month, so that they can track their spending better.

4
Advanced Functionality with the Expenses App

In the last chapter, we began working on an expense tracking app simply titled `Expenses`. After getting some basic functionality written for the app, our next goal is to continue working on the app and add new features to it that will make the app feature-complete. This chapter will cover the following topics:

- Utilizing the `react-native-vector-icons` library to utilize icons in our app
- Learning how to use the `Picker` component to render a dropdown, such as an interface that can accept any array of items for user selection
- Updating our list view to show the expense category icons and show the current amount spent with a progress bar
- Creating a second view that renders the previous months' expenses
- Using the `Icon.TabBarIOS` component to toggle between the current month's and the previous month's view
- Allowing deletion of added expenses for both the current month and the previous ones

 Due to the extensive features in this chapter, the section on making modifications for this app to run on an Android device has been moved to `Chapter 9`, *Additional React Native Components*.

Using vector icons

In Chapter 3, *Our Second Project - The Budgeting App*, we mentioned that upon tapping that button, the user should be shown a modal that allows them to input details for their expenses: the name, amount, date the purchase was made on, and an icon to categorize the item. The modal should `allow` the user to either cancel or save the entry they make.

For our first exercise, we should do the following things:

- Begin by writing a utilities file for handling icons:
  - This file should contain an object that contains the stringified names of categories and their icon names from our vector icon library.
  - This file should also contain a method that takes in the name, desired size, and color of an icon and returns that icon as a component. Treat this as a stateless functional component.

Let's look at how we can utilize the vector icon library that we installed in the last chapter.

We can import `react-native-vector-icons` with the following statement:

```
import Icon from '
react-native-vector-icons/FontAwesome';
```

This maps a reference of `Icon` to a component that uses the Font Awesome icon set.

To utilize it, you can render an `Icon` component like this:

```
<Icon name="rocket" size={ 30 } color="#900" />
```

The `name` property tells the library which icon to pull from its collection. You can find a list of all the icons that Font Awesome contains at `http://fontawesome.io`.

Our app will contain the following 12 icons:

- `home`
- `shopping-cart`
- `cutlery`
- `film`
- `car`
- `coffee`
- `plane`

- shopping-bag
- book
- beer
- gamepad
- plug

The categories that these icons represent will be (in order) the following ones:

- Home
- Grocery
- Restaurant
- Entertainment
- Car
- Coffee
- Travel
- Shopping
- Books
- Drinks
- Hobby
- Utilities

With these in mind, we should create a helper file that will let us render an icon.

Icon methods

The `iconMethods` file will be a lot simpler than our previous helper methods. With `iconMethods`, our goal is to keep an object that maps category names and icons and then, export a function that will help us return the `react-native-vector-icon` components.

```
import React from 'react';

import Icon from 'react-native-vector-icons/FontAwesome';

const expenses = [
  { amount: '4', category: 'coffee', description: 'Latte' },
  { amount: '1.50', category: 'books', description: 'Sunday Paper' },
  { amount: '35', category: 'car', description: 'Gas' },
  { amount: '60', category: 'restaurant', description: 'Steak dinner' }
];
```

The `categories` object lets us quickly access both the category and icon name:

```
export const getIconComponent = (categoryName, size, color) => {
  return (
    <Icon
      name={ categories[categoryName].iconName }
      size={ size || 30 }
      color={ color || '#3D4A53' }
    />
  );
}
```

Here, we have a stateless function, `getIconComponent`, that accepts the `name` of a category along with an optional `size` and `color`, then returns an `Icon` component for our app.

Now that we have our `iconMethods` file built out, it's time to create a `Picker` component to select a category.

Picker

So far in this book, we have used `DatePickerIOS` and `DatePickerAndroid` for users to select dates. Each platform also has access to a native `Picker` component, where we can populate an array of choices and allow our users to interact with it.

Building a `Picker` is easy. We start by writing a `Picker` in the `render` method of a component and populate it with `Picker.Item` children:

```
<Picker>
  <Picker.Item
    label='Hello'
    value='hello'
  />
</Picker>
```

Then, we can give the `Picker` some props. The following ones are used in this exercise:

- `onValueChange`: This is a callback fired when an item has been selected. It passes two arguments: `itemValue` and `itemPosition`
- `selectedValue`: This is a reference to the current value of the `Picker` list

Selecting a category

We will modify our existing `AddExpensesModal` component to add the following functionality:

- Create a `Button` right below the `ExpandableCell/DatePickerIOS` component to select a category for our expense.
- On press, that button should render a `Picker` component for the user to interact with. This `Picker` should have the following features:
  - Contain the list of twelve categories that we are using in our app as `Picker` items by mapping the array instead of hardcoding each of the twelve categories.
  - Have a callback that sets the selected value as the selected category for our expense. Next:
    - Render this `Picker` as a child of an `ExpandableCell` component within `AddExpensesModal` so that it can be collapsed when not in use.
    - Render the preceding `ExpandableCell` component between the date and save/cancel buttons within `AddExpensesModal`.
    - Use the `getIconComponent` function from `iconMethods` to render the selected category's icon, if applicable, and style it so that it appears on the page in the same row as the `ExpandableCell` for our `Picker` component.
    - Modify `AddExpensesModal` so that its submit button is also disabled if a category has not been set by the user.

The `AddExpensesModal` component and its styles underwent a significant number of changes since the last time we looked at them in the last chapter.

```
// Expenses/app/components/AddExpensesModal/index.js

...
import {
  ...
  Picker,
  ...
} from 'react-native';
...
import * as iconMethods from '../../utils/iconMethods';
...
export default class AddExpensesModal extends Component {
  ...
  constructor (props) {
    super (props);

    this.state = {
      amount: '',
      category: undefined,
      categoryPickerExpanded: false,
      date: new Date(),
      description: '',
      datePickerExpanded: false
    }
  }
```

The `expanded` key is replaced by two separate Booleans for each `ExpandableCell`.

The `expandableCellTitle` is replaced by one string for each `ExpandableCell`:

```
render () {
  const expandableCellDatePickerTitle = ...
  const expandableCellCategoryPickerTitle = 'Category: ' +
    (this.state.category ? iconMethods.categories
    [this.state.category].name : 'None (tap to change)')
```

The rendering of the original `ExpandableCell` has been modified to accommodate the changes in variable and function names to make it more specific to its child component:

```
return (
  <Modal
    animationType={ 'slide' }
    transparent={ false }
    visible={ this.props.modalVisible }
  >
```

```
<ScrollView style={ styles.modalContainer }>
  ...
  <View style={ [styles.expandableCellContainer,
  { height: this.state.datePickerExpanded ? this.state.
  datePickerHeight : 40 }]}>
    <ExpandableCell
      expanded={ this.state.datePickerExpanded }
      onPress={ () => this._onDatePickerExpand() }
      title={ expandableCellDatePickerTitle }>
      <DatePickerIOS
        date={ this.state.date }
        mode={ 'date' }
        onDateChange={ (date) => this._onDateChange(date) }
        onLayout={ (event) => this._getDatePickerHeight(event)
        }
      />
    </ExpandableCell>
  </View>
  <View style={ [styles.expandableCellContainer,
  { height: this.state.categoryPickerExpanded ? 200 : 40 }]}>
    <View style={ styles.categoryIcon }>
      { this.state.category && iconMethods.
      getIconComponent(this.state.category) }
    </View>
```

This is the newly-added `ExpandableCell` component, rendering a `Picker` underneath it:

```
    <ExpandableCell
      expanded={ this.state.categoryPickerExpanded }
      onPress={ () => this._onCategoryPickerExpand() }
      title={ expandableCellCategoryPickerTitle }>
        <Picker
        onValueChange={ (value, index) =>
        this._setItemCategory(value) }
        selectedValue={ this.state.category }>
        { this._renderCategoryPicker() }
      </Picker>
    </ExpandableCell>
  </View>
```

The `Button` component used to save an expense has been modified to check for the presence of a category to allow its saving:

```
<Button
  color={ '#86B2CA' }
  disabled={ !(this.state.amount &&
  this.state.description && this.state.category) }
  onPress={ () => this._saveItemToBudget() }
  title={ 'Save Expense' }
/>
  ...
  </ScrollView>
  </Modal>
)
}
```

The `_clearFieldsAndCloseModal` method has been updated for the new fields:

```
...
_clearFieldsAndCloseModal () {
  this.setState({
    amount: '',
    category: undefined,
    categoryPickerExpanded: false,
    date: new Date(),
    datePickerExpanded: false,
    description: ''
  });

  this.props.toggleModal()
}
```

The `_onDatePickerExpand` method is just a renaming of the old `_onExpand` method, while `_onCategoryPickerExpand` is specific to the `Picker` category:

```
...
_onCategoryPickerExpand () {
  this.setState({
    categoryPickerExpanded: !this.state.categoryPickerExpanded
  })
}

_onDatePickerExpand () {
  this.setState({
    datePickerExpanded: !this.state.datePickerExpanded
  });
}
```

Render each `Picker.Item` by mapping the array of category names to a new element:

```
_renderCategoryPicker () {
  var categoryNames = Object.keys(iconMethods.categories);

  return categoryNames.map((elem, index) => {
    return (
      <Picker.Item
        key={ index }
        label={ iconMethods.categories[elem].name }
        value={ elem }
      />
    )
  })
}
```

The `_setItemCategory` function is fired in the `onValueChange` callback of our `Picker` category:

```
_setItemCategory (category) {
  this.setState({
    category
  });
}
```

Save the `category` property to storage as part of `_saveItemToBudget`:

```
async _saveItemToBudget () {
  const expenseObject = {
    amount: this.state.amount,
    category: this.state.category,
    date: moment(this.state.date).format('ll'),
    description: this.state.description
  };

  await storageMethods.saveItemToBudget(this.props.month,
  this.props.year, expenseObject);

  this._clearFieldsAndCloseModal();
  }
}
```

This is how the new `Picker` component should look:

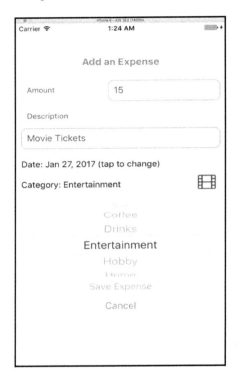

I added styling for `categoryIcon`:

```
// Expenses/app/components/AddExpensesModal/styles.js

import { Dimensions, Navigator, StyleSheet } from 'react-native';

const styles = StyleSheet.create({
  ...
  categoryIcon: {
    flex: 1,
    marginLeft: Dimensions.get('window').width - 50,
    position: 'absolute'
  },
```

The preceding code uses the `Dimensions` API to set `marginLeft` to the width of the screen minus `50` pixels.

```
  ...
  expandableCellContainer: {
    flex: 1,
    flexDirection: 'row'
  },
  ...
});

export default styles;
```

The preceding code has updated styling to contain a `flexDirection` of `row`.

Updating CurrentMonthExpenses and ExpenseRow

Up to this point, we have been rendering the `CurrentMonthExpenses` and `ExpenseRow` components without a category as one did not exist previously. Let's update them with the following goals in mind:

- `CurrentMonthExpenses` should access each item's category and pass it to `ExpenseRow`
- `ExpenseRow` should render the appropriate category's assigned icon in the row of expenses so that our users can quickly visualize what it is that they spent part of their budget on

- We should use the `resetAsyncStorage` method created in `StorageMethods` to clear any current list of expenses before modifying `ExpenseRow` so that the previous expenses without a category assigned will not cause any issues

Once you have updated these components, check out my solution, which is as follows:

```
// Expenses/app/App.js

...
export default class App extends Component {
  ...
  componentWillMount () {
    storageMethods.resetAsyncStorage();
    ...
  }
```

```
    . . .
}
```

The preceding code used one time (and not saved in the file afterwards) to clear storage.

Then, I updated the `CurrentMonthExpenses` component to pass in the `category` an expense was assigned as a prop to the `ExpenseRow` component:

```
// Expenses/app/components/CurrentMonthExpenses/index.js

. . .
export default class CurrentMonthExpenses extends Component {
  . . .
  _renderRowData (rowData, rowID) {
    if (rowData) {
      return (
        <ExpenseRow
          amount={ rowData.amount }
          category={ rowData.category }
          description={ rowData.description }
        />
      )
    }
  }
  . . .
};
```

After that, I created a new `View` to render the category icon:

```
// Expenses/app/components/ExpenseRow/index.js

. . .
import * as iconMethods from '../../utils/iconMethods';
. . .
export default (props) => {
  return (
    <View style={ styles.expenseRowContainer }>
      <View style={ styles.icon }>
        { iconMethods.getIconComponent(props.category) }
      </View>
      . . .
    </View>
  )
}
```

For styling, the following `icon` property was added:

```
// Expenses/app/components/ExpenseRow/styles.js

const styles = StyleSheet.create({
  ...
  icon: {
    flex: 1,
    marginLeft: 10
  }
});
```

Here is how your app should look after icons have been added:

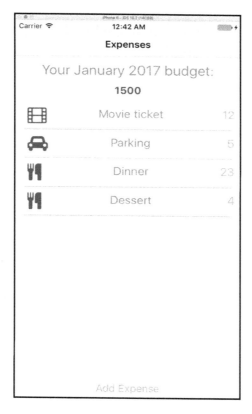

Great job on the updates! In the next section, we should give the user a visualization of their remaining budget using a progress indicator.

Updating App.js with ProgressViewIOS

When planning this app in the last chapter, we wrote that this list should also prominently display the user's set budget for the month along with a progress indicator showing how close they are to hitting their budget.

Using `ProgressViewIOS`, we can depict our user's progress toward their monthly limit. The following props will be used in this project:

- `progress`: This is a number between 0 and 1 that tracks the value of the progress bar
- `progressTintColor`: This is a string that sets the color of the progress bar

You can render a `ProgressViewIOS` component like this:

```
<View>
  <ProgressViewIOS
    progress={ 0.75 }
    progressTintColor={ '#86B2CA' }
  />
</View>
```

In this section, we should update `Expenses` to do the following things:

- First, we should modify the `checkCurrentMonthBudget` function from `storageMethods` to also return the amount spent for the month
- Then, `App.js` should have its `_updateBudget` function updated to account for the amount spent being returned by `checkCurrentMonthBudget`
- Finally, add a `ProgressViewIOS` component to `CurrentMonthExpenses`:
    - It should have a function to calculate its `progress` prop
    - It should also show the dollar amount currently spent as a string

ProgressViewIOS example

To begin, we will need to make an addition to our `storageMethods` file to grab the current month's spent amount so that we can calculate the `progress` prop for `ProgressViewIOS`. This can be done by modifying `checkCurrentMonthBudget`:

```
// Expenses/app/utils/storageMethods.js

export const checkCurrentMonthBudget = async () => {
  let year = dateMethods.getYear();
  let month = dateMethods.getMonth();

  let response = await getAsyncStorage();

  if (response === null || !response.hasOwnProperty(year) ||
  !response[year].hasOwnProperty(month)) {
    return false;
  }

  let details = response[year][month];

  return {
    budget: details.budget,
    spent: details.spent
  }
}
```

Here, we are returning an object containing both the `budget` and `spent` amounts as opposed to just the `budget`. This means that we will also need to modify how the `App` component's `_updateBudget` method receives our response data.

The following addition to the `App` component just shows the `_updateBudget` asynchronous method since it is the only part modified to accommodate `storageMethods`' `checkCurrentMonthBudget` method's changes:

```
// Expenses/app/App.js

...
  async _updateBudget () {
    let response = await storageMethods.checkCurrentMonthBudget();

    if (response !== false) {
      this.setState({
        budget: response.budget,
        spent: response.spent
      });
```

```
        return;
    }

    this._renderEnterBudgetComponent();
}
```

The text block that renders the budget as a string has been modified to display the current amount spent:

```javascript
// Expenses/app/components/CurrentMonthExpenses/index.js

...
import {
  ProgressViewIOS,
  ...
} from 'react-native';
...
export default class CurrentMonthExpenses extends Component {
  ...
  render () {
    ...
    return (
      <View style={ styles.currentMonthExpensesContainer }>
        <View style={ styles.currentMonthExpensesHeader }>
          ...
          <Text style={ styles.subText }>
            { this.props.spent } of { this.props.budget } spent
          </Text>
```

A `ProgressViewIOS` component is also mounted right after the preceding text block, pointing its `progress` prop to a function called `_getProgressViewAmount`, which calculates it for us:

```javascript
        <ProgressViewIOS
          progress={ this._getProgressViewAmount() }
          progressTintColor={ '#A3E75A' }
          style={ styles.progressView }
        />
      </View>
      ...
    </View>
  )
}
```

The following code is a simple division to grab the percentage:

```
_getProgressViewAmount () {
  return this.props.spent/this.props.budget;
}
...
};
```

Set `margin` to `10` so that it does not reach the edge of the screen:

```
// Expenses/app/components/CurrentMonthExpenses/styles.js

...
const styles = StyleSheet.create({
  ...
  progressView: {
    margin: 10
  },
  ...
});

export default styles;
```

Reduce the `fontSize` of both the properties to `16` and set `alignSelf` to `center`:

```
// Expenses/app/components/ExpenseRow/styles.js

...
const styles = StyleSheet.create({
  amountText: {
    alignSelf: 'center',
    color: '#86B2CA',
    flex: 1,
    fontSize: 16,
    marginRight: 10,
    textAlign: 'right'
  },

  descriptionText: {
    alignSelf: 'center',
    color: '#7D878D',
    fontSize: 16,
    textAlign: 'left'
  },
});

export default styles;
```

As a result of these changes, your app should now have a progress indicator showing the user how close they are to hitting their budget for the month.

Thanks to the _updateCurrentMonthExpenses function in App.js, saving new expenses for the month will result in the amount spent and progress indicator being updated accordingly without any new logic having to be written:

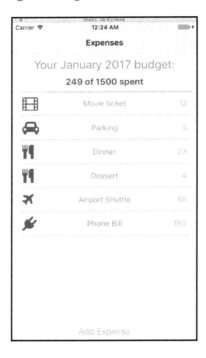

This looks great! Our next step is to create a second view that will let us look at all the months' expenses, which in turn will have us using a TabBar to toggle between the two.

A view for prior months' expenses

Our view for the previous months' expenses should be one that renders a list of the existing months in our budget. It should give us the month, the budget allocated for the month, and have the years separated by some sort of a header. Then, on tap, it should go to the summary for each month to show us our previous months' expenses that were input.

We should create some functions in a new utilities file, named `mockDataMethods`, to help us mock the data for the previous months and populate our app:

```
// Expenses/app/utils/mockDataMethods.js

import { setAsyncStorage } from './storageMethods';

const years = ['2017', '2016', '2015'];
const months = ['1', '2', '3', '4', '5', '6', '7', '8', '9', '10', '11',
'12'];

const expenses = [
  { amount: '4', category: 'coffee', description: 'Latte' },
  { amount: '1.50', category: 'books', description: 'Sunday Paper' },
  { amount: '35', category: 'car', description: 'Gas' },
  { amount: '60', category: 'restaurant', description: 'Steak dinner' }
];
```

Above, arrays for years, months, and expenses are created and populated with data.

```
const mockObject = {
  budget: 500,
  expenses: expenses,
  spent: 100.5
};
```

I created a mocked object to be assigned to each month:

```
export const mockPreviousMonthExpenses = async () => {
  let mockedPreviousMonthsExpensesObject = {};
  years.forEach((year) => {
    mockedPreviousMonthsExpensesObject[year] = {};

    months.forEach((month) => {
      if (year === '2017' && (parseInt(month) > 1)) {
        return;
      }

      mockedPreviousMonthsExpensesObject[year][month] =
      Object.assign({}, mockObject);
    });
  });

  setAsyncStorage(mockedPreviousMonthsExpensesObject);
}
```

This function loops through the `years` array and creates an empty object within that year's property. It then does another loop within it to create a similar object for the `month` within that `year` and assigns the `mockObject` to it. Along the way, it also stops the function if we attempt to create any mocked expenses for months past January 2017.

Then, we use our `setAsyncStorage` function to assign our mocked expenses object to be the source of truth for our application:

```
// Expenses/app/App.js

import { mockPreviousMonthExpenses } from './utils/mockDataMethods';
...
export default class App extends Component {
  ...
  componentWillMount () {
    mockPreviousMonthExpenses();
    storageMethods.logAsyncStorage();
    ...
  }
  ...
}
```

Within the `componentWillMount` life cycle of `App.js`, we can call on the `mockPreviousMonthExpenses` function we created in `mockDataMethods` to populate our local storage with this mocked data.

Additionally, we use the `logAsyncStorage` method from `storageMethods` in order to log the information to the console so that we can see that our mocked data has been saved to storage for later use.

Once this step is completed, you should remove the `mockPreviousMonthExpenses` function from `App.js` since it does not need to be continuously called. Here is how our mocked expenses will look. You can view your own results by calling `console.table` on the object and opening up Chrome developer tools:

```
                                                                                      storageMethods.js:100
(inde…  1       2       3       4       5       6       7       8       9       10      11      12
2015    Object  Object  Object  Object  Object  Object  Object  Object  Object  Object  Object  Object
2016    Object  Object  Object  Object  Object  Object  Object  Object  Object  Object  Object  Object
2017    Object
▼ Object
  ▼ 2015: Object
    ▼ 1: Object
        budget: 500
      ▼ expenses: Array[4]
        ▼ 0: Object
            amount: "4"
            category: "coffee"
            description: "Latte"
          ▶ __proto__: Object
        ▶ 1: Object
        ▶ 2: Object
        ▶ 3: Object
          length: 4
          ▶ __proto__: Array[0]
        spent: 100.5
        ▶ __proto__: Object
    ▶ 2: Object
    ▶ 3: Object
    ▶ 4: Object
    ▶ 5: Object
    ▶ 6: Object
    ▶ 7: Object
    ▶ 8: Object
    ▶ 9: Object
    ▶ 10: Object
    ▶ 11: Object
    ▶ 12: Object
    ▶ __proto__: Object
  ▶ 2016: Object
  ▶ 2017: Object
  ▶ __proto__: Object
```

After this step has been completed, we should create a new component that will show these details. Since we want a list that contains some sort of headers to separate the years, we will be rendering a `ListView` and using the `renderSectionHeader` prop to create sections in our app.

ListView with section headers

To set up our `ListView` to accommodate section headers, we need to make some modifications to the way we've been creating `ListViews`.

First, when we instantiate a new `ListView DataSource`, we'll be passing it a second callback, `sectionHeaderHasChanged`. Like `rowHasChanged`, this one checks to see whether a section header has changed. In your code, it looks something like this:

```
this.state = {
  ds: new ListView.DataSource({
  rowHasChanged: (r1, r2) => r1 !== r2,
  sectionHeaderHasChanged: (s1, s2) => s1 !== s2
    }),
  }
```

Then, instead of calling `cloneWithRows`, we call the similarly named `cloneWithRowsAndSections` function:

```
const dataSource = this.state.ds.cloneWithRowsAndSections
(this.state.listOfExpenses);
```

Finally, your `ListView` component should now accept a function as its `renderSectionHeader` prop, which will render the section header for your application:

```
<ListView
  ...
  renderSectionHeader={ (sectionData, sectionID) =>
  this._renderSectionHeader(sectionData, sectionID) }
/>

_renderSectionHeader (sectionData, sectionID) {
  return (
    <View>
      <Text>{ sectionID }</Text>
    </View>
  )
}
```

Now that you have an overview of how to apply a section header to your `ListView` component, it's time to apply that knowledge. Let's create a new component, `PreviousMonthsList`. This component should do the following things:

- For the time being, replace the rendering of `CurrentMonthExpenses` in App.js with your `PreviousMonthsList` component so that you can view your progress while writing the component.
- Grab the list of expenses from `AsyncStorage` and save it to the component state

- Render a `ListView` with section headers, which displays the name of the month as a string along with that month's numerical budget and a section header for each year that our `mocked` expenses provided
- Style the rows and section headers to have a different look from each other

Once you have built your version of this component, check for the one that I built:

```
// Expenses/app/App.js

...
import PreviousMonthsList from './components/PreviousMonthsList';

export default class App extends Component {
  ...
  render () {
    return (
      <View style={ styles.appContainer }>
        <PreviousMonthsList />
        ...
      </View>
    )
  }
  ...
}
```

The first thing I did was import `PreviousMonthsList` into `App.js` and replace where `CurrentMonthExpenses` was being mounted in its `render` method with `PreviousMonthsList` instead. This made it simpler for me to work on the component, knowing that any changes I made would be immediately noticeable.

After this component was completed, I reverted `App.js` back to its original state (before the `PreviousMonthsList` component was created):

```
// Expenses/app/components/PreviousMonthsList/index.js

import React, { Component } from 'react';

import {
  ListView,
  Text,
  View
} from 'react-native';

import styles from './styles';
import * as dateMethods from '../../utils/dateMethods';
import * as storageMethods from '../../utils/storageMethods';
```

```
export default class PreviousMonthsList extends Component {
  constructor (props) {
    super (props);

    this.state = {
      ds: new ListView.DataSource({
        rowHasChanged: (r1, r2) => r1 !== r2,
        sectionHeaderHasChanged: (s1, s2) => s1 !== s2
      }),
      listOfExpenses: {}
    };
  }
```

The DataSource instance saved into component state has the new
sectionHeaderHasChanged function passed into it.

During the componentWillMount life cycle event, I am asynchronously calling the
getAsyncStorage function from storageMethods and saving its result into the
listOfExpenses property in the component state:

```
async componentWillMount () {
  let result = await storageMethods.getAsyncStorage();

  this.setState({
    listOfExpenses: result
  });
}
```

The dataSource constant is being assigned with the cloneWithRowsAndSections
method of the ListView.DataSource instance saved in the component state so that the
section header for our list of expenses is available in the app:

```
render () {
  const dataSource = this.state.ds.cloneWithRowsAndSections
  (this.state.listOfExpenses);

  return (
    <View style={ styles.previousMonthsListContainer }>
      <ListView
        automaticallyAdjustContentInsets={ false }
        dataSource={ dataSource }
        renderRow={ (rowData, sectionID, rowID) => this._
        renderRowData(rowData, rowID) }
        renderSectionHeader={ (sectionData, sectionID) => this._
        renderSectionHeader(sectionData, sectionID) }
        renderSeparator={ (sectionID, rowID) => this._
        renderRowSeparator(sectionID, rowID) }
```

```
        />
      </View>
    )
  }
```

There is nothing special in the three stateless functions that handle the rendering of our row data, section header, and separator.

```
  _renderRowData (rowData, rowID) {
    return (
      <View style={ styles.rowDataContainer }>
        <Text style={ styles.rowMonth }>
          { dateMethods.getMonthString(rowID) }
        </Text>
        <Text style={ styles.rowBudget }>
          { rowData.budget }
        </Text>
      </View>
    )
  }

  _renderRowSeparator (sectionID, rowID) {
    return (
      <View
        key={ sectionID + rowID }
        style={ styles.rowSeparator }
      />
    )
  }

  _renderSectionHeader (sectionData, sectionID) {
    return (
      <View style={ styles.sectionHeader }>
        <Text style={ styles.sectionText }>
          { sectionID }
        </Text>
      </View>
    )
  }
}
```

The `rowDataContainer` style is given a `flexDirection` property set to `row` so that the two strings being rendered within it are on the same line:

```
// Expenses/app/components/PreviousMonthsList/styles.js

import { StyleSheet } from 'react-native';

const styles = StyleSheet.create({
  previousMonthsListContainer: {
    flex: 1
  },
  rowBudget: {
    color: '#86B2CA',
    flex: 1,
    fontSize: 20,
    marginRight: 10,
    textAlign: 'right'
  },
  rowDataContainer: {
    flex: 1,
    flexDirection: 'row',
    marginTop: 10,
    height: 30
  },
```

The `sectionHeader` gets its own styling so that a specified `height` and `backgroundColor` can be set to visually distinguish it from the rows of data in the `PreviousMonthsList` component:

```
  rowMonth: {
    color: '#7D878D',
    flex: 1,
    fontSize: 20,
    marginLeft: 10,
    textAlign: 'left'
  },
  rowSeparator: {
    backgroundColor: '#7D878D',
    flex: 1,
    height: StyleSheet.hairlineWidth,
    marginLeft: 15,
    marginRight: 15
  },
  sectionHeader: {
    height: 20,
    backgroundColor: '#86B2CA'
  },
```

```
  sectionText: {
    color: '#7D878D',
    marginLeft: 10
  }
});

export default styles;
```

At this point, by temporarily rendering `PreviousMonthsList` to where `CurrentMonthExpenses` previously belonged, we have a view that looks like this:

The previous month's expenses

The next step that we want to carry out is to create a view that shows us the expenses for each month and then allows the user to enter that view by tapping on one of these months. This view should be navigated to when the user long presses on a month in the `PreviousMonthsList` component.

Thankfully, we already have a component that can handle this for us. In the last chapter, we built the `CurrentMonthExpenses` component that renders the expenses for a given month.

So far in our app, `CurrentMonthExpenses` is being rendered in just one place--`App.js`. The container that it renders within has a top margin offset to accommodate the navigation bar.

If we want to reuse the `CurrentMonthExpenses` component to render any month's expenses, we should build some logic to selectively include a top margin offset equal to the navigation bar's height if the component is being navigated to by `PreviousMonthsList`.

This can be achieved by having `CurrentMonthExpenses` accept an optional Boolean as a prop to then append its `currentMonthExpensesContainer` style with its top margin being set to the navigation bar's height:

```
// Expenses/app/components/CurrentMonthExpenses/index.js

...
import {
  ...
  Navigator,
} from 'react-native';
...
export default class CurrentMonthExpenses extends Component {
  static propTypes = {
    ...
    isPreviousMonth: PropTypes.bool,
  }

  ...
  render () {
    ...
    return (
      <View style={ [styles.currentMonthExpensesContainer,
        this.props.isPreviousMonth ? {marginTop: Navigator.
        NavigationBar.Styles.General.TotalNavHeight} : {}] }>
        ...
      </View>
    )
  }
  ...
};
```

The `Navigator` is being imported so that we have access to its navigation bar height. The `CurrentMonthExpenses` component's `propTypes` have been updated to expect an optional Boolean titled `isPreviousMonth`.

Then, the `render` method of `CurrentMonthExpenses` checks to see whether the `isPreviousMonth` Boolean has been passed to the component. If it has, it adds the `marginTop` property to the `currentMonthExpensesContainer` style equal to the height of the navigation bar.

Now it is time to link each row from `PreviousMonthsList` to navigate to the `CurrentMonthExpenses` component. Modify your `PreviousMonthsList` component so that it does the following things:

- Importing and wrapping a `TouchableHighlight` component over each row being rendered.
- When one of the rows is pressed, your app should navigate to `CurrentMonthExpenses`.
- As part of this navigation to `CurrentMonthExpenses`, your app's navigator should pass it all the props that it expects (as specified in the `propTypes` object of `CurrentMonthExpenses`), along with the optional `isPreviousMonth` prop set to `true`.

When you complete this step, check out the solution that I came up with:

```
// Expenses/app/components/PreviousMonthsList/index.js

...
import {
  ...
  TouchableHighlight,
} from 'react-native';

import CurrentMonthExpenses from '../CurrentMonthExpenses';
...

export default class PreviousMonthsList extends Component {
  ...
  _renderRowData (rowData, sectionID, rowID) {
    return (
      <View style={ styles.rowDataContainer }>
        <TouchableHighlight
          onPress={ () => this._renderSelectedMonth(rowData,
          sectionID, rowID) }
          style={ styles.rowDataTouchableContainer }>
```

```
         . . .
         </TouchableHighlight>
       </View>
     )
   }
```

I modified the _renderRowData method of PreviousMonthsList to wrap a
TouchableHighlight component around the row of text. Since TouchableHighlight
can only accept one immediate child component, I wrapped the two text elements around a
View.

The _renderSelectedMonth method pushes CurrentMonthExpenses to the navigator
and passes it all the expected props for that component. I used the Number.toString
prototype method to convert the rowData.budget number to a string
as CurrentMonthExpenses expects a string as its budget prop:

```
    . . .
    _renderSelectedMonth (rowData, sectionID, rowID) {
      this.props.navigator.push({
        component: CurrentMonthExpenses,
        title: dateMethods.getMonthString(rowID) + ' ' + sectionID,
        passProps: {
          budget: rowData.budget.toString(),
          expenses: rowData.expenses,
          isPreviousMonth: true,
          month: rowID,
          spent: rowData.spent,
          year: sectionID
        }
      })
    }
  }
```

I gave the rowDataTouchableContainer style a height of 30 pixels and set the
flexDirection property of textRow to row so that the two Text components within it
will render properly:

```
  // Expenses/app/components/PreviousMonthsList/styles.js

  . . .
  const styles = StyleSheet.create({
    . . .
    rowDataTouchableContainer: {
      flex: 1,
      height: 30
    },
```

```
  . . .
    textRow: {
      flex: 1,
      flexDirection: 'row'
    }
});
  . . .
```

When the user presses on the name of a previous month, they will now see the following view:

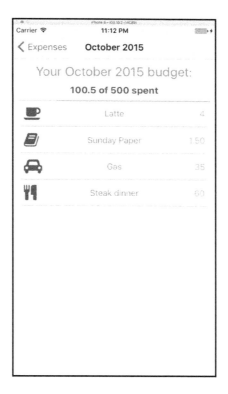

Now, we have two different paths for our users to take in the app: they can view add expenses to the current month's list in App.js, or they can view the archives of all of their previous months' expenses. In the next section, we will learn how to implement a tab bar to show these two views.

Implementing TabBarIOS

TabBarIOS renders a tabbed navigation bar at the bottom of the screen. The bar can contain multiple icons, each responsible for a different view.

The different tabs that TabBarIOS renders are considered items of the tab bar. They are declared as TabBarIOS.Item components and are nested as children within TabBarIOS.

However, with the react-native-vector-icons library we imported, we would like to use Font Awesome icons for our navigation. Instead of rendering the TabBarIOS.Item components as children for our TabBarIOS component, we will substitute them for Icon.TabBarItemIOS.

Icon.TabBarItemIOS is a component that behaves in the exact same way that TabBarIOS.Item does, but with a couple of extra props that are specific to it. We will be using the following props for our implementation:

- onPress: This is a callback that fires when the tab is tapped on by the user. This should always at least set the selected component to a Boolean in your state.
- selected: This is a Boolean that determines whether a specific tab is in the forefront of the application or not.
- title: This is a string that shows the text that appears underneath your icon.
- iconName: This is a string that maps to the icon you wish to display.
- iconSize: This is a number that dictates the size of the icon.

The iconColor and selectedIconColor will need to have renderAsOriginal set to true so that these child-level settings override the parent TabBarIOS component's tintColor and unselectedTintColor props.

Here's how a sample TabBarIOS component can look:

```
<TabBarIOS>
  <Icon.TabBarItemIOS
    iconName={ 'home' }
    iconSize={ 20 }
    onPress={ () => this._setSelectedTab('home') }
    selected={ this.state.selectedTab === 'home' }
    title={ 'home' }
  >
    { this._renderHomeView() }
  </Icon.TabBarItemIOS>
</TabBarIOS>
```

As you can see, TabBarIOS wraps around the Icon.TabBarItemIOS child components. Each of these child components handle their own icon type, size, and title. They also wrap around a function that renders their respective views.

Now, it's time for you to give it a try. Let's build a TabBarIOS component into our app by doing the following things:

- Separate the app into *current month* and *previous month's* expenses using TabBarIOS. Choose a suitable icon for each one!
- Adjust styling as you see fit to adjust any dimensions needed to accommodate TabBarIOS.
- Give each PreviousMonthsList its own NavigatorIOS component so that the TabBarIOS component does not disappear when PreviousMonthsList navigates to a previous month's list of expenses.
- Remove the navigation bar from the root-level NavigatorIOS component found in index.ios.js so that the navigation components for PreviousMonthsList do not render a second navigation bar.

Once you have built tabbed navigation for the app, come back and check out the version I wrote:

```
// Expenses/index.ios.js

...
export default class Expenses extends Component {
  render() {
    return (
      <NavigatorIOS
        ...
        navigationBarHidden={ true }
      />
    );
  }
}
...
```

The only change made to the index.ios.js root file is the addition of the navigationBarHidden prop for our root NavigatorIOS component, set to true so that the navigation bar does not appear.

```
// Expenses/app/App.js

...
import {
```

```
    NavigatorIOS,
    ...
} from 'react-native';
```

  . . .

In the `App.js` component, I am now explicitly setting items in state to default values so that components that are dependent on that prop don't throw an error when the prop is not defined. Additionally, the `expenses` key has been modified to be an object--this will be the full object returned by the `getAsyncStorage` method in `StorageMethods`, not just for the current month:

```
export default class App extends Component {
  constructor (props) {
    super();

    this.state = {
      budget: '',
      expenses: {},
      selectedTab: 'currentMonth',
    }
  }
```

The entire `expenses` object will be passed into `PreviousMonthsList`, allowing it to render all expense data and update whenever a new item is added to a previous month through the `AddExpenses` component.

The old `expenses` array, which references just the current month, is now explicitly labeled as `currentMonthExpenses`.

There is also a new item in the component's state--`selectedTab`. This defaults to `currentMonth`, which is the leftmost tab that we intend on rendering.

```
    componentWillMount () {
      this.setState({
        spent: 0,
        currentMonthExpenses: [],
        month: dateMethods.getMonth(),
        year: dateMethods.getYear()
      });

      ...
    }
```

The render method for `App.js` has been completely overhauled. It now returns a `TabBarIOS` component and two `Icon.TabBarItemIOS` children components that render a different view each:

```
render () {
  return (
    <TabBarIOS>
      <Icon.TabBarItemIOS
        iconName={ 'usd' }
        iconSize={ 20 }
        onPress={ () => this._setSelectedTab('currentMonth') }
        title={ 'Current Month' }
        selected={ this.state.selectedTab === 'currentMonth' }
      >
        { this._renderCurrentMonthExpenses(this.state.
        currentMonthExpenses) }
      </Icon.TabBarItemIOS>
      <Icon.TabBarItemIOS
        iconName={ 'history' }
        iconSize={ 20 }
        onPress={ () => this._setSelectedTab('previousMonths') }
        title={ 'Previous Months' }
        selected={ this.state.selectedTab === 'previousMonths' }
      >
        { this._renderPreviousMonthsList(this.state.expenses) }
      </Icon.TabBarItemIOS>
    </TabBarIOS>
  )
}
```

The `_renderCurrentMonthExpenses` method contains the old `render` method for this component:

```
_renderCurrentMonthExpenses () {
  return (
    <View style={ styles.appContainer }>
      <CurrentMonthExpenses
        budget={ this.state.budget }
        expenses={ this.state.currentMonthExpenses }
        month={ this.state.month }
        spent={ this.state.spent }
        year={ this.state.year }
      />
      <AddExpenses
        month={ this.state.month }
        updateExpenses={ () => this._updateExpenses() }
        year={ this.state.year }
      />
```

```
        </View>
    )
}
```

The _renderPreviousMonthsList method returns a NavigatorIOS component whose initial route is PreviousMonthsList. The expenses key in App.js' state is passed in to PreviousMonthsList via passProps:

```
...
_renderPreviousMonthsList () {
  return (
    <NavigatorIOS
      initialRoute={{
        component: PreviousMonthsList,
        title: 'Previous Months',
        passProps: {
          expenses: this.state.expenses
        }
      }}
      style={ styles.previousMonthsContainer }
    />
  )
}
```

The _setSelectedTab function changes the selectedTab property in the App.js' component state to the argument passed to it. This is the callback fired by the onPress props of the Icon.TabBarItemIOS:

```
...
_setSelectedTab (selectedTab) {
  this.setState({
    selectedTab
  });
}
```

The last change is that _updateCurrentMonthExpenses now calls getAsyncStorge from storageMethods.js instead of getMonthObject and has been renamed as _updateExpenses to reflect its new functionality:

```
...
async _updateBudget () {
    ...
    this._updateExpenses();
    ...
  }
  ...
}
```

```
async _updateExpenses () {
  let response = await storageMethods.getAsyncStorage();

  if (response) {
    let currentMonth = response[this.state.year][this.state.month];

    this.setState({
      budget: currentMonth.budget,
      currentMonthExpenses: currentMonth.expenses,
      expenses: response,
      spent: currentMonth.spent
    });
  }
}
}
```

The `previousMonthsContainer` style is applied to the `NavigatorIOS` instance that renders `PreviousMonthsList`. It does not contain a top margin equal to the navigation bar's height since this will cause the navigation bar itself to have a top margin equal to its own height:

```
// Expenses/app/styles.js

...
const styles = StyleSheet.create({
  ...
  previousMonthsContainer: {
    flex: 1,
    marginBottom: 48
  }
});

export default styles;
```

Minor changes to `PreviousMonthsList` are that I'm now checking for the `expenses` object to be passed to it and the `cloneWithRowsAndSections` call in the `render` method is now updated to reflect this.

Additionally, the `componentWillMount` life cycle has been entirely removed since we are now getting all our data as a prop.

```
// Expenses/app/components/PreviousMonthsList/index.js

import React, { Component, PropTypes } from 'react';
...
export default class PreviousMonthsList extends Component {
  static propTypes = {
    expenses: PropTypes.object.isRequired
  }
  ...
  render () {
    const dataSource = this.state.ds.cloneWithRowsAndSections
    (this.props.expenses);
    ...
  }
  ...
}
```

The `marginTop` property for `previousMonthsListContainer` in this component has been set to the navigation bar height:

```
// Expenses/app/components/PreviousMonthsList/styles.js

import { Navigator, StyleSheet } from 'react-native';

const styles = StyleSheet.create({
  previousMonthsListContainer: {
    ...
    marginTop: Navigator.NavigationBar.Styles.General.TotalNavHeight,
  },
  ...
});

export default styles;
```

Finally, the `AddExpenses` component has been tweaked to reflect changing the `_updateCurrentExpenses` function name to `_updateExpenses`:

```
// Expenses/app/AddExpenses/index.js

...
export default class AddExpenses extends Component {
  static propTypes = {
    ...
    updateExpenses: PropTypes.func.isRequired,
    ...
```

```
  }
  ...
  _toggleModal (boolean) {
    ...
    this.props.updateExpenses();
  }
}
```

Here is how your app should look with `TabBarIOS` implemented:

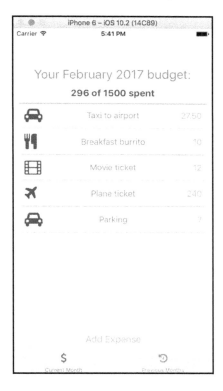

There is one last thing we should do with the app, and it is to let users delete expenses.

Deleting expenses

For users to delete expenses from any month, we need to do the following things:

- Add a method to `storageMethods` to update an `expenses` object. It should accept the month, year, and array of expenses. Then, it should override the array of expenses for that specific month and year combination in `AsyncStorage` with this new array, and recalculate the amount spent.
- Wrap a `TouchabbleHighlight` component around each row that, when long pressed, opens an alert that asks the user whether they wish to delete the item.
- If the user confirms that they would like to delete the item, then we should delete it. A new array of expenses for the current month should be created without the deleted item, and it should be saved using the `storageMethods` function we made.
- When an expense is deleted, we should update the current view to reflect the item being deleted and the updated spent amount.
- If the user cancels, the alert should close and no changes should be made.

Take some time to build this feature; when you're finished, check out the code I wrote for this part.

First, I modified the `StorageMethods` file:

```
// Expenses/app/utils/StorageMethods.js

...
export const saveItemToBudget = async (month, year, expenseObject) => {
  let response = await getAsyncStorage();

  let newExpensesArray = [
    ...response[year][month].expenses,
    expenseObject
  ];

  return updateMonthExpensesArray(month, year, newExpensesArray);
}

export const updateMonthExpensesArray = async (month, year, array) => {
  let response = await getAsyncStorage();

  let newTotal = getTotalSpentForMonth(array);

  response[year][month].expenses = array;
  response[year][month].spent = newTotal;
```

```
    await setAsyncStorage(response);
    return true;
}
```

The first thing I did was write the `updateMonthExpensesArray` method. As I was writing it, I noticed that much of the code was similar to what `saveItemToBudget` was executing, so I refactored `saveItemToBudget` to call the new `updateMonthExpensesArray` method. This allows me to reuse some code in my file instead of writing it twice.

When the `CurrentMonthExpenses` component deletes an item, `App.js` `_updateExpenses` method should be executed so that `AsyncStorage` is updated with a new array for the month and year that does not contain the deleted expense:

```
// Expenses/app/App.js

...
export default class App extends Component {
  ...
  _renderCurrentMonthExpenses () {
    return (
      <View style={ styles.appContainer }>
        <CurrentMonthExpenses
          ...
          updateExpenses={ () => this._updateExpenses() }
        />
        ...
      </View>
    )
  }
```

The `_updateExpenses` method is also passed into the `PreviousMonthsList` component so that it can propagate it down to its own rendering of `CurrentMonthExpenses` for the previous months:

```
  _renderPreviousMonthsList () {
    return (
      <NavigatorIOS
        initialRoute={{
          ...
          passProps: {
            ...
            updateExpenses: () => this._updateExpenses()
          }
        }}
      />
    )
```

```
    }
    ...
}
```

The `PreviousMonthsList` gets a minor tweak to support the addition of the `updateExpenses` function:

```
// Expenses/app/components/PreviousMonthsList/index.js

...
export default class PreviousMonthsList extends Component {
  static propTypes = {
    ...
    updateExpenses: PropTypes.func.isRequired
  }
  ...
  _renderSelectedMonth (rowData, sectionID, rowID) {
    this.props.navigator.push({
      ...
      passProps: {
        ...
        updateExpenses: () => this.props.updateExpenses(),
      }
    });
  }
}
```

The `render` method has been changed to set the `dataSource` constant of `ListView` to accept the expenses value of the `CurrentMonthExpenses` state in case it is present--this will be used to visually update the component to exclude a deleted item once a deletion occurs.

This is necessary because `PreviousMonthsList` is the initial route of its own `NavigatorIOS` instance and therefore does not receive updated props from `App.js`:

```
// Expenses/app/components/CurrentMonthExpenses/index.js

...
import {
  Alert,
  ...
} from 'react-native';
...
export default class CurrentMonthExpenses extends Component {
  static propTypes = {
    ...
    updateExpenses: PropTypes.func.isRequired,
```

```
  }
  ...
  render () {
    const dataSource = this.state.ds.cloneWithRows
    (this.state.expenses || this.props.expenses || []);
    ...
  }
```

The _cancelAlert method closes the Alert dialogue that appears:

```
  ...

  _cancelAlert () {
    return false;
  }
```

The following conditional blocks deal with the possibility that a user may want to delete more than one item from a list:

```
async _deleteItem (rowID) {
  let newExpensesArray;

  if (this.state.expenses) {
    newExpensesArray = [...this.state.expenses];
  }

  if (!this.state.expenses) {
    newExpensesArray = [...this.props.expenses];
  }
```

The _deleteItem method takes in the ID of the row being deleted, clones the expenses array, uses the splice method of the Array prototype to remove that specific index from it, and then removes it from AsyncStorage with the updateMonthExpensesArray method I created in the StorageMethods file.

Then, I set an expenses value in the local state to equal the new expenses array and call the updateExpenses method from App.js to update the data in the app:

```
newExpensesArray.splice(rowID, 1);

await storageMethods.updateMonthExpensesArray
(this.props.month, this.props.year, newExpensesArray);

this.setState({
  expenses: newExpensesArray
});
```

```
        this.props.updateExpenses();
    }
```

Each `ExpenseRow` component will be passed in this `_onLongPress` method, which takes in its `rowID` and creates an alert prompt for the user. Based on the selected option, it either cancels the alert or deletes the row selected:

```
...
_onLongPress (rowID) {
    const alertOptions = [
        {text: 'Cancel', onPress: () => this._cancelAlert() },
        {text: 'Delete', style: 'destructive', onPress: () =>
        this._deleteItem(rowID)}
    ];

    Alert.alert('Delete Item', 'Do you wish to delete
    this item?', alertOptions)
}
```

The `_renderRowData` method has been changed to pass in the `onLongPress` prop to `ExpenseRow`:

```
_renderRowData (rowData, rowID) {
    if (rowData) {
        return (
            <ExpenseRow
                ...
                onLongPress={ () => this._onLongPress(rowID) }
            />
        )
    }
}
...
};
```

The `TouchableHighlight` component of `ExpenseRow` has been updated to add an `onLongPress` callback that executes the `onLongPress` method passed into it as a prop from `CurrentMonthExpenses`. This is how the alert is triggered, giving the user the option to delete an added expense:

```
// Expenses/app/components/ExpenseRow/index.js

...
export default (props) => {
    return (
        <TouchableHighlight
            onLongPress={ () => props.onLongPress() }
```

```
      . . .
    >
      . . .
    </TouchableHighlight>
  )
}
```

This concludes our work on the iOS version of this app! Since this was a large app to build, I don't wish to drag you through the Android modifications in this chapter. Instead, the modifications I will make to this app to build it on an Android device can be found at the end of Chapter 9, *Additional React Native Components*.

In the next chapter, we will begin working on an entirely new project.

Summary

In this chapter, we finished building our expense tracking app by utilizing the vector icon library we installed earlier to visually display the user's expenses. We also built a second view to look at the previous months' expenses and wrote a function to mock the data needed to visually verify that our app worked as intended. Then, we separated these two views using tabbed navigation and allowed users to delete expenses from the app.

5
Third Project - The Facebook Client

Until now, we've mainly built applications that deal only with information provided by a user. However, lots of applications tend to send and receive data from other sources around the web. For our third and final project in this book, we will build an app that accesses the external Facebook API so that users can access their profile.

In this chapter, you will do the following things:

- Plan `Friends`, our Facebook application, by deciding what key factors it should have
- Gain access to the Facebook API and install the official SDK for both iOS and Android
- Use the Facebook API's **Login** SDK to grant the app appropriate permissions
- Grab information from the Facebook API using `GraphRequest` and `GraphRequestManager`
- Utilize an `ActivityIndicator` to let the user visually know that data is currently loading
- Begin building the essential features of our Facebook application

Planning the app

Friends will be the first full-fledged example we build of just how powerful React Native is. It will deal with a lot of moving parts, so it's good to plan out the app in depth. On a basic level, accessing the Facebook **Graph** API gives us the following permissions:

- Signing in
- Viewing your feed
- Viewing the list of posts on your feed along with its comments and likes
- Adding new posts and comments on your feed
- Browsing the photos that you've uploaded to your Facebook profile along with their comments and likes
- Viewing the events that you have RSVPd
- Rediscovering the list of pages that you have liked

As in the previous chapters, we want to break this off into bite-sized accomplishments. By the end of this chapter, Friends should do the following things:

- Prompt the user to sign in to Facebook, if they haven't already, and save their authentication token automatically with the SDK
- While the feed is loading, show a spinning animation to visualize that data is loading
- Show the user their feed
- For each post on the feed, render the contents of the post along with the number of comments and likes on the post
- Upon tapping, load and show just the comment chain of that specific post
- Allow the reader to respond to comments on a specific post or create a new post

About the Facebook API

Before we proceed further, a note about the level of access we can gain with the Facebook API--you will only be able to gain information about the user who is logged in. The specific user's friend list is inaccessible through Facebook's API, but a small subset of friends who have also installed the same app is available. Since it's not very useful in our project, I'm purposefully omitting it.

While the user's posts and photos will certainly have a list of comments along with the names and pictures of the people who posted them, accessing those friends' profiles is not possible using the current iteration of the Facebook API.

Obtaining Facebook API credentials

This looks like a great starting point. However, before we can begin, we need to register our app with Facebook. Head over to Facebook's developer site and select **Add a New App**. At the time of writing, the URL is `https://developers.facebook.com`.

Once you have your application registered, download the Facebook SDK for iOS at `https://developers.facebook.com/docs/ios/` and unzip its contents to your `Documents` folder, naming it `FacebookSDK`. Keep this folder open; we will need it shortly.

After that, go to the dashboard of your application and take note of the **App ID**. You'll also need this in a moment. You can find it here:

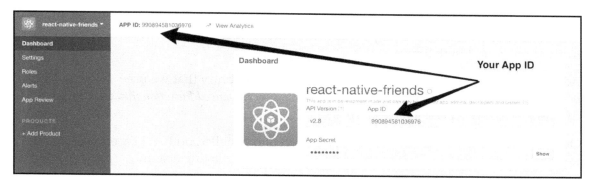

In the following section, we'll look at how to install the official Facebook SDK for React Native.

Installing the Facebook SDK on iOS and Android

Initialize a new React Native project using the following command line:

```
react-native init Friends
```

Afterwards, navigate to the new project you just created using a command line.

The Facebook SDK for React Native is available through npm in a package called react-native-fbsdk. We'll install it as such:

```
npm install --save react-native-fbsdk
```

Now link the SDK, as follows:

```
react-native link react-native-fbsdk
```

Now, follow the detailed instructions on the react-native-fbsdk repo on GitHub found at https://github.com/facebook/react-native-fbsdk. Since the installation instructions are prone to being changed at any given time, I highly recommend that you use the instructions found in that repo.

Afterward, install the react-native-vector-icons library that we used in Expenses using the process we saw earlier (refer to Chapter 4, *Advanced Functionality with the Expenses App*, if you need a refresher).

Once you have initialized the app for this project and installed both the Facebook SDK and react-native-vector-icons library, it's time to start playing around.

Logging in with the Facebook SDK

The first thing we can try in our app is logging in the user. The FBSDK has access to a built-in component called LoginButton that, on press, will send the user to a login screen using a WebView while being within the app. If the login is successful, an access token will be saved for your app to make use of, without you needing to personally track it.

Start by adding the `LoginButton` snippet found in the FBSDK repository's `README` to your app's `index` file. You'll get something like this:

```
// Friends/index.ios.js

import React, { Component } from 'react';
import {
  AppRegistry,
  StyleSheet,
  View
} from 'react-native';

import {
  AccessToken,
  LoginButton
} from 'react-native-fbsdk';
```

Import the `AccessToken` and `LoginButton` modules from the `react-native-fbsdk` repo, using destructuring notation.

```
export default class Friends extends Component {
  render() {
    return (
      <View style={ styles.container }>
        <LoginButton
          readPermissions={["public_profile", "user_photos",
          "user_posts", "user_events", "user_likes"]}
```

The `readPermissions` prop accepts an array of strings and asks the user for specific read-only permissions equal to the array passed in.

The Facebook API has a lot of different permissions you can request, and for the purposes of this project, we will ask for the following:

- `public_profile`: This provides access to a subset of items that are part of the user's public Facebook profile. This includes their ID, name, profile picture, and more.
- `user_events`: This is a list of events that a person is either hosting or has RSVPd to.
- `user_likes`: This is the collection of Facebook pages that the user has clicked **Like** on.
- `user_photos`: These are the user's uploaded or tagged photos.
- `user_posts`: These are the posts on the user's timeline.

The `onLoginFinished` method is written to be asynchronous:

```
            async onLoginFinished={
              async (error, result) => {
                if (error) {
                } else if (result.isCancelled) {
                  alert("login is cancelled.");
                } else {
                    const data = await AccessToken.getCurrentAccessToken()
                    alert(data);
                }
              }
            }
            onLogoutFinished={() => alert("logout.")}
          />
        </View>
      );
    }
}

const styles = StyleSheet.create({
  container: {
    flex: 1,
    justifyContent: 'center',
    alignItems: 'center',
    backgroundColor: '#F5FCFF',
  }
});

AppRegistry.registerComponent('Friends', () => Friends);
```

While there are some other props available for `LoginButton`, the three presented in the preceding code are the only ones we will worry about. Here's what each of these props refer to:

- `publishPermissions`: This represents the publishing permissions to request from the logged-in user when the button is pressed
- `onLoginFinished`: This is a callback that gets invoked when a login request has either been completed or produces an error
- `onLogoutFinished`: This is another `callback` that invokes itself when a logout request has been completed

If everything works out, you will see the following screen with the Facebook log in button--
Log in with Facebook, in the center:

By tapping on this logo, you will be taken to a login page within a `WebView` component that
handles Facebook login.

After logging in, the user will see a prompt that asks for read-only permissions equal to the ones we asked for in the `readPermissions` array passed in as a prop to the `LoginButton` component:

Once your user is authorized, you'll be able to grab data from Facebook's Graph API.

Using the Facebook Graph API

The FBSDK lets us make requests to the Facebook Graph API using the `GraphRequest` and `GraphRequestManager` classes to create those requests and execute them.

`GraphRequest` is used to create a request to the Graph API, while `GraphRequestManager` is called to execute that request.

GraphRequest

To instantiate a new `GraphRequest`, we can pass up to three arguments:

- `graphPath`: This is a string pertaining to the endpoint in the Graph API that we wish to hit. For example, to get information about the logged-in user, a `graphPath` of `/me` will be used.
- `config`: This is an optional object that can configure the request. The props that this object accepts are all optional:
    - `httpMethod`: This is a string that describes the HTTP method for this request, for example, `GET` or `POST`.
    - `version`: This is a string that describes the specific Graph API version to use.
    - `parameters`: This is an object containing the request's parameters.
    - `accessToken`: This is a stringified version of the access token used by this request.
- `callback`: This is a callback function that is fired once the request has either been completed or has failed.

A sample `GraphRequest` instance will look like this:

```
const requestMyPhotos = new GraphRequest('/me/photos/uploaded',
  null, this._responseInfoCallback);

_responseInfoCallback (error, result) {
  if (error) {
    console.log('Error fetching data: ' + error.toString())
  } else {
    console.log(result);
  }
}
```

For this request to be executed, we will use `GraphRequestManager`.

GraphRequestManager

The GraphRequestManager queue requests the Facebook Graph API and executes it when told to do so.

It has access to the following methods:

- addRequest: This is a function that accepts an instance of GraphRequest and pushes the request into the queue of GraphRequestManager. It also pushes the callback into a separate requestCallbacks queue for execution once the request has been completed or failed.
- addBatchCallback: This accepts an optional callback to be executed once the entire batch of requests has been completed. Each instance of GraphRequestManager can only accept up to one callback, and the invocation of that callback does not indicate that every graph request in the batch was successful--the only thing it is indicative of is that the entire batch has completed execution.
- start: This accepts an optional number equal to a timeout value. The timeout value defaults to 0 if it's not passed in. When GraphRequestManager.start is invoked, the GraphRequestManager makes a series of requests to the Facebook Graph API on a first-in, first-out basis and executes the callbacks for each request made, if applicable.

Adding to the preceding example, a GraphRequestManager request looks something like this:

```
new GraphRequestManager().addRequest(requestMyPhotos).start();
```

This request creates a new instance of GraphRequestManager complete with its own new batch, adds the preceding requestMyPhotos task to the batch, and then starts it. From here, the Facebook Graph API will return some form of data.

The callback passed into the instance of requestMyPhotos in GraphRequest will then execute, logging either an error or the result of the request.

Creating our first request

It's time to create our first request to verify that the access token we've received has worked.

Within your `Friends` component in `index.ios.js`, let's do the following things:

- Create a method, called `_getFeed`, that creates a `GraphRequest` to your Facebook feed. This method should grab data at the `/me/feed` endpoint and reference a callback to be executed when that `GraphRequest` is complete. You can skip the optional `config` object that `GraphRequest` can optionally accept.
- In the same `_getFeed` function, create a new `GraphRequestManager` and add the `GraphRequest` instance to it; then start the `GraphRequestManager`.
- For the callback referenced by `_getFeed`, have it log either the error or the result that it receives when your `GraphRequest` is completed.
- Call `_getFeed` as part of the `onLoginFinished` callback in `LoginButton`.

When you have finished, the result should look somewhat like this:

```
// Friends/index.ios.js

...
import {
  ...
  GraphRequest,
  GraphRequestManager,
} from 'react-native-fbsdk';

export default class Friends extends Component {
  render() {
    return (
      <View style={ styles.container }>
        <LoginButton
          ...
          onLoginFinished={
            async (error, result) => {
              ...
              } else {
                await AccessToken.getCurrentAccessToken();
                this._getFeed();
```

Rather than alerting the access token, I am calling _getFeed.

```
                }
              }
            }
            ...
          />
        </View>
      );
    }
```

Create a new instance of GraphRequest by passing it the endpoint desired along with the callback to be fired once the request is complete:

```
_getFeed () {
  const infoRequest = new GraphRequest ('/me/feed', null,
  this._responseInfoCallback);
```

Now, create a new instance of GraphRequestManager, add the infoRequest object to it, and then start the request:

```
  new GraphRequestManager ().addRequest (infoRequest).start ();
}
```

When the request is completed, it will log either the result or an error if one was encountered:

```
_responseInfoCallback (error, result) {
  if (error) {
    console.log('Error fetching data: ', error.toString());
    return;
  }

  console.log(result);
 }
}
...
```

With your iOS simulator and remote debugging opened, check out your browser's console as you log in:

```
▼ Object                                                    index.ios.js:78
  ▼ data: Array[25]
    ▶ 0: Object
    ▶ 1: Object
    ▶ 2: Object
    ▶ 3: Object
    ▶ 4: Object
    ▶ 5: Object
    ▶ 6: Object
    ▶ 7: Object
    ▶ 8: Object
    ▶ 9: Object
    ▶ 10: Object
    ▶ 11: Object
    ▶ 12: Object
    ▶ 13: Object
    ▶ 14: Object
    ▶ 15: Object
    ▶ 16: Object
    ▶ 17: Object
    ▶ 18: Object
    ▶ 19: Object
    ▶ 20: Object
    ▶ 21: Object
    ▶ 22: Object
    ▶ 23: Object
    ▶ 24: Object
      length: 25
    ▶ __proto__: Array[0]
  ▶ paging: Object
  ▶ __proto__: Object
```

This is great! It shows that we are linked up with the Graph API and that it accepts the access token we've given it. Now, let's create a separate `graphMethods.js` utility file that we can use in different components.

GraphMethods

The goal of this file is to create some commonly used methods that interact with the Facebook Graph API and export them so that we can use them in different components throughout the app.

Like the utility files we created for `Expenses`, this `graphMethods` file should live inside a `utils` folder, nested inside an `app` folder that rests at the root level of our project:

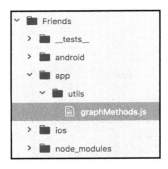

Create this utilities file and have it do the following things:

- Create a function called `makeSingleGraphRequest` that accepts a request as an argument, creates a new instance of `GraphRequestManager`, passes in the request to `GraphRequestManager`, and then calls the `start` method of `GraphRequestManager`.
- Create and export a function, called `getFeed`, that accepts a callback, creates a new `GraphRequest` pointing to `/me/feed` with that callback, and then calls `makeSingleGraphRequest` with it.

Once your version is complete, check out mine below:

```
// Friends/app/utils/graphMethods.js

import {
  GraphRequest,
  GraphRequestManager
} from 'react-native-fbsdk';

const makeSingleGraphRequest = (request) => {
  return new GraphRequestManager().addRequest(request).start();
}

export const getFeed = (callback) => {
  const request = new GraphRequest('/me/feed', null, callback);

  makeSingleGraphRequest(request)
}
```

NavigatorIOS and App component

Now, let's create an App component using an `App.js` file. Create this within the `app` folder of your project:

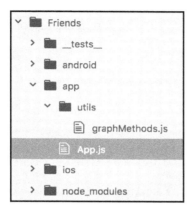

This component should contain logic similar to what we had in `index.ios.js` previously--we will replace the `index.ios.js` file with a `NavigatorIOS` component shortly.

Your new App component should be a reflection of the `index.ios.js` file you wrote earlier in this chapter, except that it should import and use the `graphMethods` file instead of the component-specific `_getFeed` method.

Once you have completed this task, refer to my version:

```
// Friends/app/App.js

import React, { Component } from 'react';
import {
  View
} from 'react-native';

import {
  AccessToken,
  LoginButton
} from 'react-native-fbsdk';
```

Since `GraphRequest` and `GraphRequestManager` are being imported within `graphMethods`, I can omit them from the `import` statement in the preceding code.

I am using destructuring notation to import just the `getFeed` method from `graphMethods`. This will come in handy in the future as that file is populated with more helper methods:

```
import { getFeed } from './utils/graphMethods';
```

Since the callback for `GraphRequest` contains the `error` and `result` arguments, I pass them in so that `_responseInfoCallback` can make use of them:

```
import styles from './styles';

export default class App extends Component {
  render() {
    return (
      <View style={ styles.container }>
        <LoginButton
        readPermissions={["public_profile", "user_photos",
        "user_posts", "user_events", "user_likes"]}
          onLoginFinished={
            async (error, result) => {
              if (error) {
              } else if (result.isCancelled) {
                alert("login is cancelled.");
              } else {
                  await AccessToken.getCurrentAccessToken();
                  getFeed((error, result) =>
                  this._responseInfoCallback(error, result))
              }
            }
          }
          onLogoutFinished={() => alert("logout.")}
        />
      </View>
    );
  }

  _responseInfoCallback (error, result) {
    if (error) {
      console.log('Error fetching data: ', error.toString());
      return;
    }

    console.log(result);
  }
}
```

Here is the basic styling for our `App` component:

```
// Friends/app/styles.js

import { StyleSheet } from 'react-native';

const styles = StyleSheet.create({
  container: {
    flex: 1,
    justifyContent: 'center',
    alignItems: 'center',
    backgroundColor: '#F5FCFF',
  }
});

export default styles;
```

Great work! The next step is to refactor `index.ios.js` at your project's root to do the following things:

- Import `NavigatorIOS` from the React Native SDK as well as the `App` component you just created
- Render the root `NavigatorIOS` component, passing it the `App` component as its initial route

When you have finished this part, feel free to check out my solution:

```
// Friends/index.ios.js

import React, { Component } from 'react';
import {
  AppRegistry,
  NavigatorIOS,
  StyleSheet,
} from 'react-native';

import App from './app/App';

export default class Friends extends Component {
  render() {
    return (
      <NavigatorIOS
        initialRoute={{
          component: App,
          title: 'Friends'
        }}
        style={ styles.container }
```

```
      />
    );
  }
}

const styles = StyleSheet.create({
  container: {
    flex: 1,
    backgroundColor: '#F5FCFF',
  }
});

AppRegistry.registerComponent('Friends', () => Friends);
```

Now it's time to create a login prompt for the user so that they only see the `LoginButton` component when they are not logged in.

Creating a login prompt

The first thing we should do is think about how our app will behave. When it's launched, we should check for an available access token using the FBSDK `AccessToken` API. If it's not available, then our user isn't logged in and we should show them the **Log In** button, just like we required a budget in our previous project, `Expense`.

If/when the user is logged in, we should grab their feed data, load it into the component state, and then log it to the console to show that we have it.

The first thing we should do is modify the `App` component so that:

- On the `componentWillMount` event, we use the `AccessToken` API's `getCurrentAccessToken` method to check and see whether the user is logged in.
  - If the user is not logged in, we should alert the user that they are not logged in. In the next section, we will replace this part with the login screen that we will create.
  - If the user is logged in, we should call the `getFeed` method of `graphMethods`.
- Also, it should no longer render the `LoginButton`--this will go into a different component in a moment. Instead, let's have the `App` component render a string that says `'Logged In'` for the time being.

Take the time you need to make these changes, then check the code below for my working example:

```
// Friends/app/App.js

...
import {
  Text,
  ...
} from 'react-native';

import {
  ...
} from 'react-native-fbsdk';
```

I removed the import of LoginButton to App since it will be broken off into a different component.

The componentWillMount logic calls the _checkLoginStatus method:

```
...
export default class App extends Component {
  componentWillMount () {
    this._checkLoginStatus();
  }
```

The LoginButton component in the render method of App has been replaced with a Text block for the time being. The _responseInfoCallback function has not been changed nor removed:

```
  render() {
    return (
      <View style={ styles.container }>
        <Text>Logged In</Text>
      </View>
    );
  }
```

The async _checkLoginStatus function is similar to the onLoginFinished callback of the LoginButton component we previously rendered:

```
  async _checkLoginStatus ( ){
    const result = await AccessToken.getCurrentAccessToken();

    if (result === null) {
      alert('You are not logged in!');
      return;
```

```
    }

    getFeed((error, result) => this._responseInfoCallback(error,
    result));
  }
  ...
}
```

If the user is not logged in when they refresh the app, they will see this message:

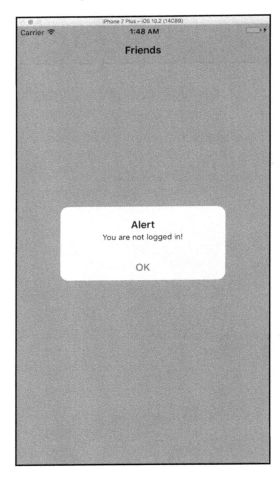

Great job on your progress! For the next step, create a `components` folder within the `app` folder, within which create a `LoginPage` folder that contains both an `index` and a `styles` file:

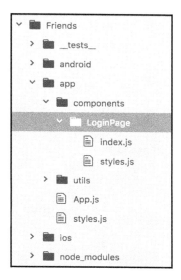

Now, let's modify the `App` component again while we create the `LoginPage`. The `App` component should do the following things:

- Import the `LoginPage` component
- Use the `push` method of the navigator to push the `LoginPage` component when the user is not logged in; replace the part in your code that alerts the user that they are not logged in with this logic
- Pass the `_checkLoginStatus` callback to the `LoginPage` component so that, when the user is logged in, we can check the login status with the `App` component and log their list of posts within `/me/feed`

The `LoginPage` component should do the following things:

- Contain a view that wraps around the `LoginButton` component that we rendered previously in this chapter.
- Have an `onLoginFinished` callback that does the following things:
    - Logs an error to the console if the login action is cancelled
    - Calls the `getFeed` callback that was passed to it along with the `pop` method of the navigator if the login action is successful

When you are finished, your result should look something like this:

```
// Friends/app/App.js

...
import LoginPage from './components/LoginPage';

export default class App extends Component {
  ...
  async _checkLoginStatus ( ){
    ...
    if (result === null) {
      this.props.navigator.push({
        component: LoginPage,
        title: 'Log In to Facebook',
        navigationBarHidden: true,
        passProps: {
          getFeed: () => getFeed()
        }
      });
      return;
    }
    ...
  }
  ...
}
```

Rather than alerting the user that they are not logged in, I'm now pushing the `LoginPage` component via the app's navigator if the user is not logged in. This is how I wrote the `LoginPage` component:

```
// Friends/app/components/LoginPage/index.js

import React, { Component } from 'react';
import {
  View
} from 'react-native';

import {
  LoginButton
} from 'react-native-fbsdk';

import styles from './styles';

export default class LoginPage extends Component {
  render() {
    return (
      <View style={ styles.container }>
```

```
<LoginButton
readPermissions={["public_profile", "user_photos",
"user_posts", "user_events", "user_likes"]}
  onLoginFinished={
    (error, result) => {
      if (error) {
        console.log('Error logging in: ', error.toString());
        return;
      }
```

The preceding part logs an error if one occurred during login.

In the following code we log the fact that the user cancelled the login process:

```
      if (result.isCancelled) {
        console.log('login was cancelled');
        return;
      }
```

However, we call the `getFeed` and `navigator.pop` methods if the login was successful:

```
      this.props.getFeed();
      this.props.navigator.pop();

    }
  }
  onLogoutFinished={() => alert("logout.")}
/>
</View>
);
}
}
```

The stylesheet for `LoginPage` is the exact same as the one found in `Expenses/app/styles.js`, so I left it out for the sake of brevity.

Great progress! In the next section, we will create some storage methods to handle the rate limit for Facebook's Graph API.

Optimizing for the API

The current rate limit for Facebook's Graph API is 200 calls per hour per user. This means that if your app has 100 users, you can make 20,000 calls per hour. The limit is in aggregate, meaning that any single user could take up all 20,000 calls in that given hour.

To reduce the number of network calls we make to the API, we should tweak our App component to save feed data within AsyncStorage and only refresh its data when manually prompted to do so by the user.

We can begin by creating methods for AsyncStorage, which are similar to the ones we had in Expenses:

```
// Friends/app/utils/storageMethods.js

import { AsyncStorage } from 'react-native';

export const getAsyncStorage = async (key) => {
  let response = await AsyncStorage.getItem(key);
  let parsedData = JSON.parse(response) || {};

  return parsedData;
}

export const setAsyncStorage = async (key, value, callback) => {
  await AsyncStorage.setItem(key, JSON.stringify(value));

  if (callback) {
    return callback();
  }

  return true;
}
```

For this app, we will be storing different key-value pairs within AsyncStorage; so, we want to explicitly pass the getAsyncStorage and setAsyncStorage methods a key.

The resetAsyncStorage and logAsyncStorage methods remain the same from when we used them in Expenses:

```
export const resetAsyncStorage = (key) => {
  return setAsyncStorage(key, {});
}

export const logAsyncStorage = async (key) => {
  let response = await getAsyncStorage(key);

  console.log('Logging Async Storage');
  console.table(response);
}
```

Next, modify the _checkLoginStatus method in App.js so that it does the following things:

- Calls the getAsyncStorage method in storageMethods to check for the existence of data within the feed property if the user is logged in.
  - If the feed property exists, we should save its results to the App component's state under the same name. We will not call getFeed if this is the case.
  - If the key does not exist, we should call getFeed.

Now, let's modify the _requestInfoCallback method in App.js so that if it does not contain an error, it will do the following things:

- Save the response.data array using the setAsyncStorage method from storageMethods, using feed as the key that is passed in.
- Save the same array to the App component's local state.

Here's how my version looks:

```
// Friends/app/App.js

...
import { getAsyncStorage, setAsyncStorage } from './utils
/storageMethods';
...
export default class App extends Component {
  ...
  async _checkLoginStatus () {
    ...
    const feed = await getAsyncStorage('feed');

    if (feed && feed.length > 0) {
      this.setState({
        feed
      });
      return;
    }
```

If the feed array exists, set it to local state.

Otherwise, call getFeed:

```
getFeed((error, result) => this._responseInfoCallback
(error, result));
```

```
    }

  _responseInfoCallback (error, result) {
    ...
    setAsyncStorage('feed', result.data);
    this.setState({
      feed: result.data
    });
  }
}
```

This change first checks for any feed data that we have saved in the app before resorting to making an external API call for that data. In the next chapter, we will explore a component that will allow us to refresh this data on demand.

The next step we should take is to give the user an indication that data is being loaded so that they don't have a static screen for too long. We will use the ActivityIndicator component to do so.

Using ActivityIndicator

The ActivityIndicator component displays a circular loading indicator that lets you visualize a *loading* action for the user. It's helpful for the overall user experience since your users shouldn't feel like their actions aren't accomplishing their intentions.

The two ActivityIndicator props we will use in this app are as follows:

- animating: This is a Boolean that either shows or hides the component. It defaults to true.
- size: This is the physical size of the component. On iOS, your options are one of two strings: small and large. On Android, in addition to those two strings, you can pass it a number. This prop defaults to small.

We should modify our app to show this ActivityIndicator when data hasn't been loaded from the Graph API.

Let's modify the App component so that it conditionally renders the ActivityIndicator component when data has not yet been saved into the feed property of the App component's state.

The solution I came up with is as follows:

```
// Friends/app/App.js

...
import {
  ActivityIndicator,
  ...
} from 'react-native';
...
export default class App extends Component {
  constructor (props) {
    super (props);

    this.state = {
      feed: undefined,
      spinning: true
    }
  }
```

Set the `feed` and `spinning` values in the `App` component's state upon initialization.

Call the new `_renderView` method to conditionally determine what to render:

```
  ...
  render() {
    return (
      <View style={ styles.container }>
        { this._renderView() }
      </View>
    );
  }
```

Modify `_checkLoginStatus` to set the `spinning` property to `false` when loading data:

```
  async _checkLoginStatus () {
    ...
    if (feed && feed.length > 0) {
      this.setState({
        feed,
        spinning: false
      });
      return;
    }
    ...
  }
```

Check to see whether the `ActivityIndicator` should still be spinning. If so, return the `ActivityIndicator` component. If not, return the original `Text` component instead:

```
_renderView () {
  if (this.state.spinning) {
    return (
      <ActivityIndicator
        animating={ this.state.spinning }
        size={ 'large' }
      />
    );
  }

  return (
    <Text>Logged In</Text>
  )
}
```

Like `_checkLoginStatus`, modify `_responseInfoCallback` to set `spinning` to `false`:

```
_responseInfoCallback (error, result) {
  ...
  setAsyncStorage('feed', result.data);
  this.setState({
    feed: result.data,
    spinning: false
  });
}
}
```

Now, we should take the data we received and display it within a `ListView`.

Creating a standard ListView

The next step is to take the data received from the Graph API and render it into the view.

Right now, the `feed` array in the `App` component state contains 25 objects. Each object contains the following key-value pairs:

- `created_time`: This is the date and time this post was made
- `id`: This is an identifier that will let us grab the details of the post
- `story`: This an optional post description that adds context, such as whether the post contained a location-based check-in, whether it was a shared memory or link, and so on

- `message`: This an optional message that the user personally wrote for this post

Each post contains several edges, just like a node on a graph data structure. For `Friends`, we will access these following edges:

- `/likes`: This is a list of users who like this specific post
- `/comments`: These are the comments made to this post
- `/attachments`: These are the media attachments associated with the said post

Before we can access the edges, we should render a `ListView` component that displays these 25 posts in a coherent manner. Take some time to create a `ListView` that does the following things:

- Renders the 25 posts in individual rows
- Has conditional logic to show the story and message only if they exist

If you have gone through the first two projects in this book, the `ListView` is nothing new to you.

Create a new component titled `FeedList` within your `components` folder. In this file, create a `ListView` component that takes its array from a prop passed into it and renders a standard `ListView`.

Then, create a new helper file, called `dateMethods`. It should contain a function that accepts a date string and returns a formatted date. I like to use the MomentJS for things like this, but feel free to do this however you like.

Additionally, create another component titled `FeedListRow`, which will be responsible for rendering each individual row of the `FeedList`.

Afterward, in `App.js`, import the `FeedList` component you created and render it where the `Text` component is currently placed within _renderData. Ensure that you pass it the `feed` array so that it has data to render. Render the `FeedList` instead of the old `Text` component:

```
// Friends/app/App.js

...
import FeedList from './components/FeedList';
...
```

`Text` is no longer imported:

```
export default class App extends Component {
  ...
  _renderView () {
    if (this.state.spinning) {
      ...
    }

    return (
      <FeedList
        feed={ this.state.feed }
        navigator={ this.props.navigator }
      />
    );
  }
  ...
}
```

Next, the `FeedList` component takes in the `feed` array from the `App` component state and renders a standard `ListView`, explicitly passing in each post's details:

```
// Friends/app/components/FeedList/index.js

import React, { Component } from 'react';
import {
  ListView,
  View
} from 'react-native';

import FeedListRow from '../FeedListRow';

import styles from './styles';

export default class FeedList extends Component {
```

Instantiate a new `ListView.DataSource` object:

```
constructor (props) {
  super (props);

  this.state = {
    ds: new ListView.DataSource({
      rowHasChanged: (r1, r2) => r1 !== r2
    })
  }
}
```

Use the `feed` array passed in from `App` to render the `ListView`, as illustrated:

```
render () {
  const dataSource = this.state.ds.cloneWithRows
  (this.props.feed || []);
```

Render a `ListView` component using `FeedListRow` for each individual row, as follows:

```
    return (
      <View style={ styles.container }>
        <ListView
          automaticallyAdjustContentInsets={ false }
          dataSource={ dataSource }
          renderRow={ (rowData, sectionID, rowID) =>
            <FeedListRow
              createdTime={ rowData.created_time }
              message={ rowData.message }
              navigator={ this.props.navigator }
              postID={ rowData.id }
              story={ rowData.story }
            />

          }
          renderSeparator={ (sectionID, rowID) =>
            <View
              key={ rowID }
              style={ styles.separator }
            />
          }
        />
      </View>
    )
  }
}
```

The `separator` gets its own styling for separating each post, as shown:

```
// Friends/app/components/FeedList/styles.js

import { StyleSheet } from 'react-native';

const styles = StyleSheet.create({
  container: {
    flex: 1,
    marginTop: 65
  },
  separator: {
    flex: 1,
```

```
    height: StyleSheet.hairlineWidth,
    marginLeft: 15,
    marginRight: 15,
    backgroundColor: '#1d2129'
  }
});

export default styles;
```

Use the date string taken from the Facebook API and then format it with `moment`:

```
// Friends/app/utils/dateMethods.js

import moment from 'moment';

export const getDateTimeString = (date) => {

  return moment(date).format('lll');
}
```

In `FeedListRow`, import the `getDateTimeString` method from the `dateMethods` file that was just created:

```
// Friends/app/components/FeedListRow/index.js

import React, { Component } from 'react';
import {
  Text,
  TouchableHighlight,
  View
} from 'react-native';

import { getDateTimeString } from '../../utils/dateMethods';
```

Wrap a `TouchableHighlight` component around for future navigation purposes, as illustrated:

```
import styles from './styles';

export default class FeedListRow extends Component {
  render () {
    return (
      <View style={ styles.container }>
        <TouchableHighlight
          onPress={ () => this._navigateToPostView() }
          underlayColor={ '#D3D3D3' }
        >
          <View>
```

```
            <Text style={ styles.created }>
              { this._renderCreatedString() }
            </Text>
              { this._renderStoryString() }
            <Text style={ styles.message }>
              { this._renderMessageString() }
            </Text>
          </View>
        </TouchableHighlight>
      </View>
    )
  }
```

Placeholder function for now, we will modify this later.

```
  _navigateToPostView () {
    // TODO: Push to navigator
    console.log('pushed');
  }
```

Methods to render certain parts of the post's data.

```
  _renderCreatedString () {
    return 'Posted ' + getDateTimeString(this.props.createdTime);
  }

  _renderMessageString () {
    return this.props.message
  }

  _renderStoryString () {
    if (this.props.story) {
      return (
        <Text style={ styles.story }>
          { this.props.story }
        </Text>
      )
    }
  }
}
```

This is the styling I built for FeedListRow:

```
// Friends/app/components/FeedListRow/styles.js

import { StyleSheet } from 'react-native';

const styles = StyleSheet.create({
```

```
    container: {
      flex: 1,
      margin: 10
    },
    created: {
      color: '#365899',
      fontWeight: 'bold',
      marginBottom: 5
    },
    story: {
      marginBottom: 5,
      textDecorationLine: 'underline'
    }
  });

  export default styles;
```

You'll notice that this component's _navigateToPostView method has a commented task to take care of. This is the basis for the next step in this exercise, and we will jump right to it in the next chapter.

Summary

This was a long chapter, so thank you for staying with me! In this chapter, we obtained access to the Facebook Graph API, installed the Facebook SDK for iOS and Android, and began using the Facebook SDK to log the user into the app and use their access token to grab their feed data and render it onto the screen.

Along the way, you also used an ActivityIndicator component to visually communicate to the user that we are currently loading data.

We will ramp up a lot more in the next chapter. See you there.

6
Advanced Facebook App Functionality

Now that we have gained access to Facebook's Graph API, it's time to finish building our app.

In this chapter, we will:

- Continue building `Friends`, our Facebook-connected application, by grabbing additional data from the Graph APIs, such as media attachments, comments, and number of likes from each existing post in our feed
- Add a pull-to-refresh mechanism for our app to allow the user to reload data
- Learn about the `Image` component, which will allow us to render images in our application
- Discover WebView, to open links in a locally available `View` component
- Include a log out screen for the app
- Make changes to the app in order to build an Android version

Let's continue where we left off from the last chapter and work on the extension of our `FeedListRow` component.

Creating a PostView

At the end of `Chapter 5`, *Third Project - The Facebook Client*, we created a `FeedListRow` component with a `TouchableHighlight` that fired the following function when pressed:

```
// Friends/app/components/FeedListRow/index.js

...
  _navigateToPostView () {
    console.log('pushed');
  }
...
```

We will build a `PostView` component that our users will navigate to when the `TouchableHighlight` component is pressed in `FeedListRow` and replace the current login within this _navigfateToPostView function to handle that navigation.

This `PostView` component should, upon loading, look in `AsyncStorage` for this post's details and load them if it exists. If it does not, then it should make a request to the Facebook Graph API for the post's details and save them into `AsyncStorage` for future use.

The details that we are interested in, are the post's attachments, comments, and likes. Since each post on Facebook is assigned a unique post ID, we can also save an object containing the attachments, comments, and likes data under that post ID as its key in `AsyncStorage`.

First, we will start by creating a new function in `storageMethods.js` that performs the following functions:

- Accepts a post ID and batch callback to execute as arguments
- Makes three separate `GraphRequest` instances, one for each of the three edges we will be obtaining (attachments, comments, and likes), saving its return data into an object
- Starts one `GraphRequestManager`, chaining the three `GraphRequest` instances and passing in the batch callback, thus passing in the return data object to the batch callback function

Then, create a `PostView` component that does the following:

- It renders the same created story and message strings that `FeedListRow` created so that the user retains the context of what they tapped on.

- It uses a storage method to check for the existence of data pertaining to that specific post's ID. If it exists, then `PostView` will use it. If not, then it should use our new storage method to grab the attachments, comments, and likes from that post's ID.
- The batch callback passed into our new storage method should include the saving of its results into `AsyncStorage` under the same key as the post ID.
- It visually displays the number of comments and likes the post has, into a row.

Finally, modify the `FeedListRow` component so that it uses its existing `_navigateToPostView` method to navigate to `PostView`, passing any necessary props.

Create a `resultsObject` to store the results of each unique `GraphRequest`:

```
// Friends/app/utils/graphMethods.js

...
export const getPostDetails = (id, batchCallback) => {
  let resultsObject = {
    attachments: undefined,
    comments: undefined,
    likes: undefined
  }
```

For each of the three `GraphRequest` instances in the preceding code, use the post ID given to it and call its corresponding `attachments`, `comments`, and `likes` edges from the API. Then, save those results into the `resultsObject` under their corresponding key:

```
const attachmentsRequest = new GraphRequest('/' + id +
'/attachments', null, (error, response) => {
  if (error) {
    console.log(error);
  }
  resultsObject.attachments = response.data;
});

const commentsRequest = new GraphRequest('/' + id + '/comments',
null, (error, response) => {
  if (error) {
    console.log(error);
  }
  resultsObject.comments = response.data;
});

const likesRequest = new GraphRequest('/' + id + '/likes', null,
(error, response) => {
  if (error) {
```

```
      console.log(error);
   }
   resultsObject.likes = response.data;
});
```

Finally, create a new `GraphRequestManager` instance, and add all three requests to it along with the `batchCallback` given to this function as an argument. Pass `resultsObject` into the `batchCallback` to give that callback access to the data obtained from the `attachments`, `comments`, and `likes` edges:

```
new GraphRequestManager()
  .addRequest(attachmentsRequest)
  .addRequest(commentsRequest)
  .addRequest(likesRequest)
  .addBatchCallback(() => batchCallback(resultsObject))
  .start();
}
```

Then, import various different helper methods that will be used in this component, as follows:

```
// Friends/app/components/PostView/index.js

import React, { Component } from 'react';
import {
  ActivityIndicator,
  Text,
  TouchableHighlight,
  View
} from 'react-native';

import { getAsyncStorage, setAsyncStorage } from
'../../utils/storageMethods';
import { getDateTimeString } from '../../utils/dateMethods';
import { getPostDetails } from '../../utils/graphMethods';
import styles from './styles';
```

Set the `loading` Boolean in state to `true` for `ActivityIndicator`:

```
export default class PostView extends Component {
  constructor (props) {
    super (props);

    this.state = {
      loading: true
    }
  }
```

During `componentWillMount`, grab the object in storage under this post's ID key. Check for the existence of data: If no data exists, `getAsyncStorage` is configured to return an empty object. Call `_getPostDetails` if this is `true`; otherwise, save the details to local state:

```
async componentWillMount () {
  const result = await getAsyncStorage(this.props.postID);

  if (Object.keys(result).length === 0) {
    this._getPostDetails();
    return;
  }
  this._savePostDetailsToState(result);
}
```

Just like `FeedListRow`, render the created date, story, and message if applicable. Conditionally, call `_renderActivityIndicator` or `_renderDetails` depending on the loading Boolean. At the end, render a separator in anticipation of adding comments to this component:

```
render () {
 return (
   <View style={ styles.container }>
     <View>
       <Text style={ styles.created }>
         { this._renderCreatedString() }
       </Text>
         { this._renderStoryString() }
       <Text>
         { this._renderMessageString() }
       </Text>
     </View>
     <View>
       { this.state.loading ? this._renderActivityIndicator() :
       this._renderDetails() }
     </View>
     <View style={ styles.separator } />
   </View>
  )
}
```

Call the `getPostDetails` method we just created in `graphMethods` and pass it a callback that uses the results object from `getPostDetails` to save its contents to state; then save it to `AsyncStorage` under a key equal to this post's ID:

```
async _getPostDetails () {
  await getPostDetails(this.props.postID, (result) => {
    this._savePostDetailsToState(result);
    setAsyncStorage(this.props.postID, result);
  });
}
```

Render an `ActivityIndicator` component:

```
_renderActivityIndicator () {
  return (
    <ActivityIndicator
      animating={ this.state.spinning }
      size={ 'large' }
    />
  )
}
```

Render the number of `Likes` and `Comments` this post has, as follows:

```
_renderCreatedString () {
  return 'Posted ' + getDateTimeString(this.props.createdTime);
}

_renderDetails () {
  return (
    <View style={ styles.detailsContainer }>
      <Text style={ styles.detailsRow }>
        { this.state.likes.length } Likes, {
        this.state.comments.length } Comments
      </Text>
    </View>
  )
}
```

The `_renderCreatedString`, `_renderMessageString`, and `_renderStoryString` methods are unchanged from `FeedListRow`:

```
_renderMessageString () {
  return this.props.message
}

_renderStoryString () {
  if (this.props.story) {
```

```
      return (
        <Text style={ styles.story }>
          { this.props.story }
        </Text>
      )
    }
  }
```

Save data from this post's `attachments`, `comments`, and `likes` edges into state and turn off the spinning `ActivityIndicator`:

```
  _savePostDetailsToState (data) {
    this.setState({
      attachments: data.attachments,
      comments: data.comments,
      likes: data.likes,
      loading: false
    });
  }
}
```

Here is the styling for `PostView`:

```
// Friends/app/components/PostView/index.js

import { StyleSheet } from 'react-native';

const styles = StyleSheet.create({
  container: {
    flex: 1,
    margin: 10,
    marginTop: 75,
  },
  created: {
    color: '#365899',
    fontWeight: 'bold',
    marginBottom: 5
  },
  detailsContainer: {
    flexDirection: 'row',
    justifyContent: 'space-between'
  },
  detailsRow: {
    color: '#365899',
    marginBottom: 15,
    marginTop: 15,
    textAlign: 'left'
  },
```

```
  separator: {
    height: 2,
    marginLeft: 15,
    marginRight: 15,
    backgroundColor: '#365899'
  },
  story: {
    marginBottom: 5,
    textDecorationLine: 'underline'
  }
});

export default styles;
```

Finally, change the _navigateToPostView function in FeedListRow:

```
// Friends/app/components/FeedListRow/index.js

...
export default class FeedListRow extends Component {
  ...
  _navigateToPostView () {
    this.props.navigator.push({
      component: PostView,
      passProps: {
        createdTime: this.props.createdTime,
        message: this.props.message,
        postID: this.props.postID,
        story: this.props.story
      }
    });
  }
  ...
}
```

Next, we will add a ListView to populate the comments of that post and render it below the separator line in PostView.

Adding comments to PostView

In this next step, we will edit PostView so that it includes a ListView to render all its comments. Since PostView will have the comments data saved into its state once the information has been loaded by the componentWillMount life cycle, we can use that data to render the comments.

Start by creating a component to house this `ListView`; let's call it `CommentList`. It should do the following:

- Contain a list of comments, passed to it by `PostView` as a prop
- Render a `ListView` using those comments
- The rows should be rendered by a child component, `CommentListRow`

Your `CommentListRow` component should do the following:

- Each row should contain its poster's name and the message they wrote
- Separate each comment with a `ListView` component

Finally, update `PostView` so that it renders `CommentList` directly beneath the separator in the `render` method of `PostView`. Instantiate a new `ListView.DataSource` instance:

```
// Friends/app/components/CommentList/index.js

import React, { Component } from 'react';
import {
  ListView,
  Text,
  View
} from 'react-native';

import CommentListRow from '../CommentListRow';
import styles from './styles';

export default class CommentList extends Component {
  constructor (props) {
    super (props);
    this.state = {
      ds: new ListView.DataSource({
        rowHasChanged: (r1, r2) => r1 !== r2
      })
    }
  }
```

Set the `dataSource` constant, passing in the `comments` prop or an empty array:

```
  render () {
    const dataSource = this.state.ds.cloneWithRows(this.props.comments ||
[]);
```

Each row should be a new `CommentListRow` component:

```
return (
  <View style={ styles.container }>
    <ListView
      automaticallyAdjustContentInsets={ false }
      dataSource={ dataSource }
      renderRow={ (rowData, sectionID, rowID) =>
        <CommentListRow
          message={ rowData.message }
          name={ rowData.from.name } />
      }
```

Render a separator for each comment:

```
      renderSeparator={ (sectionID, rowID) =>
        <View
          key={ rowID }
          style={ styles.separator } />
      } />
    </View>
  )
}
}
```

This is the styling for the `CommmentList` styles block:

```
// Friends/app/components/CommentList/styles.js

import { StyleSheet } from 'react-native';

const styles = StyleSheet.create({
  container: {
    flex: 1
  },
  separator: {
    flex: 1,
    height: StyleSheet.hairlineWidth,
    marginLeft: 15,
    marginRight: 15,
    backgroundColor: '#1d2129'
  }
});

export default styles;
```

Next, let's look at CommentListRow:

```
// Friends/app/components/CommentListRow/index.js

import React, { Component } from 'react';
import {
  Text,
  View
} from 'react-native';

import styles from './styles';

export default (props) => {
  return (
    <View style={ styles.container }>
      <View style={ styles.header }>
        <Text style={ styles.name }>
          { props.name }
        </Text>
      </View>
      <View style={ styles.body }>
        <Text style={ styles.comment }>
          { props.message }
        </Text>
      </View>
    </View>
  )
}
```

A simple stateless functional component returns the comment row with the poster's name and their comment. The following block contains styling for CommentListRow:

```
// Friends/app/components/CommentListRow/styles.js

import { StyleSheet } from 'react-native';

const styles = StyleSheet.create({
  body: {
    marginBottom: 20,
    marginLeft: 30,
    marginRight: 30,
    marginTop: 10,
  },
  comment: {
    color: '#1d2129'
  },
  container: {
    flex: 1
```

```
  },
  header: {
    marginTop: 5,
    marginLeft: 10,
    marginRight: 10
  },
  name: {
    color: '#1d2129',
    fontWeight: 'bold'
  }
});

export default styles;
```

Finally, let's take a look at the change made to `PostView`:

```
// Friends/app/components/PostView/index.js

...
import CommentList from '../CommentList';

export default class PostView extends Component {
  ...
  render () {
    return (
      <View style={ styles.container }>
        ...
        <View style={ styles.separator } />
        <View style={ styles.commentListContainer }>
          <CommentList comments={ this.state.comments } />
        </View>
      </View>
    )
  }
  ...
}
```

The preceding code imports and renders `CommentList` right below the separator.

The `commentListContainer` style looks like this:

```
// Friends/app/components/PostView/styles.js

  commentListContainer: {
    flex: 1,
    marginTop: 20
  }
```

At this point, we should continue to flesh out `PostView` with the other features we described at the beginning of this chapter. In the next section, we will look at how to refresh the existing data we already have in the event that more data is added to the user's feed or single post.

Reloading data with RefreshControl

The pull-to-refresh interaction was conceived with **Tweetie**, a popular Twitter iOS application created in 2008. This interaction involves the user pulling down their screen until it reaches a certain threshold, then releasing it to signify their intent to refresh the contents of the screen.

With the React Native SDK, we can use `RefreshControl` to gain that same pull-to-refresh interaction and let our users reload data in the app at their will.

Here are the `RefreshControl` props that we will use in this chapter:

- `onRefresh`: This is a function that is called when the refresh action is executed
- `refreshing`: This is a Boolean that indicates whether the view should be animated

- `tintColor`: This is the color of the refreshing indicator
- `title`: This is a string that is displayed underneath the refresh indicator
- `titleColor`: This is the color of the title

To use a `RefreshControl`, render it into a `ListView` or `ScrollView` component under its `refreshControl` prop.

For our implementation, we want to start by modifying `App.js` so that it does the following:

- Contains a `refreshControlSpinning` Boolean in its state
- Modifies the current `_checkLoginStatus` function to move the logic for getting feed data from storage into its own function, `_getFeedData`; the new `_getFeedData` function should also switch the `refreshControlSpinning` Boolean to `false` once complete

- Includes a function, _refreshFeedList, to refresh the feed that sets refreshControlSpinning to true, then calls the new _getFeedData function
- Passes the refreshControlSpinning Boolean and the _refreshFeedList function to the FeedList component that it renders

Then, modify FeedList so that it does the following:

- Renders a RefreshControl component into the refreshControl prop of its ListView
- Points its spinning prop to the refreshControlSpinning Boolean of App.js
- Points its onRefresh prop to the _refreshFeedList function of App.js.

Here are my modifications to the App component:

```
// Friends/app/App.js

...
export default class App extends Component {
  constructor (props) {
    ...
    this.state = {
      ...
      refreshControlSpinning: false
    }
  }
}
```

We added a new refreshControlSpinning Boolean to state. The old spinner Boolean for the ActivityIndicator component is renamed as activityIndicatorSpinning. The last line in _checkLoginStatus is broken down to its own method for reusing it later in the following snippet. Also, update the getFeed prop being pushed to LoginPage to reflect the new, broken out method:

```
async _checkLoginStatus () {
  ...
  if (result === null) {
    this.props.navigator.push({
      ...
      passProps: {
        getFeed: () => _getFeed()
      }
    });
    ...
  }

  this._getFeed();
```

```
  }

  _getFeed () {
    getFeed((error, result) => this._responseInfoCallback
    (error, result));
  }
```

Let's pass `refreshControlSpinning` and `_refreshFeedList` to `FeedList`:

```
  _renderView () {
    ...
    return (
      <FeedList
        ...
        refreshControlSpinning={ this.state.refreshControlSpinning }
        refreshFeedList={ () => this._refreshFeedList() }
      />
    );
  }
```

Set the `refreshControlSpinning` Boolean to `true` and call `_getFeed`:

```
  _refreshFeedList () {
    this.setState({
      refreshControlSpinning: true
    });

    this._getFeed();
  }
```

Set `refreshControlSpinning` to `false` once data has been loaded into state and `AsyncStorage`:

```
  _responseInfoCallback (error, result) {
    ...
    this.setState({
      refreshControlSpinning: false
      ...
    });
  }
}
```

Add a `refreshControl` prop to `ListView`, which points to `_renderRefreshControl`:

```
// Friends/app/components/FeedList/index.js

import {
  ...
  RefreshControl,
} from 'react-native';
...
export default class FeedList extends Component {
  ...
  render () {
    ...
    return (
      <View style={ styles.container }>
        <ListView
          refreshControl={ this._renderRefreshControl() }
          ...
        />
      </View>
    )
  }
}
```

Return the `RefreshControl` component. Its `onRefresh` prop points to the `_refreshFeedList` method in `App.js`, and it refreshes Boolean points to the `refreshControlSpinning` property from `App.js` as well:

```
  _renderRefreshControl () {
    return (
      <RefreshControl
        onRefresh={ () => this.props.refreshFeedList() }
        refreshing={ this.props.refreshControlSpinning }
        tintColor={ '#365899' }
        title={ 'Refresh Feed' }
        titleColor={ '#365899' }
      />
    )
  }
}
```

The next step is to render any image attachments into `PostView`.

Rendering images

To show an image with React Native, we use the Image component. It lets us display images from both local and remote sources. Styles can also be added to an image, the same way you would stylize any other React component.

We will use the following props for our Image components in this chapter:

- resizeMode: We will use one of the following strings:
  - cover: This scales the image uniformly and maintains its aspect ratio so that both the width and height of the image will be equal to or larger than the view that encapsulates the Image component.
  - contain: This string also scales the image uniformly and maintains its aspect ratio so that both the width and height of the image will be equal to or less than the view that encapsulates the Image component.
  - stretch: This scales the width and height independently and can change the aspect ratio of the source image.
  - repeat: This repeats the image to cover the entire frame of the encapsulating view. This option also keeps the original size and aspect ratio on iOS, but not on Android.
  - center: This centers the image.

- source: This will be either a remote URL or local path to the image being rendered.
- style: This is a styles object.

On a basic level, you can load static image resources like this:

```
<Image source={ require('../images/my-icon.png') } />
```

Also, you can do the same for remote ones:

```
<Image
  source={{ uri: 'https://www.link-to-my-image.com/image.png' }}
  style={{
    width: 400,
    height: 400
  }} />
```

Every post on the user's feed that has an image attached to it can have that very image rendered using the `Image` component.

The way images are structured from the Facebook Graph API is like this:

```
attachments: [{
  media: {
    image: {
      height: 400,
      src: 'https://www.link-to-my-image.com/image.png',
      width: 400
    }
  }
}]
```

With this in mind, let's start by creating a new utilities file called `imageMethods`. This file should do the following:

- Import the `Dimensions` API from React Native.
- Export the `getHeightRatio` function that takes in the height and width of an image and returns the height that the image should have. We can calculate this by performing the following:
  - Grabbing the dimensions of the width of the user's device and subtracting an amount from it to accommodate a left and right margin.
  - Using this margin offset and dividing it by the image's original width to get a desired ratio.
  - Returning the result of multiplying the height by the ratio for the correct image height.
    - Export another function, `getWidthOffset`, which takes the width of the user's device and returns it, subtracting an amount to accommodate a left and right margin. For code reusability, we should use this as part of the first bullet point for `getHeightRatio`.

Modify `PostView` so that it does the following:

- The top-level `View` should be replaced by a `ScrollView` component in consideration of longer images.
- It renders the first image in a post's `attachments` array if the post has finished loading and if the `attachments` array has any images.

- The Image component should set its resizeMode prop to contain so that the image does not go off the screen. It should have some sort of left and right margin so that it does not meet the edge of the screen, and the width and height should be calculated by the imageMethods file.
- This rendering should be placed below the details of the post (time, message, and story), but above the number of likes and comments it has.

Grab the gridWidthOffset, divide it by the image's width, and then divide the image's height by this result, as follows:

```
// Friends/app/utils/imageMethods.js

import { Dimensions } from 'react-native';

export const getHeightRatio = (height, width) => {
  return height * (getWidthOffset()/width);
}
```

Grab the width of the user's device and then subtract 20 pixels from it:

```
export const getWidthOffset = () => {
  return Dimensions.get('window').width - 20;
}
```

Import the Image, ScrollView, and imageMethods into the PostView component:

```
// Friends/app/components/PostView/index.js

import {
  ...
  Image,
  ScrollView,
} from 'react-native';

import { getHeightRatio, getWidthOffset } from '../../utils/imageMethods';
```

Replace the top-level view with a ScrollView in anticipation of longer posts. Add conditional logic to fire _renderAttachments, placing it before the call to _renderDetails:

```
...
export default class PostView extends Component {
  ...
  render () {
    return (
      <ScrollView style={ styles.container }>
```

```
    . . .
    <View>
      { !this.state.loading && this._renderAttachments() }
    </View>
    . . .
  </ScrollView>
  )
}
```

Assign `subattachments` for a very specific fringe case involving certain photos/albums:

```
. . .
_renderAttachments () {
  let attachment = this.state.attachments[0]
  let media;

  if (attachment && attachment.hasOwnProperty('subattachments')) {
    attachment = attachment.subattachments.data[0];
  }
}
```

Check for the existence of the `media` property, as follows:

```
  if (attachment && attachment.hasOwnProperty('media')) {
    media = attachment.media;
  }
```

If the `media` property exists and it contains an `image` property, then render the `Image`:

```
  if (media && media.image) {
```

Return an `Image` component with determined props:

```
    const imageObject = media.image;

    return (
      <Image
        resizeMode={ 'contain' }
        source={{ uri: imageObject.src }}
        style={{
          marginRight: 10,
          marginTop: 30,
          width: getWidthOffset(),
          height: getHeightRatio(imageObject.height,
          imageObject.width)
        }}
      />
    )
  }
```

```
    }
    ...
}
```

The `container` style for `PostView` has been changed to omit the `marginTop` property:

```
// Friends/app/components/PostView/styles.js

  commentListContainer: {
    flex: 1,
    marginTop: 20
  }
```

The `commentListContainer` style accompanies the new `ScrollView` component.

Now that the images have been rendered, we should deal with the other type of attachment--links.

Rendering links with WebView

When your users select a link, it's beneficial to render that link within your application so that your user doesn't get thrown out of the app and into their browser. To accomplish this task with React Native, we will use the `WebView` component.

The `WebView` component renders Web content within a native, app-contained view. For this app, we will use just one of its many props:

- `source`: This loads either a URI with optional headers or static HTML into the `WebView`.

Rendering a `WebView` component is simple:

```
import {
  WebView
} from 'react-native';

class WebViewSample extends Component {
  render () {
    return (
      <WebView
        source={{uri: 'https://www.google.com'}} />
    )
  }
}
```

Not all posts contain links in their attachments. When they do, the hierarchy looks like this:

```
attachments: [{
title: 'Link to Google'
  url: 'https://www.google.com'
}]
```

Let's make some changes to accommodate a WebView. First, create a new component titled WebViewComponent; it should be a stateless function that returns a WebView along with its source set to whatever link it receives as a prop.

Then, modify PostView so that it does the following functions:

- Renders a button directly below where an image would be rendered if one was included in the post.
- That button should only be rendered if the first attachment of the post has a link associated with it. The button should contain the title of the link and, when clicked on, navigate to your WebViewComponent to open the link.

 Unsecured HTTP links are automatically blocked by iOS' App Transport Security as of iOS 9. You can whitelist these on a case-by-case basis within the Info.plist file of your project in Xcode. Apple does not recommend this and will require that all apps submitted adhere to this new policy in the near future.

The following is a stateless functional component that just returns a WebView with a source URI:

```
// Friends/app/components/WebViewComponent/index.js

import React, { Component } from 'react';

import {
  WebView
} from 'react-native';

export default (props) => {
  return (
    <WebView
      source={{ uri: props.url }}
    />
  )
}
```

Import the `Button` and `WebViewComponent` dependencies:

```
// Friends/app/components/PostView/index.js

import {
  Button,
  ...
} from 'react-native';

import WebViewComponent from '../WebViewComponent';
```

Conditionally call `_renderLink` if `PostView` has finished loading:

```
...
export default class PostView extends Component {
  ...
  render () {
    return (
      <ScrollView style={ styles.container }>
        ...
        <View>
          { !this.state.loading && this._renderLink() }
        </View>
        ...
      </ScrollView>
    )
  }
```

Grab the first attached object:

```
...
_renderLink () {
  let attachment = this.state.attachments[0];
  let link;
  let title;
```

Check for `subattachments` again:

```
if (attachment && attachment.hasOwnProperty('subattachments')) {
  attachment = attachment.subattachments.data[0];
}
```

If the `title` is an empty string or not defined, generically name it `Link`:

```
if (attachment && attachment.hasOwnProperty('url')) {
  link = attachment.url;
  title = attachment.title || 'Link';
```

Render a `Button` that calls `_renderWebView` when pressed:

```
    return (
      <Button
        color={ '#365899' }
        onPress={ () => this._renderWebView(link) }
        title={ title }
      />
    )
  }
}
```

Navigate the user to the `WebViewComponent`, sending it the URL provided.

```
  _renderWebView (url) {
    this.props.navigator.push({
      component: WebViewComponent,
      passProps: {
        url
      }
    });
  }
  ...
}
```

We have one last finishing touch to make on this app, and it involves letting the user sign out of the application.

Signing out with TabBarIOS

Our final step involves adding a sign out page for the user. Using the `TabBarIOS` component and the `react-native-vector-icons`, we will create a tabbed view that allows the user to sign out.

Let's make some modifications for this to happen. We need to first modify `App.js` so that it does the following functions:

- Imports the `TabBarIOS` and `react-native-vector-icons` dependencies
- Returns a `TabBarIOS` component in its `_renderView` method if the activity indicator is not spinning
- Add a `selectedTab` string in the `App` component's state to track which tab is currently chosen, defaulting to the `FeedList` component

- Has separate functions to render the `FeedList` and `LoginPage` components without navigation
- Passes the `LoginPage` a callback that executes the `_checkLoginStatus` method
- Modifies its `container` style to no longer justify nor align any items to the center

Then, modify the `LoginPage` component so that its `onLogoutFinished` callback will execute `_checkLoginStatus`. Import new dependencies to the project:

```
// Friends/app/App.js

import {
  TabBarIOS,
  ...
} from 'react-native';
...
import Icon from 'react-native-vector-icons/FontAwesome';
```

Store the `selectedTab` string in state, defaulting it to `feed`:

```
...
export default class App extends Component {
  constructor (props) {
    ...
    this.state = {
      ...
      selectedTab: 'feed'
    }
  }
```

Render the `FeedList` component using the same logic from earlier:

```
  ...
  _renderFeedList () {
    return (
      <FeedList
        feed={ this.state.feed }
        navigator={ this.props.navigator }
        refreshControlSpinning={ this.state.refreshControlSpinning }
        refreshFeedList={ () => this._refreshFeedList() }
      />
    )
  }
```

Render the `LoginPrompt` component, passing it the `_checkLoginStatus` method:

```
_renderLoginPrompt () {
  return (
    <LoginPage checkLoginStatus={ () => this._checkLoginStatus() } />
  )
}
```

This will cause the app to navigate back to the `LoginPage` when the user is signed out using the following code:

```
_renderView () {
  ...
  return (
    <View style={ styles.container }>
      <TabBarIOS>
        <Icon.TabBarItemIOS
          title={ 'Feed' }
          selected={ this.state.selectedTab === 'feed' }
          iconName={ 'newspaper-o' }
          iconSize={ 20 }
          onPress={ () => this._setSelectedTab('feed') }
        >
          { this._renderFeedList() }
        </Icon.TabBarItemIOS>
        <Icon.TabBarItemIOS
          title={ 'Sign Out' }
          selected={ this.state.selectedTab === 'signOut' }
          iconName={ 'sign-out' }
          iconSize={ 20 }
          onPress={ () => this._setSelectedTab('signOut') }
        >
          { this._renderLoginPrompt() }
        </Icon.TabBarItemIOS>
      </TabBarIOS>
    </View>
  )
}
```

Rendering of the `TabBarIOS` component is where the contents of `_renderFeedList` existed earlier within `_renderView`.

```
...
_setSelectedTab (selectedTab) {
  this.setState({
    selectedTab
  });
}
}
```

The preceding code sets the `selectedTab` property in state to whichever tab is tapped on by the user:

```
// Friends/app/styles.js

container: {
  flex: 1,
  backgroundColor: '#F5FCFF',
}
```

The preceding code removed all other stylings from the `container` property so that the tab bar's icons aren't forced to the center of the screen:

```
// Friends/app/components/LoginPage/index.js

...
export default class LoginPage extends Component {
  render() {
    return (
      <View style={ styles.container }>
        <LoginButton
          ...
          onLogoutFinished={() => this.props.checkLoginStatus() }
        />
      </View>
    );
  }
}
```

The previous alert call in the `onLogoutFinished` prop of `LoginButton` has been replaced to fire `checkLoginStatus` instead.

Great job on all your progress in this app! The next step is to make modifications for Android development.

Porting to Android

The Android modifications we will make for this app are similar to the changes made for Expenses, which will be discussed later in Chapter 9, *Additional React Native Components*. The modifications we are making for Friends is as follows:

- Swapping out TabBarIOS for DrawerLayoutAndroid and ToolbarAndroid
- Creating Drawer and DrawerRow components to support DrawerLayoutAndroid
- Using Navigator in the root-level index.android.js file
- Creating an Android-specific version of the App component
- Updating FeedList for Android-specific styling
- Modifying FeedListRow to support Android navigation
- Adding BackAndroid and Navigator support to PostView

 In-depth explanations for DrawerLayoutAndroid and ToolbarAndroid can be found in Chapter 9, *Additional React Native Components*.

Adding DrawerLayoutAndroid and ToolbarAndroid

Let's begin by adding Toolbar/Drawer-based navigation for the Android version of Friends. We will need to start by creating a component called Drawer, which performs the following functions:

- This accepts an array of routes as a prop.
- This returns a ListView containing each route as a row to render. Each row should contain a TouchableHighlight component that, when clicked on, will call a prop called navigateTo, which we will eventually pass into Drawer.

We should also break the row that is rendered by Drawer into its own component titled DrawerRow. This component should do the following things:

- Accept the name of the row as a prop and render that name in a Text element
- Call setNativeProps so that its parent TouchableHighlight component will render this custom component

Instantiate a new `ListView.DataSource`:

```
// Friends/app/components/Drawer/index.js

import React, { Component } from 'react';

import {
  ListView,
  Text,
  TouchableHighlight,
  View
} from 'react-native';

import DrawerRow from '../DrawerRow';
import styles from './styles';

export default class Drawer extends Component {
  constructor (props) {
    super (props);
    this.state = {
      ds: new ListView.DataSource({
        rowHasChanged: (r1, r2) => r1 !== r2
      })
    }
  }
```

Render a `ListView` component, complete with a separator. Delegate the rendering of our rows to the `_renderDrawerRow` method:

```
  render () {
    const dataSource = this.state.ds.cloneWithRows
    (this.props.routes || []);
    return (
      <View style={ styles.container }>
        <ListView
          automaticallyAdjustContentInsets={ false }
          dataSource={ dataSource }
          enableEmptySections={ true }
          renderRow={ (rowData, sectionID, rowID) =>
          this._renderDrawerRow(rowData, sectionID, rowID) }
          renderSeparator={ (sectionID, rowID) =>
            <View
              key={ rowID }
              style={ styles.separator } />
          } />
      </View>
    )
  }
```

Wrap a TouchableHighlight around the custom DrawerRow component, passing it the name of the route. Call the navigateTo method from props in the onPress method of TouchableHighlight, passing it the index of the row:

```
_renderDrawerRow (rowData, sectionID, rowID) {
  return (
    <View>
      <TouchableHighlight
        style={ styles.row }
        onPress={ () => this.props.navigateTo(rowData.index) }>
        <DrawerRow
          routeName={ rowData.title } />
      </TouchableHighlight>
    </View>
  )
}
```

Next, the DrawerRow component was created:

```
// Friends/app/components/Drawer/styles.js

import { StyleSheet } from 'react-native';

const styles = StyleSheet.create({
  container: {
    flex: 1
  },
  separator: {
    height: StyleSheet.hairlineWidth,
    marginLeft: 10,
    marginRight: 10,
    backgroundColor: '#000000'
  }
})

export default styles;
```

The following code calls setNativeProps since DrawerRow is wrapped around TouchableHighlight:

```
// Friends/app/components/DrawerRow/index.js

import React, { Component } from 'react';

import {
  Text,
  View
```

```
} from 'react-native';

import styles from './styles';

export default class DrawerRow extends Component {
  setNativeProps (props) {
    this._root.setNativeProps(props)
  }
```

Render the name of the route:

```
  render () {
    return (
      <View
        style={ styles.container }
        ref={ component => this._root = component }
        { ...this.props }>
        <Text style={ styles.rowTitle }>
          { this.props.routeName }
        </Text>
      </View>
    )
  }
}
```

Here is the styling I created for `DrawerRow`:

```
// Friends/app/components/DrawerRow/styles.js

import { StyleSheet } from 'react-native';

const styles = StyleSheet.create({
  container: {
    flex: 1,
    height: 40,
    padding: 10
  },
  rowTitle: {
    fontSize: 20,
    textAlign: 'left'
  }
})

export default styles;
```

Integrating Drawer with Friends

Next, we will modify the root `index.android.js` file so that it does the following:

- Renders a `DrawerLayoutAndroid` component wrapped around `Icon.ToolbarAndroid` and `Navigator`.
- Imports and sets the `renderNavigationView` of `DrawerLayoutAndroid` to the `Drawer` component we created.
- Creates a callback to open `DrawerLayoutAndroid`.
- Writes a callback named `_navigateTo` that navigates to a given index. Pass this to `LoginPage` as a prop.
- Imports and renders the `App`, `LoginPage`, `PostView`, and `WebViewComponent` components using the `renderScene` callback in `Navigator`:

```
// Friends/index.android.js

import React, { Component } from 'react';
 import {
   AppRegistry,
   DrawerLayoutAndroid,
   Navigator,
   StyleSheet,
   View
} from 'react-native';

import App from './app/App';
import Drawer from './app/components/Drawer';
import LoginPage from './app/components/LoginPage';
import PostView from './app/components/PostView';
import WebViewComponent from './app/components/WebViewComponent';

import Icon from 'react-native-vector-icons/MaterialIcons';
```

Let's import all necessary dependencies, including React Native SDK components/APIs, each custom component being rendered by the `Navigator`, and the Material Icons pack from `react-native-vector-icons`.

```
export default class Friends extends Component {
  constructor (props) {
    super (props);

    this.state = {
      visibleRoutes: [
        { title: 'My Feed', index: 0 },
        { title: 'Log Out ', index: 1 }
```

```
        ]
    }
  }
```

Establish the array of visible routes to be passed into the `Drawer` component.

```
render() {
  const routes = [
    { title: 'My Feed', index: 0 },
    { title: 'Sign In/Log Out', index: 1 },
    { title: 'Post Details', index: 2 },
    { title: 'Web View', index: 3 }
  ];

  return (
    <View style={styles.container}>
      <DrawerLayoutAndroid
        drawerLockMode={ 'unlocked' }
        ref={ 'drawer' }
        renderNavigationView={ () => this._renderDrawerLayout() }
      >
```

Render a `DrawerLayoutAndroid` component, with its `renderNavigationView` prop being delegated to _renderDrawerLayout; set a `ref` of `drawer` to the component so we can refer to it in _openDrawer.

```
        <Icon.ToolbarAndroid
          titleColor="#fafafa"
          navIconName="menu"
          height={ 56 }
          backgroundColor="#365899"
          onIconClicked={ () => this._openDrawer() }
        />
```

Render the `Icon.ToolbarAndroid` component to contain the hamburger menu. Its onIconClicked callback executes _openDrawer.

```
        <Navigator
          initialRoute={{ index: 0 }}
          ref={ 'navigator' }
          renderScene={ (routes, navigator) =>
            this._renderScene(routes, navigator) }
        />
      </DrawerLayoutAndroid>
    </View>
  );
}
```

Render the `Navigator`, setting its initial route to the `index` for the `App` component. Delegate `renderScene` to the `_renderScene` method. Give a `ref` of `navigator` so we can reference it in `_navigateTo`.

```
_checkLoginStatus () {
  this._navigateTo(0);
}
```

The preceding code navigates to the `App` component, which triggers its checking of the user's login status.

```
_openDrawer () {
  this.refs['drawer'].openDrawer();
}
```

The `_openDrawer` method calls `openDrawer` on our `DrawerLayoutAndroid` component.

```
_navigateTo (index) {
  this.refs['navigator'].push({
    index,
    passProps: {
      checkLoginStatus: () => this._checkLoginStatus()
    }
  });
  this.refs['drawer'].closeDrawer();
}
```

The `_navigateTo` method pushes the given `index` to the `navigator`. Given a prop of `checkLoginStatus`, which will be used for the `LoginPage` component. It closes the `drawer` at the end.

```
_renderDrawerLayout () {
  return (
    <Drawer
      navigateTo={ (index) => this._navigateTo(index) }
      routes={ this.state.visibleRoutes }
    />
  );
}
```

The _renderDrawerLayout method renders the Drawer component, passing it the _navigateTo method as a prop along with the array of routes.

```
_renderScene (route, navigator) {
  if (route.index === 0) {
    return (
      <App
        title={ route.title }
        navigator={ navigator }
      />
    );
  }
```

The _renderScene method is responsible for rendering all four available routes.

```
  if (route.index === 1) {
    return (
      <LoginPage
        title={ route.title }
        navigator={ navigator }
        { ...route.passProps }
      />
    );
  }

  if (route.index === 2) {
    return (
      <PostView
        title={ route.title }
        navigator={ navigator }
        { ...route.passProps }
      />
    );
  }

  if (route.index === 3) {
    return (
      <WebViewComponent
        title={ route.title }
        navigator={ route.navigator }
        { ...route.passProps }
      />
    );
  }
}

}
```

```
const styles = StyleSheet.create({
  container: {
    flex: 1,
    backgroundColor: '#F5FCFF',
  }
});
```

```
AppRegistry.registerComponent('Friends', () => Friends);
```

Creating an Android version of App.js

Now, we should create an Android-specific App component for Friends. Start by renaming the existing App.js file found at Friends/app/App.js as App.ios.js and create a new file titled App.android.js.

This file should contain similar logic to App.ios.js, but any references to iOS-specific components, such as TabBarIOS, should be removed. Additionally, any navigation events should be updated to support Navigator logic.

Here's how I did it:

```
// Friends/app/App.android.js

...
```

The following three items were removed from the import statements: NavigatorIOS, TabBarIOS, and LoginPage:

```
export default class App extends Component {
  constructor (props) {
    ...
  }
```

The selectedTab property in state was removed from the constructor:

```
  ...
  async _checkLoginStatus () {
    ...
    if (result === null) {
      this.props.navigator.push({
        index: 1,
        passProps: {
          getFeed: () => this._getFeed()
        }
      });
```

```
            return;
        }
        . . .
    }
```

The `componentWillMount` and `render` methods stayed the same as in the iOS version. The navigation method in `_checkLoginStatus` was modified to pass an `index` instead of the `LoginPage` component:

```
    . . .
    _renderView () {
        . . .
        return this._renderFeedList();
    }
```

The `_getFeed`, `_renderFeedList`, and `_renderLoginPrompt` methods were not modified either. Instead of returning `TabBarIOS` in `_renderView`, I return a call to `_renderFeedList` instead.

```
        . . .
    }
```

Finally, `_refreshFeedList` and `_responseInfoCallback` methods were also left unchanged. However, `_setSelectedTab` was removed from `App.android.js` since it was a `TabBarIOS`-specific method.

Modifying FeedList

The styling for `FeedList` needs to change conditionally on Android so that its `container` style does not contain the `marginTop` property. Modify `FeedList` so that it does the following functions:

- Imports the `Platform` API from React Native.
- Conditionally checks for the user's platform and serves them either the container style on iOS devices or a new Android-specific style that does not include the `marginTop` property.

Here are my `FeedList` modifications for Android:

```
// Friends/app/components/FeedList/index.js

. . .
import {
  Platform,
```

```
  ...
} from 'react-native';
  ...
export default class FeedList extends Component {
  ...
  render () {
    ...
    return (
      <View style={ Platform.OS === 'ios' ? styles.container :
      styles.androidContainer }>
        ...
      </View>
    )
  }
  ...
}
```

I imported the Platform API and used a ternary operator to run a check for the user's operating system, assigning the top-level View component in the render method of FeedList an applicable style depending on that check's results:

```
// Friends/app/components/FeedList/styles.js

androidContainer: {
  flex: 1
},
```

I added the androidContainer style to the StyleSheet of FeedList.

Supporting Navigator in FeedListRow

Next, we have to update FeedListRow to do the following:

- Import the Platform API
- Modify the navigateToPostView to check for the user's operating system and use the appropriate syntax to push the PostView for each one

I created the propsObject to store the object assigned to passProps so that I did not have to rewrite it for a second time:

```
// Friends/app/components/FeedListRow/index.js

...
import {
  Platform,
```

```
  . . .
} from 'react-native';
  . . .
export default class FeedListRow extends Component {
  . . .
  _navigateToPostView () {
    const propsObject = {
      createdTime: this.props.createdTime,
      message: this.props.message,
      postID: this.props.postID,
      story: this.props.story
    };
```

Here we look at conditional logic for iOS:

```
if (Platform.OS === 'ios') {
  this.props.navigator.push({
    component: PostView,
    passProps: propsObject
  });
  return;
}
```

Since the iOS logic ends the function with the `return` statement, `push` with the `Navigator` if on Android.

```
    this.props.navigator.push({
      index: 2,
      passProps: propsObject
    });
  }
  . . .
}
```

Adding PostView navigator and BackAndroid support

Now, let's modify the `PostView` component with the following changes:

- Import the `Platform` and `BackAndroid` APIs
- Add and remove listeners for `BackAndroid` during `componentWillMount` and `componentWillUnmount`

- Write a callback in the component to handle back button presses on Android, calling `pop` on the navigator as a result
- Create conditional logic similar to `FeedListRow` to push the `WebViewComponent`

I created an event listener for `BackAndroid` in the `componentWillMount` lifecycle:

```
// Friends/app/components/PostView/index.js

...
import {
  BackAndroid,
  Platform,
  ...
} from 'react-native';
...
export default class PostView extends Component {
  ...
  async componentWillMount () {
    BackAndroid.addEventListener('hardwareButtonPress', () =>
    this._backButtonPress());
    ...
  }
```

Likewise, I remove that event listener during `componentWillUnmount`:

```
componentWillUnmount () {
  BackAndroid.removeEventListener('hardwareButtonPress', () =>
  this._backButtonPress())
}
```

This method calls `pop` on the `navigator` and is fired when the back button is pressed:

```
...
_backButtonPress () {
  this.props.navigator.pop();
  return true;
}
```

The conditional logic for pushing `WebViewComponent` on an iOS is as follows:

```
...
_renderWebView (url) {
  if (Platform.OS === 'ios') {
    this.props.navigator.push({
      component: WebViewComponent,
      passProps: {
        url
```

```
        }
      });
      return;
    }
```

The conditional logic for the same thing, but on Android is as follows:

```
    this.props.navigator.push({
      index: 3,
      passProps: {
        url
      }
    });
  }
}
```

Summary

Congratulations! You have successfully built three React Native applications throughout the course of this book. In this chapter, you learned to add a pull-to-refresh interaction into the application, letting users of your apps quickly refresh their data using a well-known gesture. Then, you utilized the `Image` component, rendering remote images into your application. Next, you created a `WebView` component for the application, allowing users to view Web-related content without shuffling them out of the app and into the system browser. Finally, you made the required modifications to create an Android version of the application.

7
Redux

Now that we have had a chance to get our feet wet with React Native, it's time to dive into some serious architecture. One of the things that you might have encountered with our previous apps is that our components ended up encapsulating a large amount of logic in them and that some files ran several hundred lines. In this chapter, we're going to introduce a new architecture for our apps to reduce bloat in our components. In this chapter, we will do the following:

- Learn about Redux, the architecture that will help manage our React Native apps' state and data flow
- Install the dependencies for Redux in our application
- Refactor `Tasks`, our to-do list app, to use Redux

Introducing Redux

Redux is a very popular library that many developers use to help write their React applications. On its GitHub repo, Redux bills itself as *a predictable state container for JavaScript apps*. Rather than having each component manage its own independent state, Redux proposes that your entire React application is governed by one single state. This single state is then proliferated through each component and allows the majority of your app's logic to live in reusable functions.

The three principles of Redux

You can describe Redux by referring to three key principles regarding the state: it needs to be the single source of truth for your application, be read-only, and be modifiable only by pure functions.

Single state tree

In Redux, rather than having each component manage its own state, we deal with one single-state tree that contains all the logic in our application. For example, for the Tasks app we built in the first two chapters, you can visualize it as follows:

```
{
  cellExpanded: false,
  tasks: [
    {
      title: 'Buy Milk',
      completed: false,
      dueDate: undefined
    },
    {
      title: 'Walk Dog',
      completed: true,
      dueDate: undefined
    }
  ],
}
```

This helps make our app a lot easier to debug, since we're only dealing with one object tree when looking at the information it contains.

State is read-only

The application state should never be modified directly. Instead, it should only be modified as the result of actions being dispatched and reducers interacting with it.

Changes are made with pure functions

The idea of a pure function comes from functional programming, and can be summarized as follows:

- Given the same arguments, a pure function always returns the same result
- Regardless of our application state, a pure function is able to execute
- Variables outside of a pure function's scope cannot be modified by it

These three principles correlate with three major parts of the Redux ecosystem: actions, reducers, and store.

Actions are how we can indirectly modify our read-only state. Reducers are the pure functions that perform that modification. The single store in Redux is where our state exists.

Actions

Actions are simple objects containing information that sends data from your app over to the app's store. All the logic that your app handles will pass through the action - your store never receives any data from sources that aren't actions.

An action requires a `type` property, which defines the type of user action that has occurred. Types of actions are represented in a stringified form. They can be hardcoded into the object itself or passed in as a constant. For example:

```
export function addTask(taskName) {
  return {
    type: 'ADD_TASK',
    taskName: taskName
  }
}

// With constants

const ADD_TASK = 'ADD_TASK';

export function addTask(taskName) {
  return {
    type: ADD_TASK,
    taskName: taskName
  }
}
```

These functions will be made available as props to all the components in your application and can be called at any time. When an action is called, the store then dispatches the action to every reducer in your application. Only the right reducer, chosen with conditional logic, will fire at this time, and will execute code that changes your application's state.

Reducers

In Vanilla JavaScript, there's an array prototype method called `reduce`. The purpose of this native reduce function is to return one single reduced value after running a callback and initial value through an entire array's contents.

In Redux, a reducer is a function that takes in your application's state and relevant information passed to it from an action, and then returns one single reduced value for your application's state after executing the code.

Reducers should, as a good practice, be restricted to one reducer per file, for clarity.

There are two really important things we need to know about reducers with Redux:

- Your application state is never mutated. Instead, a copy is returned with any changed values.
- Since each reducer will fire when an action happens in order to decide if that action is relevant to it, we have to return the previous application state in the event that any unknown (to that specific reducer) actions are fired.

Working from the preceding example, this is how a reducer would look for an ADD_TASK action:

```
const task = (state = [], action) => {
```

Using ES6's default arguments syntax to give us an empty array if a state does not exist, the action object is passed in from the action creator:

```
switch(action.type) {
    case 'ADD_TASK':
      return [
        ...state,
        {
          taskName: action.taskName
        }
      ]
    default:
      return state;
  }
}
```

Stores

A store is an object that brings actions and reducers together. It does the following things for us:

- Contains the application state
- Gives access to that state, via a method called getState
- Dispatches actions, which reducers then use to modify that state

One thing to be aware of with Redux is that, in a given application, you will only ever have one store. In the event that we want to split our logic into multiple handlers, we'll actually split the reducers instead, through a method called **reducer composition** this is something we'll take a look at once we need it.

Here's how a sample store in Redux looks. Let's assume we have the task reducer from before, and another one as follows:

```
import { combineReducers, createStore, compose } from 'redux';

const defaultState = {
  task,
  dueDate
}
```

These are examples of actions:

```
const addTask = function(taskName) {
  return {
    type: 'ADD_TASK',
    taskName: taskName
  }
}

const changeDueDate = function(dueDate) {
  return {
    type: 'CHANGE_DUE_DATE',
    dueDate: dueDate
  }
}
```

These are where we would have our reducers:

```
const task = // Reducer to add a new task to the list
const dueDate = // Reducer to modify a task's due date

const rootReducer = combineReducers(task, dueDate);

const store = createStore(rootReducer, defaultState);
```

Within a component, we can simply call an action within a component as follows:

```
this.props.addTask('Buy Milk')
```

But wait, how do our components know that this action is available? Just where do we expose our props? We do it using a library called React-Redux, which contains two things we want to utilize.

The first is the `connect` method, which connects our React Native application to the Redux store. The two arguments we're interested in passing to connect are `mapStateToProps` and `mapDispatchToProps`.

`mapStateToProps`, if specified, is a function that subscribes to updates to the state tree. Any time the state tree updates, `mapStateToProps` will be called and merges its return value into your component's props. The return value needs to be an object. Here's a quick example:

```
const mapStateToProps = (state) => {
  return {
    tasks: state.tasks
  }
}
```

`mapDispatchToProps` will map our dispatch methods to our components' props. As a function, we can call `bindActionCreators` to it and pass in our action creators, as well as a dispatch call, so they can be invoked directly. Here's how it looks:

```
import { bindActionCreators } from 'redux';
import { connect } from 'react-redux';
import * as actionCreators from '../actions';

const mapDispatchToProps = (dispatch) => {
  return bindActionCreators(actionCreators, dispatch);
}
```

Then, assuming `Main` as the entry point for our app, we'll use `connect` to bring them together:

```
import Main from './Main';

const App = connect(mapStateToProps, mapDispatchToProps)(Main)
```

In order to propagate our store (and all of the actions and reducers associated with it), we'll use the `Provider` from `React-Redux` to wrap our application and pass it our store as a prop. This allows the components in our React app to inherit these props naturally. It happens at the root level, as follows:

```
return (
  <Provider store={ store }>
    <App />
  </Provider>
)
```

This is a good amount of setup, and, if you're having some doubts about its effectiveness, I would urge you to power through the rest of this chapter: Redux is incredibly useful, because it's going to let us write cleaner components that are a lot easier to maintain, and will help future contributors understand our code base better.

Our next step is to install Redux, so let's get started.

Installing Redux

We'll use npm to install Redux. There are also a couple of dependencies it needs, and we're going to install all of them at once. Make sure you're at the root directory of your project folder, and do the following:

```
npm install --save redux react-redux redux-thunk
```

Here's a brief overview of the three packages we're installing into our project:

- Redux: This is the library itself.
- React-Redux: This is a library that provides bindings for React. Redux isn't specifically tied to React, and this library will let us access the Provider component to pass down our props at the parent level with ease.
- Redux-Thunk: This is middleware that will help us make asynchronous calls with our actions, and is useful because we will be making calls to AsyncStorage.

Now that we have the three packages installed, it's time to start setting up our architecture.

Redux architecture

The architecture of our application when using Redux will be slightly modified from what we had before. At present, this is how the app directory in our project looks:

```
|app
|__components
|____DatePickerDialogue
|____EditTask
|____ExpandableCell
|____TasksList
|____TasksListCell
```

Redux requires us to think differently about how we approach our app's architecture, and we'll be adding some new folders into the app directory:

```
|app
|__containers
|__components
|__reducers
|__index.js
```

Containers in Redux

Containers are where we're going to map the dispatch methods and application state that connect to both the component and Redux. The components folder will still exist, but we are going to refactor what's inside to not rely on a component-based state.

From now on, every time we would usually render a component, we instead render its container.

Remaining folder structure

The reducers folder is going to contain a single reducer file, which handles all the logic that modifies our application state.

The index.js file found within the app folder will handle our Redux setup and be rendered by the root index files for both iOS and Android.

What you'll have at our root index.ios.js and index.android.js files are the following:

```
// TasksRedux/index.js

import Tasks from './app';
import { AppRegistry } from 'react-native';

AppRegistry.registerComponent('Tasks', () => Tasks);
```

Planning the Redux conversion

The approach we will take in converting our app to Redux will involve multiple steps:

1. First, we should begin by scaffolding a Redux project by creating a store, wrapping the AppContainer around a Provider, and creating some basic actions and reducers to handle very basic functionality--we can worry about persistent storage later.

2. Then, we will begin converting the TasksList component to Redux by creating a TasksListContainer and mapping our actions and state tree to the TasksList component. Any other components from when we built Tasks in Chapter 1, *First Project - Creating a Basic To-Do List App*, and Chapter 2, *Advanced Functionality and Styling the To-Do List App*, will remain untouched for the time being.

3. Afterwards, we will modify the TasksList component to take advantage of its container by removing all component-unspecific logic from it.

4. We will repeat this series of steps for the EditTask component.

5. Finally, we should address the asynchronous calls to the AsyncStorage API.

6. Along the way, we should take every opportunity to make changes to the Android version of Tasks to convert it to a Redux architecture.

Creating the entry point

The index file found at app/index.js will serve as the entry point into our application. Both the iOS and Android versions of Tasks will call upon it, and it's going to set up our Redux architecture. First, we'll import all the necessary dependencies. Don't worry if we haven't created any applicable files or folders for these items yet; we'll do so very shortly:

```
// TasksRedux/app/index.js

import React from 'react';
import AppContainer from './containers/AppContainer';
import { createStore, applyMiddleware } from 'redux';
import { Provider } from 'react-redux';
import thunk from 'redux-thunk';
import listOfTasks from './reducers';
```

Next, let's set up our store.

Setting up our store

To set up our store, we will need to use Redux's `createStore` method and then pass it a reducer. Here's how it looks on a high level:

```
let store = createStore(task)
```

Additionally, since we know we'll be dealing with asynchronous calls in our application, we should also set up `Redux-Thunk` to support it.

To do so, pass the `applyMiddleware` function as the second argument to `createStore`. Pass `thunk` as an argument for `applyMiddleware`:

```
let store = createStore(listOfTasks, applyMiddleware(thunk));
```

Finally, we'll export a stateless function that returns our app container wrapped around the `Provider`:

```
export default function Tasks (props) {
  return (
    <Provider store={ store }>
      <AppContainer />
    </Provider>
  )
}
```

In total, here's how our `index.js` file will look at the end of the setup:

```
// TasksRedux/app/index.js

import React from 'react';
import AppContainer from './containers/AppContainer';
import { createStore, applyMiddleware } from 'redux';
import { Provider } from 'react-redux';
import thunk from 'redux-thunk';
import listOfTasks from './reducers';

let store = createStore(listOfTasks, applyMiddleware(thunk));

export default function Tasks (props) {
  return (
    <Provider store={ store }>
      <AppContainer />
    </Provider>
  )
}
```

Now that we have created this file, let's build the app container. If you haven't already, create a `containers` folder within the `app` folder and then create separate `AppContainer` files for Android and iOS.

Building the app container

The app container is going to provide a base `NavigatorIOS` route that renders our `TasksList` container. It looks similar to what we previously had in our root index files:

```
// TasksRedux/app/containers/AppContainer.ios.js

import React, { Component } from 'react';

import {
  NavigatorIOS,
  StyleSheet
} from 'react-native';

import TasksListContainer from '../containers/TasksListContainer';

export default class App extends Component {
  render () {
    return (
      <NavigatorIOS
        initialRoute={{
          component: TasksListContainer,
          title: 'Tasks'
        }}
        style={ styles.container }
      />
    )
  }
}

const styles = StyleSheet.create({
  container: {
    flex: 1,
    backgroundColor: '#F5FCFF'
  }
});
```

The major difference between the `AppContainer` and the root index file is that it does not call `AppRegistry.registerComponent`. That part is still handled by the root index file.

Import the two routes we will use for `Navigator`:

```
// TasksRedux/app/containers/AppContainer.android.js

import React, { Component } from 'react';
import {
  Navigator,
} from 'react-native';

import TasksListContainer from './TasksListContainer';
import EditTaskContainer from './EditTaskContainer';
```

Set the `routes` array:

```
class Tasks extends Component {

  render () {
    const routes = [
      { title: 'Tasks', index: 0 },
      { title: 'Edit Task', index: 1 }
    ];
```

This function handles the logic for rendering different routes:

```
    return (
      <Navigator
        initialRoute={{ index: 0}}
        renderScene={ (routes, navigator) =>
        this._renderScene(routes, navigator) }/>
    );
  }

  _renderScene (route, navigator) {
    if (route.index === 0) {
      return (
        <TasksListContainer
          title={ route.title }
          navigator={ navigator }
        />
      )
    }

    if (route.index === 1) {
      return (
        <EditTaskContainer
          title={ route.title }
          navigator={ navigator }
        />
```

```
        )
      }
    }
  }

  AppRegistry.registerComponent('Tasks', () => Tasks);
```

Next we will move onto creating actions and reducers in anticipation of building the `TasksList` container.

Creating actions

Let's create some actions that will help us with our application. In the `Tasks` app, we had functionality for the following actions:

- Fetching tasks from `AsyncStorage`
- Creating a new task
- Editing a task's name
- Marking/unmarking a task as complete
- Showing/hiding the expandable component
- Saving changes to a task
- Clearing changes to a task
- Adding a due date
- Removing a due date

Here's an example of how an action for editing a task's name can look:

```
export function editTaskName (title, index) {
  return {
    type: 'EDIT_TASK_NAME',
    title: title,
    index: index
  }
};
```

When naming an action, we want to correlate the type of action with exactly what has happened as a result of a user interaction. In this case, the user edited the task name. This action will also pass our reducer a `title` and `index`, so the reducer can then search the state for the task with the provided `index`, and edit its `title`.

Initially, we have three actions we want to make sure work in `TasksList`: adding a task, changing its completion status, and modifying the value of `TextInput`:

```
// TasksRedux/app/actions/index.js

let currentIndex = 0;

const ADD_TASK = 'ADD_TASK';
const CHANGE_COMPLETION_STATUS = 'CHANGE_COMPLETION_STATUS';
const CHANGE_INPUT_TEXT = 'CHANGE_INPUT_TEXT';

export function addTask (text) {
  return {
    type: ADD_TASK,
    index: currentIndex++,
    text,
  . }
}
```

Each action is an exported function that returns an object with the action type as well as any other key-value pairs that contain data for our reducers to interact with:

```
export function changeCompletionStatus (index) {
  return {
    type: CHANGE_COMPLETION_STATUS,
    index
  }
}

export function changeInputText (text) {
  return {
    type: CHANGE_INPUT_TEXT,
    text
  }
}
```

These will do for now - we'll slowly build in the other actions as we convert more and more of our application to support Redux. Next up, let's build the reducers for these three actions.

Building reducers

Let's look at how we would build reducers to handle creating a new task and saving it into our list of tasks.

Assuming we're working with the following state tree:

```
{
  tasks: [
    {
      title: 'Buy Milk',
      completed: false,
      dueDate: undefined
    },
    {
      title: 'Walk Dog',
      completed: true,
      dueDate: undefined
    }
  ],
}
```

In the interest of writing a pure function, we want to make sure that we're not mutating the state and instead re-assigning our state to contain the updated changes.

In an impure function, we would simply do something like this:

 Don't do this!

```
function addTask (state, action) {
  switch(action.type) {
    case 'ADD_TASK':
      state.tasks.push({
        title: action.title,
        completed: false
      });
      return state;
    default:
      return state;
  }
};
```

What we're doing here is mutating our state tree's tasks array to push a new task into it. This can lead to problems when debugging later. Instead, what we want to do can be broken into a series of actionable steps:

1. Create a copy of the current state.
2. Create a copy of the task's property of our copied state.

3. Add our new task to the end of this copy.

4. Assign this copied array as the new task's value of our copied state.

5. Assign the copied state as our new current state.

The `singleTask` reducer handles logic that affects just one single task in the list. The results of this reducer are immediately accessed by the main `listOfTasks` reducer:

```
// TasksRedux/app/reducers/index.js

const singleTask = (state = {}, action) => {
```

In this event, we return an object containing a new task's details.

```
switch(action.type) {
  case 'ADD_TASK':
    return {
      completed: false,
      due: undefined,
      index: action.index,
      text: action.text
    }
```

The `singleTask` reducer is called during iteration in the `listOfTasks` reducer. Here, if the index of the individual task matches up with the index we want to interact with, we return the existing object using a spread operator and switch its completed status:

```
case 'CHANGE_COMPLETION_STATUS':
  if (state.index !== action.index) {
    return state;
  }
  return {
    ...state,
    completed: !state.completed
  }
```

This sets a default state to pass over to `listOfTasks`:

```
  default:
    return state;
  }
}

let defaultState = {
  listOfTasks: [],
  text: ''
}
```

The `listOfTasks` reducer is where all actions first end up firing through. It then uses a switch statement to figure out which action type is being called and returns a new state object based on that action type:

```
const listOfTasks = (state = defaultState, action) => {
```

If we want to add a task, return the state object through a spread operator containing an updated `listOfTasks` array that is built using the spread operator, calling the `singleTask` reducer with an empty object and the action object that is initially passed there:

```
switch(action.type) {
  case 'ADD_TASK':
    return {
      ...state,
      listOfTasks: [...state.listOfTasks, singleTask({}, action)],
      text: ''
    }
```

If we change a task's completion status, we call map on the `listOfTasks` array in the state and then call `singleTask` on each element in the task, passing the current task object and the action object to it:

```
  case 'CHANGE_COMPLETION_STATUS':
    return {
      ...state,
      listOfTasks: state.listOfTasks.map((element) => {
        return singleTask(element, action);
      })
    }
```

Update the `text` property of our state tree for `TextInput` components:

```
  case 'CHANGE_INPUT_TEXT':
    return {
      ...state,
      text: action.text
    }

  default:
    return state;
  }
}

export default listOfTasks;
```

To summarize, `listOfTasks` is our parent reducer and handles the overall logic of our app, while `singleTask` handles the pertinent information for one single item in our list.

Creating the TasksList container

Now that we've got our actions and reducers, we'll create the container that connects our dispatch methods and state to the `TasksList` component.

First, we'll import the `connect` module from `react-redux`, alongside any actions we intend to dispatch in `TasksList`, as well as the `TasksList` component itself:

```
// TasksRedux/app/containers/TasksListContainer/index.js

import { connect } from 'react-redux';

import {
  addTask,
  changeCompletionStatus,
  changeInputText,
} from '../../actions';

import TasksList from '../../components/TasksList';
```

Then we'll create three methods that will result in dispatching functions to our state tree using `mapDispatchToProps`:

```
const mapDispatchToProps = (dispatch) => {
  return {
    addTask: (text) => {
      dispatch(addTask(text));
    },
    changeCompletionStatus: (rowID) => {
      dispatch(changeCompletionStatus(rowID))
    },
    onChangeText: (text) => {
      dispatch(changeInputText(text));
    },
  }
}
```

Afterwards, we'll map the state we intend to pass into TasksList's prop, including the `Navigator` that we already have from the top level:

```
const mapStateToProps = (state, { navigator }) => {
  return {
    listOfTasks: state.listOfTasks || [],
    navigator: navigator,
    text: state.text || ''
  }
}
```

Finally, we will `connect` the `mapStateToProps` and `mapDispatchToProps` functions to the `TasksList` component and export it:

```
export default connect(mapStateToProps, mapDispatchToProps)(TasksList);
```

Now, let's look at how we refactor the `TasksList` component.

Redux-connected TasksList component

Components in Redux will retain their JSX markup, but any logic that isn't specific to that exact component is kept by our state tree and modified through actions and reducers:

```
// TasksRedux/app/components/TasksList/index.js

import React, { Component } from 'react';
import {
  ListView,
  Platform,
  TextInput,
  View
} from 'react-native';
```

React Native APIs and components such as `AsyncStorage` have been removed from this component, since any calls to any storage methods will be handled by our actions and reducers in the future.

Create a new `ListView.DataSource` instance, since it is specific to this component:

```
import TasksListCell from '../TasksListCell';
import styles from './styles';

export default class TasksList extends Component {
  constructor (props) {
    super (props);
```

```
        this.state = {
          ds: new ListView.DataSource({
            rowHasChanged: (r1, r2) => r1 !== r2
          }),
        };
      }
```

Create the `dataSource` constant for our `ListView` with the `listOfTasks` array in our state tree:

```
      render () {
        const dataSource =
        this.state.ds.cloneWithRows(this.props.listOfTasks);
```

Callbacks such as `onChangeText` and `onSubmitEditing` now call actions that have been mapped to the `TasksListContainer`:

```
      return (
        <View style={ styles.container }>
          <TextInput
            autoCorrect={ false }
            onChangeText={ (text) => this.props.onChangeText(text) }
            onSubmitEditing={ () => this.props.addTask(this.props.text) }
            returnKeyType={ 'done' }
            style={ Platform.OS === 'ios' ? styles.textInput :
            styles.androidTextInput }
            value={ this.props.text }
          />
```

This passes `TasksListCell`'s required `onLongPress` callback a placeholder:

```
          <ListView
            automaticallyAdjustContentInsets={ false }
            dataSource={ dataSource }
            enableEmptySections={ true }
            renderRow={ (rowData, sectionID, rowID) =>
            this._renderRowData(rowData, rowID) }
            style={ styles.listView }
          />
        </View>
      );
    }

    _renderRowData (rowData, rowID) {
      return (
        <TasksListCell
          completed={ rowData.completed }
          formattedDate={ rowData.formattedDate }
```

```
        id={ rowID }
        onLongPress={ () => alert('placeholder') }
        onPress={ () =>
        this.props.changeCompletionStatus(rowData.index) }
        text={ rowData.text }
      />
    )
  }
}}
```

Converting EditTasks to Redux

With `EditTasks`, we are introducing some new actions and reducers into the mix. These include:

- Setting the currently selected task to one that was pressed on in `TasksList`
- Handling a change when the Cancel or Save buttons are pressed in the `EditTask` screen
- Toggling the selected task as completed
- Changing the name of the selected task
- Adding, modifying, and removing the due date
- Expanding the expandable cell that shows and hides the `DatePicker` component

For the first two bullet points, those modifications will come in the form of three new actions placed in the `TasksList` container, since that's the component where these events will either happen or be defined and passed to EditTask's navigator.

Our state tree will also need to hold the following new properties:

- The formatted and unformatted dates from the DatePicker component that point to the selected task
- An object pertaining to the currently selected task in the `EditTask` screen
- An indication whether the `ExpandableCell` is visible or not
- An indication whether a date has been selected in the EditScreen view

With this in mind, let's start the conversion with our actions!

Adding actions for EditTask

Here are the additions to the actions file to accommodate `EditTask`:

```
// TasksRedux/app/actions/index.js

...
const CHANGE_CURRENTLY_EDITED_TASK = 'CHANGE_CURRENTLY_EDITED_TASK';
const CHANGE_SELECTED_TASK_COMPLETED = 'CHANGE_SELECTED_TASK_COMPLETED';
const CHANGE_SELECTED_TASK_DUE_DATE = 'CHANGE_SELECTED_TASK_DUE_DATE';
const SAVE_SELECTED_TASK_DETAILS = 'SAVE_SELECTED_TASK_DETAILS';
const EDIT_SELECTED_TASK_NAME = 'EDIT_SELECTED_TASK_NAME';
const EXPAND_CELL = 'EXPAND_CELL';
const REMOVE_SELECTED_TASK_DUE_DATE = 'REMOVE_SELECTED_TASK_DUE_DATE';
const RESET_SELECTED_TASK = 'RESET_SELECTED_TASK';
```

These are new constants that describe the different actions that the `EditTask` component will bring to the app.

These functions are straightforward, since they pass the desired action type between zero and two values for our reducers to handle:

```
...
export function changeCurrentlyEditedTask (selectedTaskObject) {
  return {
    type: CHANGE_CURRENTLY_EDITED_TASK,
    selectedTaskObject: selectedTaskObject
  }
}

export function changeSelectedTaskCompleted (value) {
  return {
    type: CHANGE_SELECTED_TASK_COMPLETED,
    value
  }
}

export function changeSelectedTaskDueDate (date) {
  return {
    type: CHANGE_SELECTED_TASK_DUE_DATE,
    date
  }
}
```

The `saveSelectedTaskDetails` action is more complex than the rest. It takes an object from the `EditTask` component and then breaks it into different properties for our reducer to work with.

```
export function editSelectedTaskName (text) {
  return {
    type: EDIT_SELECTED_TASK_NAME,
    text
  }
}

export function expandCell (currentlyExpanded) {
  return {
    type: EXPAND_CELL,
    expanded: currentlyExpanded
  }
}

export function resetSelectedTask () {
  return {
    type: RESET_SELECTED_TASK
  }
}

export function removeSelectedTaskDueDate () {
  return {
    type: REMOVE_SELECTED_TASK_DUE_DATE
  }
}

export function saveSelectedTaskDetails (object) {
  return {
    type: SAVE_SELECTED_TASK_DETAILS,
    completed: object.completed,
    date: object.due || undefined,
    formattedDate: object.formattedDate || undefined,
    index: object.index,
    text: object.text
  }
}
```

Reducers for EditTask

We should also update our reducers to handle these newly introduced actions. We should do the following:

- Expand the defaultState object, including the date, dateSelected, expanded, formattedDate, and selectedTaskObject properties
- Add a helper function to format a date with MomentJS
- Create a new switch case for the singleTask reducer to handle the SAVE_SELECTED_TASK_DETAILS action
- Build a new selectedTask reducer for temporarily storing and modifying the selectedTaskObject being edited by the user
- Extend the listOfTasks reducer to handle each of the new actions, delegating them to either the singleTask or selectedTask reducers when necessary

The defaultState object has gotten larger to accommodate new information that EditTask will be using, such as the expanded status of ExpandableCell:

```
// TasksRedux/app/reducers/index.js

import moment from 'moment';

const defaultState = {
  ...
  date: undefined,
  dateSelected: false,
  expanded: false,
  formattedDate: undefined,
  selectedTaskObject: undefined,
}
```

Format the date with MomentJS:

```
const _formatDate = (date) => {
  if (date) {
    return moment(date).format('lll');
  }
}
```

No changes were made to these two methods:

```
const singleTask = (state = {}, action) => {
  switch(action.type) {
    case 'ADD_TASK':
      ...
    case 'CHANGE_COMPLETION_STATUS':
      ...
```

This is specifically to save details for a task that has been selected for editing by the user:

```
    case 'SAVE_SELECTED_TASK_DETAILS':
      if (state.index !== action.index) {
        return state;
      }
      return {
        ...state,
        completed: action.completed,
        due: action.date,
        formattedDate: action.formattedDate,
        text: action.text
      }
```

This is a new reducer created to address the task object currently being edited by the user:

```
    default:
      return state;
  }
}

const selectedTask = (state = {}, action) => {
```

Our Redux state stores the object being edited by the user because at any given point, the user can simply decide to cancel any changes. Keeping changes in a temporary object and only saving them to the state once the user has pressed on the Save button saves us the hassle of undoing any changes the user has made:

```
  switch(action.type) {
    case 'CHANGE_SELECTED_TASK_COMPLETED':
      return {
        ...state,
        completed: action.value
      }
    case 'CHANGE_SELECTED_TASK_DUE_DATE':
      return {
        ...state,
        due: action.date || undefined,
        formattedDate: action.date ?
```

```
        _formatDate(action.date) : undefined
    }
```

Similar to the `singleTask` reducer, `selectedTask` is accessed by the main `listOfTasks` reducer:

```
    case 'EDIT_SELECTED_TASK_NAME':
      return {
        ...state,
        text: action.text
      }
    case 'REMOVE_SELECTED_TASK_DUE_DATE':
      return {
        ...state,
        due: undefined,
        formattedDate: undefined
      }
    default:
      return state;
  }
}

const listOfTasks = (state = defaultState, action) => {
  switch(action.type) {
    case 'ADD_TASK':
      ...
    case 'CHANGE_COMPLETION_STATUS':
      ...
```

No changes were made to the following two cases.

```
    case 'CHANGE_CURRENTLY_EDITED_TASK':
      const date = action.selectedTaskObject.due || new Date();
      const formattedDate = _formatDate(date);

      const hasDueDate = action.selectedTaskObject.due ? true : false
      return {
        ...state,
        date: date,
        dateSelected: hasDueDate,
        formattedDate: formattedDate,
        selectedTaskObject: action.selectedTaskObject
      }
```

This is the code for setting the `selectedTaskObject` property in our Redux state. It also sets the date, `dateSelected`, and `formattedDate` properties for the `DatePicker` component.

No changes to this case either:

```
case 'CHANGE_INPUT_TEXT':
   ...
```

This is the first time we call the `selectedTask` reducer from `listOfTasks`. It changes the completion status of the task currently being edited:

```
case 'CHANGE_SELECTED_TASK_COMPLETED':
  return {
    ...state,
    selectedTaskObject: selectedTask
    (state.selectedTaskObject, action)
  }
```

This case changes the due date of the selected task, as well as the `date`, `dateSelected`, and `formattedDate` properties:

```
case 'CHANGE_SELECTED_TASK_DUE_DATE':
  return {
    ...state,
    date: action.date,
    dateSelected: action.date ? true : false,
    formattedDate: action.date ? _formatDate(action.date) :
    undefined,
    selectedTaskObject: selectedTask
    (state.selectedTaskObject, action)
  }
```

Change the name of the selected task:

```
case 'EDIT_SELECTED_TASK_NAME':
  return {
    ...state,
    selectedTaskObject: selectedTask(state.selectedTaskObject,
    action)
  }
```

Handle the `expanded` property of `ExpandableCell`:

```
case 'EXPAND_CELL':
  return {
    ...state,
    expanded: !action.expanded
  }
```

This is what gets executed if the user presses `Cancel` in the `EditTask` screen:

```
case 'RESET_SELECTED_TASK':
  return {
    ...state,
    expanded: false,
    selectedTask: undefined,
  }
```

Remove the due date from the selected task:

```
case 'REMOVE_SELECTED_TASK_DUE_DATE':
  return {
    ...state,
    dateSelected: false,
    selectedTaskObject: selectedTask(state.selectedTaskObject,
    action)
  }
```

Finally, this saves the selected task permanently into the `listOfTasks` array:

```
case 'SAVE_SELECTED_TASK_DETAILS':
  return {
    ...state,
    expanded: false,
    listOfTasks: state.listOfTasks.map((element) => {
        return singleTask(element, action)
      })
  }

default:
  ...
  }
}

export default listOfTasks;export default listOfTasks;
```

Updating TasksListContainer to accommodate EditTask

Now we should update the `TasksListContainer` and `TasksList` component. First, `TasksListContainer` should do the following:

- Import the `changeCurrentlyEditedTask`, `resetSelectedTask`, and `saveSelectedTaskDetails` actions and add them to the `mapDispatchToProps` method
- Import the `date`, `formattedDate`, and `selectedTaskObject` properties of our Redux state and add them to the `mapStateToProps` method

Take a look at the following code:

```
// TasksRedux/app/containers/TasksListContainer

...
import {
  ...
  changeCurrentlyEditedTask,
  resetSelectedTask,
  saveSelectedTaskDetails
} from '../../actions';
```

Above, I imported three new actions.

```
...
const mapDispatchToProps = (dispatch) => {
  return {
    ...
    changeCompletionStatus: (index) => {
      dispatch(changeCompletionStatus(index));
    },
    resetSelectedTask: () => {
      dispatch(resetSelectedTask());
    },
    saveSelectedTaskDetails: (selectedTaskObject) => {
      dispatch(saveSelectedTaskDetails(selectedTaskObject));
    }
  }
}
```

Mapping the three new actions to the dispatch methods of `TasksList`.

```
const mapStateToProps = (state, { navigator }) => {
  return {
    ...
    date: state.date,
    formattedDate: state.formattedDate,
    selectedTaskObject: state.selectedTaskObject,
  }
}
...
```

Mapping three new values in the Redux state to the props of `TasksList`.

Updating the TasksList component

Next, let's make changes to `TasksList` so that it supports `EditTask`. It should do the following:

1. Import the `EditTaskContainer` for us to push to the navigator.
2. Add the `Platform` API to support Android devices.
3. Modify the `onLongPress` callback for `TasksListCell` to call a function that first adds the currently selected task to the Redux state and then navigate the user to the `EditTaskContainer`. It should contain a `Cancel` and `Save` button.
4. The `Cancel` button should fire a function that `pops` the navigator and resets the `selectedTaskObject` value in your Redux state.
5. The `Save` button should fire a function that `pops` the navigator and saves the `selectedTaskObject` into the `listOfTasks` array in your Redux state.

Here are my changes to the `TasksList` component:

```
// TasksRedux/app/components/TasksList/index.js

...
import {
  ...
  Platform,
} from 'react-native';

import EditTaskContainer from '../../containers/EditTaskContainer';
...
export default class TasksList extends Component {
  ...
```

The following code adds the `_cancelEditingTask` function to call `pop` on the navigator and then the `resetSelectedTask` action:

```
_cancelEditingTask () {
  this.props.navigator.pop();
  this.props.resetSelectedTask();
}
```

Change the onLongPress callback for TasksListCell to call the following _onLongPress function:

```
_renderRowData (rowData, rowID) {
  return (
    <TasksListCell
      ...
      onLongPress={ () => this._onLongPress(rowData) }
    />
  )
}
```

If the user is on an iOS device, push the EditTaskContainer to the navigator and pass it a string for the left and right buttons, and give them callbacks that fire when they are pressed:

```
_onLongPress (rowData) {
  this.props.changeCurrentlyEditedTask(rowData);

  if (Platform.OS === 'ios') {
    this.props.navigator.push({
      component: EditTaskContainer,
      title: this.props.selectedTaskText,
      leftButtonTitle: 'Cancel',
      rightButtonTitle: 'Save',
      onLeftButtonPress: () => this._cancelEditingTask(),
      onRightButtonPress: () => this._saveEditedTask()
    });
    return;
  }
```

On an Android device, just push the index of the route specified in AppContainer.android.js:

```
    this.props.navigator.push({
      index: 1
    });
  }
}
```

When saving the edited task, first pop the navigator and then dispatch the saveSelectedTaskDetails action:

```
  _saveEditedTask () {
    this.props.navigator.pop();
    this.props.saveSelectedTaskDetails(this.props.selectedTaskObject);
  }
}
```

Creating the EditTask container

The EditTaskContainer will be composed the same way as TasksListContainer. It will do the following:

1. Import actions relevant to the EditTask component from your actions file.
2. Import the EditTask and connect module.
3. Contain a mapDispatchToProps method to map the actions you imported.
4. Call mapStateToProps on any parts of the Redux state you wish EditTask to have access to.
5. Call connect on mapDispatchToProps, mapStateToProps, and the EditTask component.

These are the actions that EditTask will be utilizing:

```
// TasksRedux/app/containers/EditTaskContainer

import { connect } from 'react-redux';

import {
  changeSelectedTaskCompleted,
  changeSelectedTaskDueDate,
  editSelectedTaskName,
  expandCell,
  removeSelectedTaskDueDate,
  resetSelectedTask,
  saveSelectedTaskDetails
} from '../../actions';
```

The resetSelectedTask and saveSelectedTaskDetails actions are mapped to EditTaskContainer specifically for the Android version of this app:

```
import EditTask from '../../components/EditTask';

const mapDispatchToProps = (dispatch) => {
  return {
    changeCompletedStatus: (value) => {
      dispatch(changeSelectedTaskCompleted(value));
    },
    changeTextInputValue: (text) => {
      dispatch(editSelectedTaskName(text))
    },
    clearDate: () => {
      dispatch(removeSelectedTaskDueDate());
    },
```

```
      onDateChange: (date) => {
        dispatch(changeSelectedTaskDueDate(date));
      },
      onExpand: (currentlyExpanded) => {
        dispatch(expandCell(currentlyExpanded))
      },
      resetSelectedTask: () => {
        dispatch(resetSelectedTask());
      },
      saveSelectedTaskDetails: (selectedTaskObject) => {
        dispatch(saveSelectedTaskDetails(selectedTaskObject));
      }
    }
  }
```

EditTask should have access to the following data from the state tree:

```
const mapStateToProps = (state) => {
  return {
    date: state.date,
    dateSelected: state.dateSelected,
    expanded: state.expanded,
    formattedDate: state.formattedDate,
    selectedTaskObject: state.selectedTaskObject,
  }
}
```

Finally, connect everything together:

```
export default connect(mapStateToProps, mapDispatchToProps)(EditTask);
```

Modifying the EditTask component for iOS

Next, we will modify the EditTask component. It should:

- Be nearly identical to the EditTask component we had at the end of Chapter 2, *Advanced Functionality and Styling the To-Do List App*, with both an Android- and iOS-specific version
- Replace any methods that manipulate data with the actions that we can dispatch to the state tree

Since `datePickerHeight` is set during the `onLayout` event of `DatePickerIOS`, we will keep it in the local state:

```
// TasksRedux/app/components/EditTask/index.ios.js

import React, { Component } from 'react';

import {
  Button,
  DatePickerIOS,
  Switch,
  Text,
  TextInput,
  View
} from 'react-native';

import ExpandableCell from '../ExpandableCell';
import styles from './styles';

export default class EditTask extends Component {
  constructor (props) {
    super (props);

    this.state = {
      datePickerHeight: undefined
    }
  }
}
```

The `TextInput` dispatches the `changeTextInputValue` action when text is changed, and gets its value from the `selectedTaskObject` of our state tree:

```
render () {
  const noDueDateTitle = 'Set Reminder';
  const dueDateSetTitle = 'Due On ' +
  this.props.selectedTaskObject.formattedDate;

  return (
    <View style={ styles.editTaskContainer }>
      <View>
        <TextInput
          autoCorrect={ false }
          onChangeText={ (text) =>
          this.props.changeTextInputValue(text) }
          returnKeyType={ 'done' }
          style={ styles.textInput }
          value={ this.props.selectedTaskObject.text }
        />
```

The `ExpandableCell` component remains the same here, but delegates its `expanded` Boolean and `title` determination logic to our Redux state and dispatches the `onExpand` action when pressed:

```
      </View>
      <View style={ [styles.expandableCellContainer,
      { maxHeight: this.props.expanded ?
      this.state.datePickerHeight : 40 }]}>
        <ExpandableCell
          childrenHeight={ this.state.datePickerHeight }
          expanded={ this.props.expanded }
          onPress={ () => this.props.onExpand(this.props.expanded) }
          title={ this.props.due ? dueDateSetTitle : noDueDateTitle }>
```

As you can see, the only remaining component-based logic is with `_getDatePickerHeight`. All other functions are dispatched for the state tree to handle:

```
          <DatePickerIOS
            date={ this.props.date }
            onDateChange={ (date) => this.props.onDateChange(date) }
            onLayout={ (event) => this._getDatePickerHeight(event) }
          />
        </ExpandableCell>
      </View>
      <View style={ styles.switchContainer } >
        <Text style={ styles.switchText } >
          Completed
        </Text>
        <Switch
          onValueChange={ (value) =>
          this.props.changeCompletedStatus(value) }
          value={ this.props.selectedTaskObject.completed }
        />
      </View>
      <View style={ styles.clearDateButtonContainer }>
        <Button
          color={ '#B44743' }
          disabled={ this.props.dateSelected ? false : true }
          onPress={ () => this.props.clearDate() }
          title={ 'Clear Date' }
        />
      </View>
    </View>
  );
}

_getDatePickerHeight (event) {
  this.setState({
```

```
          datePickerHeight: event.nativeEvent.layout.width
      });
    }
  }
```

Modifying the EditTask component for Android

It's easiest for us to take the Android `EditTask` component from Chapter 2, *Advanced Functionality and Styling the To-Do List App*, and make changes to it. Additionally, referencing the updated iOS version of this component during these changes can also help.

Specifically, for the Android version of `EditTask`, we want to do the following:

- Swap out any references to the local state with the state tree made available via `props`
- Replace any unnecessary calls to the local methods, dispatching actions instead
- Keep the local methods for saving a task and opening both the date and time pickers
- Update the callback that pressing the back button triggers, resetting the `selectedTaskObject` in addition to calling `pop` on the navigator

The modifications that I made show the differences between `EditTask/index.android.js` and `EditTask/index.ios.js`.

I removed `ExpandableCell` from my import statements:

```
// TasksRedux/app/components/EditTask/index.android.js

...
import {
  ...
  BackAndroid,
  DatePickerAndroid,
  TimePickerAndroid,
} from 'react-native';
```

I removed the `datePickerHeight` value in the state, since the Android component does not deal with `ExpandableCell`:

```
...
export default class EditTask extends Component {
  constructor (props) {
    super (props);
  }
```

Adding and removing event listeners for the Android back button is unchanged from Chapter 2, *Advanced Functionality and Styling the To-Do List App*:

```
componentWillMount () {
  BackAndroid.addEventListener('hardwareButtonPress', () =>
  this._backButtonPress());
}

componentWillUnmount () {
  BackAndroid.removeEventListener('hardwareButtonPress', () =>
  this._backButtonPress())
}
```

No changes were made to the TextInput component.

```
render () {
  ...
  return (
    <View style={ styles.editTaskContainer }>
      <View>
        ...
      </View>
```

The Button to open DatePickerAndroid is modified to reference the selectedTaskObject due property to determine the text to render:

```
<View style={ styles.androidButtonContainer }>
  <Button
    color={ '#80B546' }
    title={ this.props.selectedTaskObject.due ?
    dueDateSetTitle : noDueDateTitle }
    onPress={ () => this._showAndroidDatePicker() }
  />
</View>
```

No changes were made to the Switch component, Clear Date Button, or Save Button. The Save Button is exclusive to the Android version of this app, since the logic to save the edited task is handled in the navigation bar on iOS:

```
<View style={ styles.switchContainer } >
  ...
</View>
<View style={ styles.androidButtonContainer }>
  ...
</View>
<View style={ styles.saveButton }>
  <Button
    color={ '#4E92B5' }
```

```
                    onPress={ () => this._saveSelectedTaskDetails() }
                    title={ 'Save Task' }
                />
            </View>
        </View>
    );
}
```

Modify the `_backButtonPress` to also dispatch the `resetSelectedTask` action:

```
_backButtonPress () {
    this.props.navigator.pop();
    this.props.resetSelectedTask();
    return true;
}
```

I also modified `_saveSelectedTaskDetails` to dispatch the `saveSelectedTasks` action:

```
_saveSelectedTaskDetails () {
    this.props.navigator.pop();
    this.props.saveSelectedTaskDetails(this.props.selectedTaskObject);
}
```

Change `_showAndroidDatePicker` to not keep the `day`, `month`, and `year` values in the state. Instead, it passes the data directly to `_showAndroidTimePicker` for immediate use:

```
...
async _showAndroidDatePicker () {
    const options = {
        date: this.props.date
    };

    const { action, year, month, day } = await
    DatePickerAndroid.open(options);

    this._showAndroidTimePicker (day, month, year);
}
```

Likewise, _showAndroidTimePicker is changed to accept those day, month, and year values. Then it creates a new Date object immediately with those three values, along with the hour and minute that TimePickerAndroid returns, and dispatches the onDateChange action with the new Date object:

```
async _showAndroidTimePicker (day, month, year) {
  const { action, minute, hour } = await TimePickerAndroid.open();

  if (action === TimePickerAndroid.dismissedAction) {
    return;
  }

  const date = new Date(year, month, day, hour, minute);

  this.props.onDateChange(date);
  }
}
```

At this point, we have almost completed our port to Redux! The only thing that remains is persisting our list of tasks as before.

Creating a StorageMethods file for asynchronous saving

Right now, any refresh or exiting of the application will wipe our list of tasks clean. That doesn't make for a very useful app, so we're now going to modify our actions to store and retrieve our list of tasks from AsyncStorage.

Let's create a `utils` folder within `app`, and then create a file titled `storageMethods.js` within `utils`:

This file will contain two functions:

- `getAsyncStorage`: This gets the `listOfTasks` item in `AsyncStorage` and returns it
- `saveAsyncStorage`: This accepts an array and saves it into `AsyncStorage` under the `listOfTasks` key

If you worked on the previous projects in this book, this part will be very familiar to you:

```
// TasksRedux/app/utils/storageMethods.js

import { AsyncStorage } from 'react-native';

export const getAsyncStorage = async () => {
  let response = await AsyncStorage.getItem('listOfTasks');
  let parsedData = JSON.parse(response) || [];

  return parsedData;
}
```

This uses asynchronous functions for readability, grabbing the `listOfTasks` value in `AsyncStorage`, parsing it to transform it back to an array, and then returning it.

```
export const saveAsyncStorage = async (listOfTasks) => {
  return AsyncStorage.setItem('listOfTasks',
  JSON.stringify(listOfTasks));
}
```

Likewise, accept an array and then set the `listOfTasks` key in `AsyncStorage` to the stringified version of the array.

Subscribing the store to changes

To update the `listOfTasks` key in `AsyncStorage` whenever a change is made to the state tree, we will call the `subscribe` method of our store. This creates a change listener to be called whenever an action has been dispatched and the state tree may have been changed.

It accepts a callback as its argument, and within that argument we can call the `getState` method of the store to access the state tree and retrieve any values we want from it.

Let's modify the index file found in the app folder so that it subscribes to changes to the store, firing a callback that calls `saveAsyncStorage` and passes it the most recent version of the `listOfTasks` array in our state tree:

```
// TasksRedux/app/index.js

...
import { saveAsyncStorage } from './utils/storageMethods';
...
store.subscribe(() => {
  saveAsyncStorage(store.getState().listOfTasks);
});
...
```

Since the rest of our application state does not have a need for persistence, `listOfTasks` is the only item being saved into `AsyncStorage`.

Creating a thunk

The `Redux-Thunk` library is a wrapper around your action creators, allowing them to perform asynchronous tasks before dispatching their intended action to the Redux store for a reducer to handle.

Here's how we will create a thunk: in the file where we create actions, we will export a function that returns a custom, asynchronous function within it, passing it the existing `dispatch` method. In this custom function, we will grab the results of a call to our `getAsyncStorage` method.

Then, within the same method, we will dispatch a private function, which we also create in the same file. That private function will return the action type, along with any parameters we wish to pass:

```
// TasksRedux/app/actions/index.js

import { getAsyncStorage } from '../utils/storageMethods';
```

I removed the `currentIndex` variable from this file, since we will no longer rely on a hardcoded number to set the index of our tasks.

First, create a constant for the action to set the list of tasks and index:

```
const SET_LIST_OF_TASKS_AND_INDEX = 'SET_LIST_OF_TASKS_AND_INDEX';
```

Create the `getListOfTasksAndIndex` action.

```
export function getListOfTasksAndIndex () {
  return async (dispatch) => {
    let response = await getAsyncStorage();

    dispatch(setListOfTasksAndIndex(response, response.length));
  }
}
```

This `setListOfTasksAndIndex` function is not exported, since it is only being called by `getListOfTasksAndIndex`. We are using the length of the array to set the index for a newly added task:

```
function setListOfTasksAndIndex (listOfTasks, index) {
  return {
    type: SET_LIST_OF_TASKS_AND_INDEX,
    index,
    listOfTasks,
  }
}
```

Modifying our reducers

We need to modify our reducers file so that it does the following:

- Adds the `currentIndex` property to its `defaultState` object
- Sets the `index` of a task when it is added to our state tree
- Increases the `currentIndex` property of our state tree by one when adding a new task
- Contains a switch case for the `SET_LIST_OF_TASKS_AND_INDEX` action, setting the `currentIndex` and `listOfTasks` properties of our state tree to the results of our `getListOfTasksAndIndex` thunk

```
// TasksRedux/app/reducers/index.js

const defaultState = {
  currentIndex: undefined,
  ...
}
...
const singleTask = (state = {}, action) => {
  switch(action.type) {
    case 'ADD_TASK':
      return {
        ...
        index: action.index,
      }
    ...
  }
}
```

The `ADD_TASK` case in the `singleTask` sub-reducer sets the index of the added task.

No changes are made to the `selectedTask` sub-reducer.

```
  ...
  const listOfTasks = (state = defaultState, action) => {
    switch(action.type) {
      case 'ADD_TASK':
        ...
        return {
          currentIndex: ++state.currentIndex,
          ...
        }
```

In the preceding code, the ADD_TASK case in the listOfTasks reducer increments the currentIndex of the state tree by one and sets it as the new currentIndex.

```
    ...
    case 'SET_LIST_OF_TASKS_AND_INDEX':
      return {
        ...state,
        currentIndex: action.index,
        listOfTasks: action.listOfTasks
      }
  }
}

export default listOfTasks;
```

In the preceding code, the SET_LIST_OF_TASKS_AND_INDEX case sets the currentIndex and listOfTasks properties in our state tree with the results of calling getAsyncStorage back in our getListOfTasksAndIndex thunk.

Updating the TasksListContainer

Next, we need to update the TasksListContainer so that it does the following:

- Maps the getListOfTasksAndIndex action and currentIndex value to its props
- Modifies the addTask action to expect and send an index argument

These are the changes I ended up with:

```
// TasksRedux/containers/TasksListContainer/index.js

...
import {
  ...
  getListOfTasksAndIndex,
} from '../../actions';

import TasksList from '../../components/TasksList';

const mapDispatchToProps = (dispatch) => {
  return {
    addTask: (text, index) => {
      dispatch(addTask(text, index));
    },
    ...
```

```
      getListOfTasksAndIndex: () => {
        dispatch(getListOfTasksAndIndex());
      },
      ...
   }
}

const mapStateToProps = (state, { navigator }) => {
   return {
      currentIndex: state.currentIndex,
      ...
   }
}
...
```

Modifying the TasksList component

Finally, we will edit `TasksList` so that it does the following:

- Dispatches the `getListOfTasksAndIndex` action during the `componentWillMount` life cycle event
- Passes in the `currentIndex` of the state tree to the `TextInput`'s `onSubmitEditing` callback as a second argument

Call `getListOfTasksAndIndex` during `componentWillMount`, making sure that `TasksList` has the most up-to-date version of the `listOftasks` array as the user opens the app:

```
// TasksRedux/app/components/TasksList/index.js

...
export default class TasksList extends Component {
   ...
   componentWillMount () {
      this.props.getListOfTasksAndIndex();
   }
}
```

Add `this.props.currentIndex` as the second argument to calling the `addTask` method, so that we explicitly give each task a unique index:

```
   render () {
      ...
      return (
         <View style={ styles.container }>
            <TextInput
```

```
            onSubmitEditing={ () => this.props.addTask
            (this.props.text, this.props.currentIndex) }
            ...
        />
        ...
      </View>
    );
  }
  ...
}
```

And there you have it! We've successfully converted Tasks, our to-do list app, to support Redux.

Summary

In this chapter, we learned the fundamentals of React development with Redux! We started by creating actions, which dispatch intent to our Redux store. Then, we wrote reducers to handle that intent and update our state tree. We also built a store that consolidated our reducers and middleware.

Afterwards, we used the Connect method to wrap a container around a React component, giving it access to any actions and parts of the state tree of our choosing.

We also converted the existing EditTask and TasksList components to be less reliant on the local state and use its logic from the state tree.

Later in the chapter, we discovered how to temporarily delay the dispatching of actions to perform necessary asynchronous calls first by using Redux-Thunk. This, in conjunction with subscribing our store to any updates, allowed us to have a fully persistent app that used AsyncStorage to keep its data.

Finally, we made sure that every step along the way kept the Android support we started the chapter with.

In the next chapter, we are going to change things a bit. We have spent all this time building applications, but no time on how to share them with the world. In the next chapter, we will learn just how to get these apps you have made onto the Apple App Store and Google Play Store.

8
Deploying Your Applications

Developers publish their apps to different marketplaces in order to distribute them to end users. For iOS, it's the Apple App Store. On Android, the primary choice is the Google Play Store.

If you're new to mobile development thanks to the power of React Native, this will seem like a new world for you. Having a background in the Web, I personally felt lost at first when it came time to publish my first mobile app-after all, we're used to deploying our apps to a server.

In this chapter, you're going to do the following things:

- Discover the requirements for submitting an app to both the Apple App Store and Google Play
- Learn about the importance of app logos and screenshots
- Write a description for our application
- For iOS, verify our app with Xcode and bundle it for submission to iTunes Connect
- Submit the iOS app for review with Apple
- Use TestFlight to create internal and external beta tests for users
- Use the Developer Console to add and submit our Android application to Google Play
- Learn how to send alpha and beta versions of our Android apps to test users

Basic requirements

At a base level, to submit your apps to either the App Store or Google Play, you will need a developer membership for the platform(s) of your choice.

For iOS, you will need an Apple Developer membership. This annual, paid membership gives you the ability to publish on all of Apple's platforms-iOS, macOS, and tvOS. It also grants you the option of sending preproduction versions of your applications to beta testers first.

With distribution to an Android device, the most popular channel is the Google Play Store. It reaches every official, Google-supported Android device and requires a Publisher Account.

For both apps, we also need to provide app icons so that our users don't install a blank icon to their devices, and screenshots so that they have a better idea of what they are downloading in advance.

Before we go any further, it should be stated that the app we've built, with the included screenshots, may not be accepted by an editorial board for sale on either App Store. We're using this project as a means to have a working app for going through the motions of actually submitting an application.

Creating developer memberships

The process for signing up for a developer membership in either store is different. Since the prerequisites and steps to do so may change at any given time, I will spare you the step-by-step details.

Enrolling in the Apple Developer Program

To sign up for an Apple Developer account, point your browser to `https://developer.apple.com`.

Joining the Apple Developer Program requires an Apple ID. As of the publishing of this book, members pay a $99 annual fee for the program.

Signing up for a Google Play Publisher account

To get started with your Publisher account, point your browser to
`https://play.google.com/apps/publish`.

To sign up for a Google Play Publisher Account, you will need a Google Account-usually, this is your Gmail address. As of the publishing of this book, the program requires a $25 one-time fee to join.

Making your app look great

In addition to having membership in the appropriate platforms' developer programs, submitting your application to either store requires that you provide it with an app logo, screenshots of the app, and a description.

Creating an icon

Icons are the gateway to your application. It's what your users will interact with to access your app. To submit an application to the appropriate marketplace of your choice, it has to have an icon.

Because an icon is your app's brand, it's increasingly not enough to simply create a solid color shade and slap some text on it-users expect more.

 Personally, I like using Sketch (`https://www.sketchapp.com/`) to design my app icons. While my design skills are not the greatest, I find it simple and intuitive to use.

There are so many ways you can procure an icon for your application. You could hire someone (either locally or online) to design one, or create one yourself using a plethora of applications.

When I need to generate different-sized app icons for submission to the App Store and Google Play, my go-to service is MakeAppIcon (`https://makeappicon.com`), which is available on the Web as a drag and drop service, as well as a standalone Mac app.

Taking app screenshots

Screenshots give your potential app customers a glimpse into how your application looks.

One quick way to create screenshots is simply to take them on your device or simulator with the application running, and then upload those to the App Store or Google Play.

You can add additional aesthetics to your screenshots using a variety of services. There happens to be one that imposes your screenshot within the photo of an iOS device, giving your potential customers a look at how the app appears on a physical device.

 To add things such as a device/background to my screenshots, LaunchKit has a great Sketch-to-App-Store plugin (`http://sketchtoappstore.com/`) that can help make this happen, though the devices available to impose your screenshots on are a bit dated-the most recent iOS device is an iPhone 6 Plus, and the only available Android device is a Nexus 5.

There are also services that help strip out the status bar in case you don't want it shown in your screenshot--especially important if you're taking that screenshot on a device with a heavily populated status bar or if your screenshots have varying times showing on the bar and you want to present them with a level of consistency.

 I like using Status Barred from the Mac App Store (`https://itunes.appl e.com/us/app/status-barred/id413853485?mt=12`) to crop the status bar from my screenshots.

Writing a description

Without a proper description, your potential customers won't know what your application does or have the relevant information to decide whether to install your app or not. Regardless of whether your app is free or paid, the lack of a proper description will be a negative strike against your application.

A simple one-liner won't do it either--you want to convey to your potential customers exactly why they want to download your app. What does it do? What features does it have that will make your users interested in it?

Always take the opportunity to write a detailed description for your application.

Combining it all

Like it or not, a good description alongside a nice app icon and screenshots does make or break your app when a potential customer decides whether to download it or not.

Once you have a developer membership, an icon, screenshots for your app, and a description, you're ready to start the process of submitting your application for the world to enjoy.

Next, we are going to go through the steps taken to submit `Friends`, our Facebook client, over to both the App Store and Google Play.

Apple App Store

The first thing we need to do is give our app an iOS App ID. In the Apple Developer portal at `https://developer.apple.com`, select **Certificates, Identifiers & Profiles**:

Once you are in the portal to manage your **Certificates, Identifiers, & Profiles**, select the option for App IDs, then press the add button in the upper-right corner:

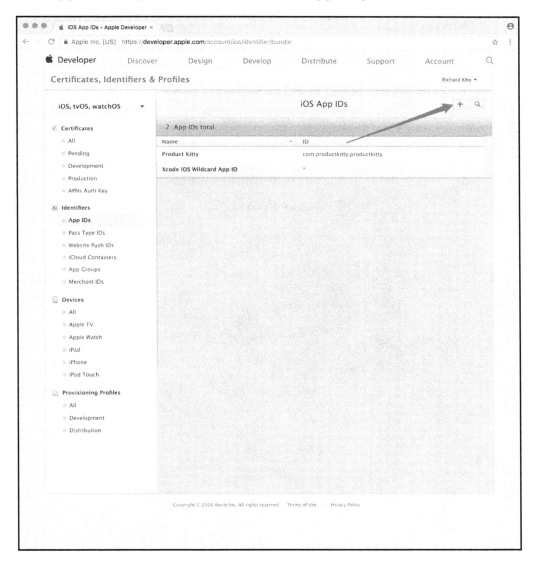

This will take you to a page that allows you to register an App ID. Give it a name (without special characters) and then decide whether you'll give the app an **Explicit App ID** or **Wildcard App ID**, followed by announcing any services that you intend to enable in your app.

An **Explicit App ID** is required if you implement app-specific services such as push notifications, in-app purchases, and Apple Pay.

If you don't plan on using any app-specific services, Apple recommends that you use a **Wildcard App ID** instead:

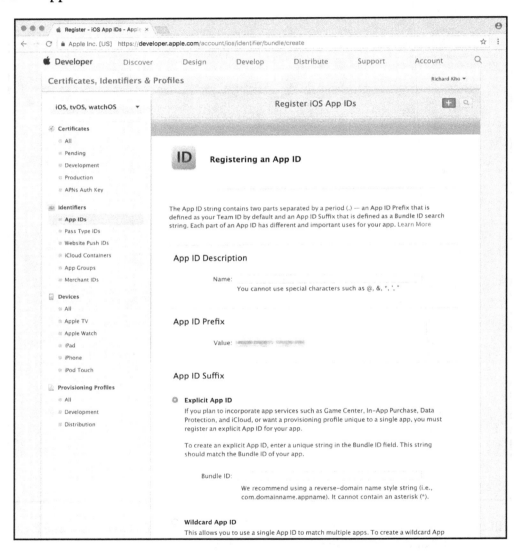

Once configured, you'll be asked to confirm your App ID. If everything looks right, hit the **Register** button to complete registration of your App ID:

With an App ID for Friends created, our next step is to open the project in Xcode and make some changes to our project.

Modifying the Bundle ID in Xcode

Open the folder where your repo for `Friends` is located, and go into the `ios` folder. Open `Friends.xcodeproj`, which will automatically launch in Xcode.

In Xcode, go to the **General** tab for your project and select the **Team** drop-down menu under **Signing**. Sign in with your Apple ID and password. Once you do so, a Signing Certificate should be automatically generated for you.

Then, under **Identity**, set your **Bundle Identifier** to the App ID you previously added in the Apple Developer Portal. After this, we'll add an icon for the app. I've added icons that you can use for this reason in the repository belonging to this chapter.

Adding app icons in Xcode

While still in the **General** tab, select the arrow to the immediate right of the **App Icons Source** drop-down menu:

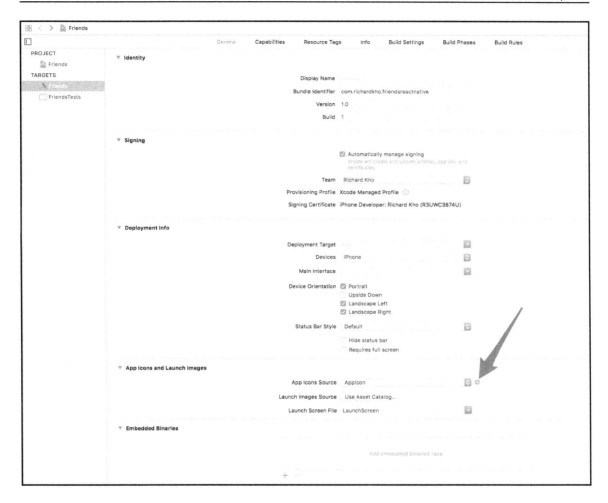

Afterwards, you will be taken to a screen that will let you drag and drop image assets to their corresponding logos. Xcode will provide warnings if you end up adding an incorrectly sized icon to the wrong drop zone:

The text underneath each drop zone's section shows the target resolution for each icon.

Once you have your app icons set up, it's time to create an archive of your application for submission to iTunes Connect.

Creating an archive

First up, let's make sure that our project's scheme settings are properly archiving the release version of our app and not the debugging one by going into the Mac Toolbar when Xcode is open and selecting **Product** | **Scheme** | **Edit Scheme**:

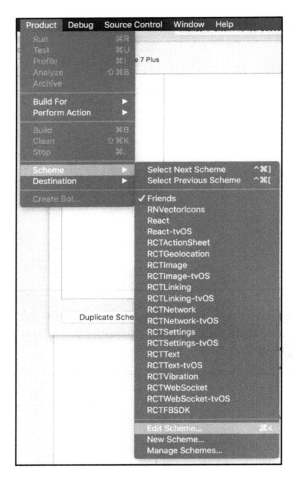

Once this pane has opened, select the **Archive** option on the left-hand column and confirm that the **Build Configuration** is set to **Release**:

Now, close this and go over to this drop-down menu, which lets you select the device to build and run your app for in Xcode:

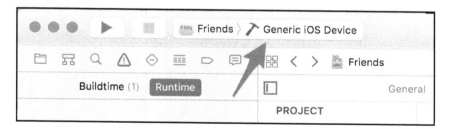

Xcode will not allow you to create an archive of an app whose target is an iOS Simulator device. If you attempt to do so, the option will simply be grayed out under the **Product** menu.

Click on this drop-down menu and select **Generic iOS Device**:

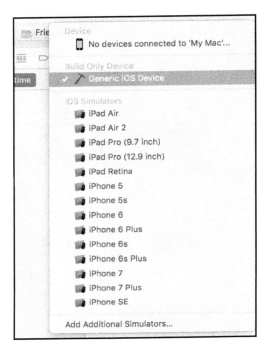

Finally, go back to the **Product** menu in Xcode and select **Archive**:

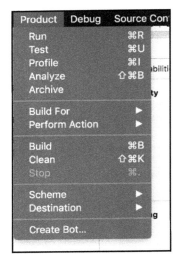

Xcode will now build and archive your app to get it ready for distribution to iTunes Connect. If everything works great, you'll see the following list of archives with some options on the right-hand side:

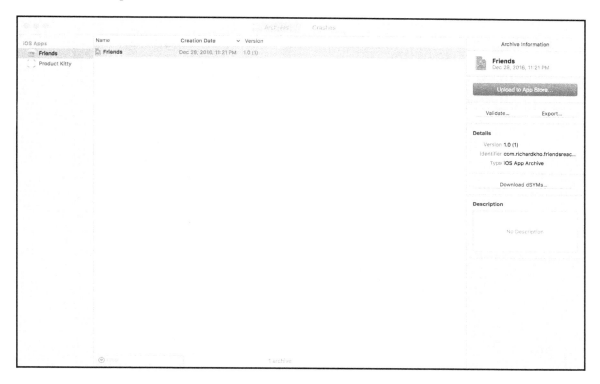

Keep this screen open, since we will need it in a moment. For now, let's go into iTunes Connect to add the app to our account.

iTunes Connect

iTunes Connect is the portal Apple developers use to submit their applications. To get there, point your browser to `https://itunesconnect.apple.com` and sign in if needed. You'll land on the iTunes Connect dashboard. On it, select **My Apps**, which is the first app on the left in the top row.

Once selected, you'll arrive at a list of apps you have submitted to iTunes Connect, and their statuses.

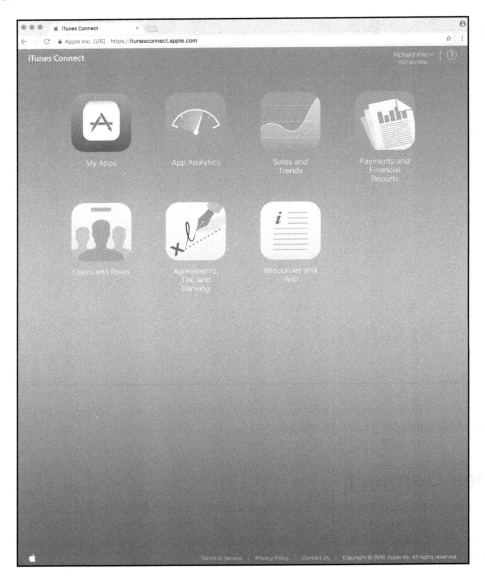

To submit a new app, choose the add symbol in the top-left corner and select **New App**:

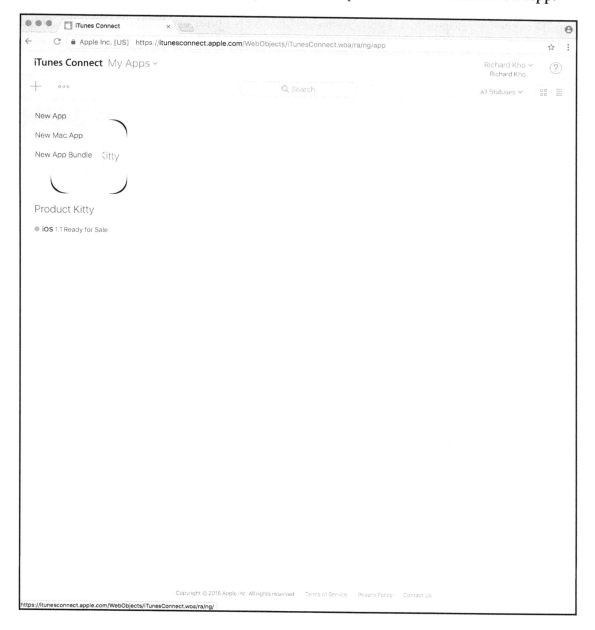

You'll be asked to fill out some details about your app in the modal that appears. Select your platform (**iOS**), give the app a name, primary language, **Bundle ID** (mapped to the App ID in the Developer Portal you created, which is also your application's **Bundle ID** in Xcode), and a unique **SKU**:

Once you complete this step, you'll be taken to a summary page about your app. Let's skip back to Xcode for now and finish the process of validating and submitting our app to iTunes Connect.

Validating our app in Xcode

Go ahead and select **Validate** in the last screen you were in with Xcode, which should result in this **Summary** screen:

Click on the **Validate** button. Let it do its work in communicating with iTunes Connect and, if everything checks out, you'll receive a Validation Successful prompt. If this is the case, hit **Done** and let's begin uploading our app.

Pressing the **Upload to App Store** button, you will be prompted with a similar request to choose your Development Team and then press **Upload**:

At this point, the archive of your project will begin the process of uploading and verifying its assets with the App Store. Give it some time and, once it's finished, you will see an Upload Successful prompt. Once you do, let's go right back to iTunes Connect.

Submitting our app for review

We have a few final steps before we can submit our app for review. First, we need to add screenshots to it. In the folder for this chapter, I have added screenshots that you can play around with.

We'll select our app under the label **1.0 Prepare for Submission** in the left-hand column, then drag our screenshots to the drop zone:

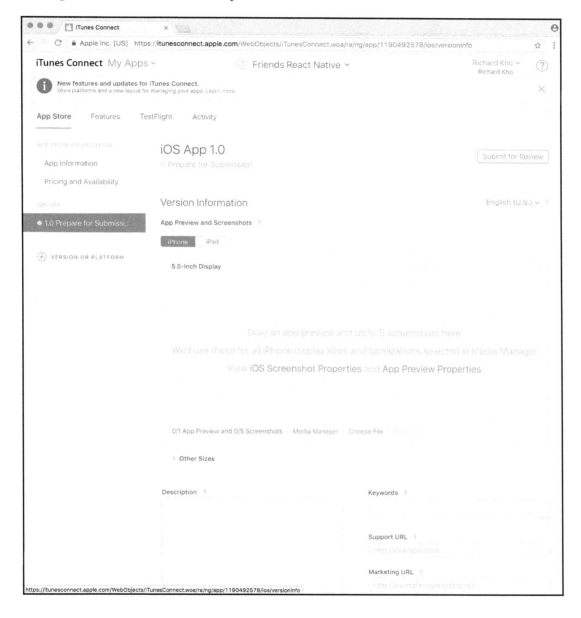

Next, give the app a **Description**, some **Keywords**, and **Support**, and **Marketing** URLs. After you've done so, scroll down and select a build to submit--this will be the one we just uploaded to the App Store through Xcode, in the previous section:

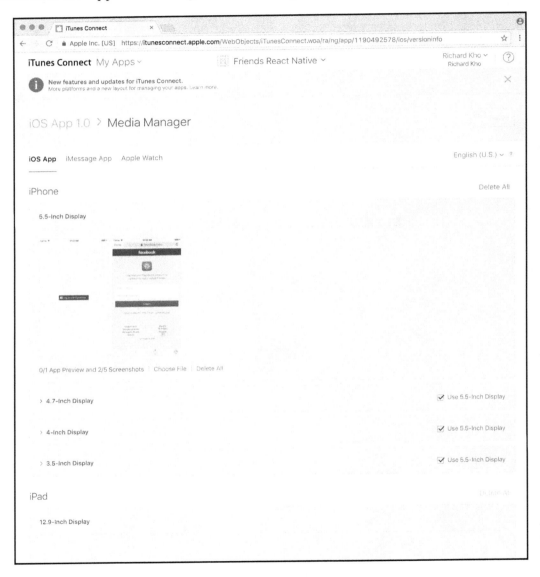

iTunes Connect automatically scales down images made for a 5.5" display so that smaller display types don't need their own unique images unless you wish to assign them yourself.

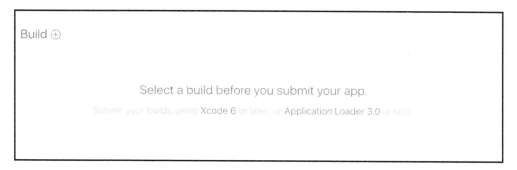

You'll find that the builds you've uploaded through Xcode are automatically populated in the modal that appears, with its corresponding version and build numbers that you've assigned in Xcode:

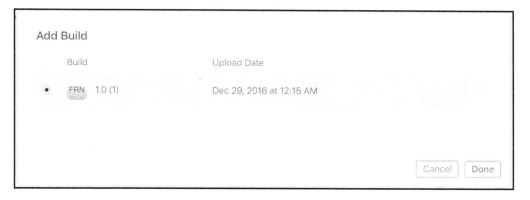

Once selected, the **Build** section in iTunes Connect will update with your app's information:

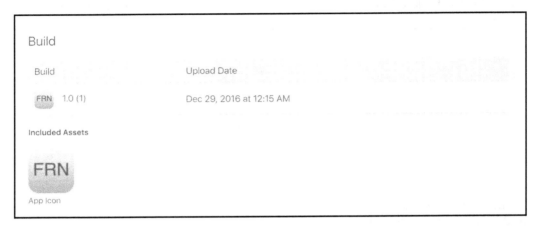

The next step is to include an app icon of 1024 × 1024 under **General App Information** and to populate it with a copyright and your contact information:

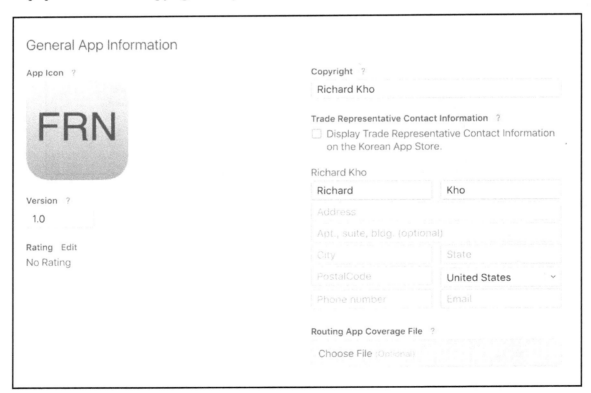

Then, provide your contact information, along with any notes you'd like the App Store reviewers to read, as well as a Demo Account if one is necessary to use all the features of the app.

Finally, decide whether you'd like your app to be released immediately or not once approved by the App Store reviewers:

Game Center

App Review Information

Contact Information ?   **Notes** ?

First name   Last name

Phone number   Email

Demo Account ?

☐ A demo account is required to use all the features
of the app.

Version Release

After your app has been approved, we can release it for you immediately. If you want to release the app yourself, choose a date or manually release it at any point after the approval. While your app is in the "Pending Developer Release," you can give out promotional codes, continue TestFlight Beta Testing, or reject the release and submit a new build. Whichever of these you choose, we have to process your app before it's made available on the App Store. While your app is in the "Processing for App Store" state, you can't get new promotional codes, invite new testers, or reject your app.

○ Manually release this version

◉ Automatically release this version

○ Automatically release this version after App Review, no earlier than   ?

Your local date and time.

▦ Dec 29, 2016   ⏲ 12:00 AM

When you've filled out all these details, press the **Submit for Review** button at the top. That's it, you're done! Pat yourself on the back and wait for Apple's review team to get back to you with either an approval or rejection.

Beta testing iOS apps with TestFlight

TestFlight is a service Apple acquired a few years ago that is fully integrated with iTunes Connect. It lets you test your iOS apps before you release them on the App Store, with a select group of beta testers.

Beta testing is important because it gives developers the ability to gather feedback on their app as it is being used in real-life situations, and discover bugs they might not have caught otherwise.

There are two kinds of tests you can run with TestFlight: **Internal** and **External** tests.

In an Internal test, users within your team who have been assigned a Developer or Admin role in iTunes Connect can privately test the app, allowing you to gain feedback from them quickly. Up to 25 users can be part of an Internal test.

For External tests, you can invite any users from outside your organization to test your app. Apps made available to an External test can accept up to 2,000 users, and the app must be reviewed by Apple before you can begin testing.

From my experience, the **Beta App Review** process takes a significantly shorter period of time than the formal App Review process for publicly releasing your app to all users.

Entering test information

The first step in making your app available via TestFlight is to log in to iTunes Connect, select one of your apps, and then choose the **TestFlight** tab. Then, fill out the **Test Information** form to provide some details about your app:

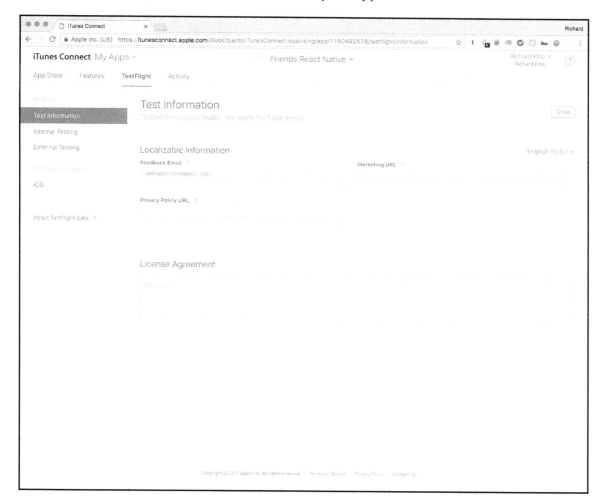

Once those details have been saved, you can begin setting up either an Internal or External test.

Creating an Internal beta test with TestFlight

To create an Internal test, select the **Internal Test** option in the sidebar and click on **Select Version to Test**, which will make the following modal visible:

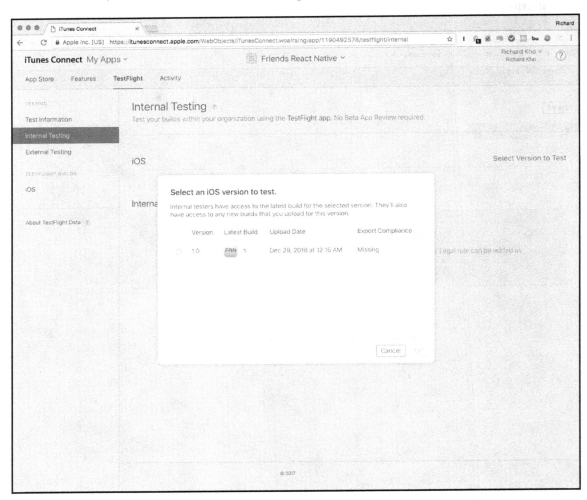

If you have uploaded multiple builds of your app, you should see them appear here. Select the one you wish to send out to your beta testers and press the **Next** button. If your app has not been previously configured to declare its **Export Compliance**, you will be brought to a second question on the modal asking if your app is designed to use, contain, or incorporate cryptography.

Next, you can click on the **Internal Testers** box to add at least one tester. This list is populated with any users you have added via iTunes Connect. If you have not added anyone to your team so far, you will only see yourself as a listed beta tester.

To change this, go back to the main iTunes Connect portal and select **Users and Roles**:

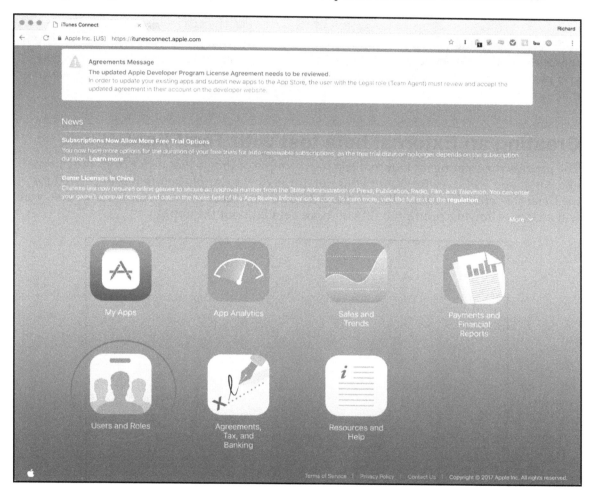

Select the + icon to add a user, and fill out the multi-page form to proceed:

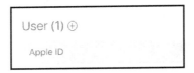

Once you have added the users you wish to send an Internal test to, you can select them in the **Internal Testing** section of the **TestFlight** tab in the app you wish to beta test. When you have selected everyone, click the **Start Testing** button and your users will receive an e-mail notification to join the test!

Creating an External beta test with TestFlight

The process for creating an External test has a couple of things that differ from the Internal one. First, you will have to submit your app for review to Apple before it is approved for the External beta. When you click on the **Add Build to Test** button for an External test, you will see the following prompt to fill out more details about the app:

This is for specifying to your users exactly what parts of the app they should be testing, along with a description for them to read. You will also need to provide an e-mail they can send feedback to, along with a marketing URL for your app.

You will then be taken to two more parts of this modal, where you are asked to provide details for the **Beta App Review** team. The first part will consist of your **Contact Information** in the event Apple would like to get in touch with you regarding your app, along with the ability to add a test account for the **Beta App Review** team to use:

Afterwards, you will be asked to provide a description of the app and what the team should be aware of as they perform a review of your app:

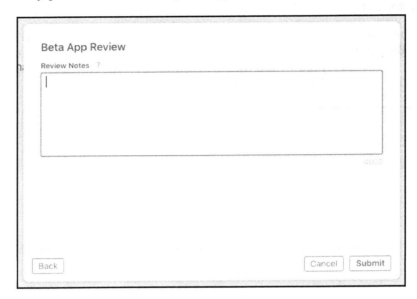

You will not be able to begin an External test until your app has cleared **Beta App Review**:

In the meantime, you can add users to the test with one of three options:

The first is to add new testers by entering their name and e-mail address, which will bring up a modal allowing you to do so:

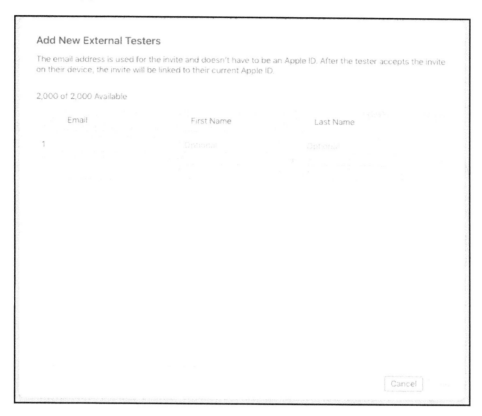

The next option lets you add existing External test users that have beta tested any apps of yours in the past. That option will give you a list along with checkboxes for you to select users to add.

The final option is to import a CSV file of your External test users.

Once you have added at least one user and your build has been approved by **Beta App Review**, you can submit the app and begin the beta test!

That's everything we are going to cover regarding the iOS App Store and iTunes Connect. In the next section, we will look at what we would do to upload Friends for Android to the Google Play Store.

Google Play Store

To submit an app to the Google Play Store, we'll have to take the following steps:

- Add an App Icon
- Give our app a unique package identifier
- Generate a signed APK file
- Upload that APK file to the Google Play developer portal
- Add screenshots and a description for our app

Adding an app icon for Android

In order to give your Android app an icon, we're going to navigate to the following folder in our repo: `android/app/src/main/res`.

Then, add an icon image renamed `ic_launcher.png` to each of the four folders with the corresponding dimensions:

- `mipmap-hdpi`: 72 × 72
- `mipmap-mdpi`: 48 × 48
- `mipmap-xhdpi`: 96 × 96
- `mipmap-xxhdpi`: 144 × 144

Once you've added these images, run the `react-native run-android` command to build your app, and you should see the icons updated on the home screen of your Android Virtual Device.

For your convenience, app icons for the Android version of Friends have been made available in the repo pertaining to this chapter's code.

Creating a unique package identifier

Your APK won't be uploaded to the Google Play Developer Console if its package name is the same as another app that already exists in the Google Play Store. To give it a unique name, we'll first open Android Studio and import the `Android` folder of our app to it.

Select **Import Project (Eclipse ADT, Gradle, etc.)** from the Android Studio welcome screen. Then navigate to the repository for your project and import just the `Android` folder within.

Afterwards, open `AndroidManifest.xml` and change the package name on the second line.

Then, right-click on your `app` folder that contains the package identifier, and select **Refactor | Rename**. Then, give your package a new name:

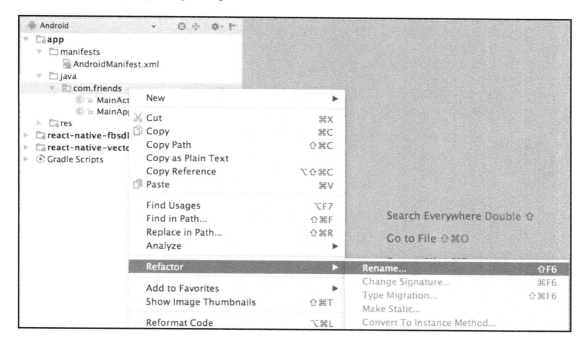

Now open up `build.gradle` within the `android/app` folder, and replace any instances of your old package identifier with your new one. The changes you've made will be applied automatically.

Generating a Signed APK file

First, in your terminal, we'll generate a private signing key:

```
$ keytool -genkey -v -keystore friends-release-key.keystore -alias
    friends -key-alias -keyalg RSA
-keysize 2048 -validity 10000
```

You'll set a password for your keystore and key. Your release key will be labeled `friends-release-key`, unless you choose otherwise.

The `validity` flag in this command sets the validity of the key for x number of days. In this case, it's `10000`, due to our command.

This `keystore` file will be located at the directory in which your terminal prompt was when you ran the command. Move it over to `android/app` in your Friends app repo.

 Important! It's not a good idea to commit your `keystore` file to Git or any other version control system. Make sure to add this file to `.gitignore`.

Then, open up your `gradle.properties` file and add the following information:

```
// Friends/android/gradle.properties
MYAPP_RELEASE_STORE_FILE=friends-release-key.keystore
MYAPP_RELEASE_KEY_ALIAS=friends-key-alias
MYAPP_RELEASE_STORE_PASSWORD=YOURPASSWORDHERE
MYAPP_RELEASE_KEY_PASSWORD=YOURPASSWORDHERE
```

Replace `YOURPASSWORDHERE` with the password you created for your release store and release key.

Next up, we're going to add the signing configuration to your app's `build.gradle` file:

```
// Friends/android/app/build.gradle

...
android {
    ...
    signingConfigs {
      release {
          storeFile file(MYAPP_RELEASE_STORE_FILE)
          storePassword MYAPP_RELEASE_STORE_PASSWORD
        keyAlias MYAPP_RELEASE_KEY_ALIAS
        keyPassword MYAPP_RELEASE_KEY_PASSWORD
```

```
        }
    }
    ...
    buildTypes {
        release {
            ...
            signingConfig signingConfigs.release
        }
    }
    ...
}
...
```

Afterwards, let's generate the APK. Back in terminal, change to the `Android` directory and run the following:

```
./gradlew assembleRelease
```

The build process can take a few minutes. Once it's finished, you'll find your generated signed APK under `android/app/build/outputs/apk/app-release.apk`.

If you'd like to test it out on an Android Virtual Device, simply change your directory back to the root of the project and run the following:

```
react-native run-android --variant=release
```

If everything looks right, then let's go and submit the app to the Google Play Store!

Submitting to Google Play

Head over to the Google Play Developer Console at `https://play.google.com/apps/publish`.

Once you're signed in with your Google account, select the **Publish an Android App on Google Play** option, which is the top-left in the quadrant of cards made visible:

You'll be prompted to give your app a **Default language** and **Title**:

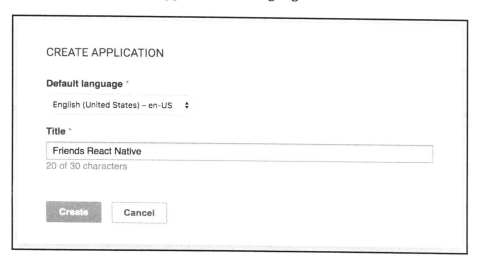

Once you create the app, you'll be taken to a page that allows you to edit the details of your application.

To submit an app, you're going to need to fill out the following information:

- A high-resolution 512 × 512 icon
- A feature graphic
- Two screenshots that are not for Android TV
- Category and content rating
- Short and full description of the app
- Upload the APK we created earlier
- Target at least one country for distribution
- A URL that points to the app's privacy policy
- Pricing information
- Declaration of whether or not the app contains advertising

Use the menu on the left-hand side to navigate between the four required tabs: **Uploading your APK**, **the listing on the Play Store**, **Content rating**, and **Pricing information**.

When all of the details have been filled out, let's navigate to the **Manage releases** section in the sidebar to begin the process of rolling out your app to the Google Play Store:

As of March 2017, Google is planning on deprecating the APK page in the sidebar and encourages everyone to start migrating over to the **Manage releases** page instead.

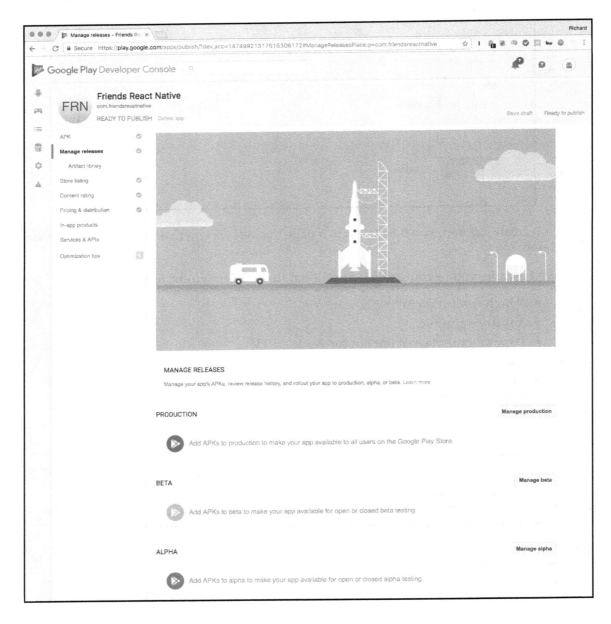

Select **Production** and you will be taken to the following page:

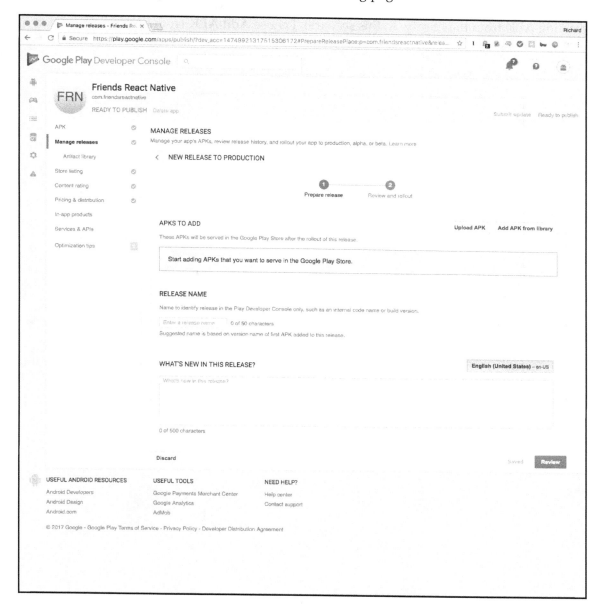

In the Google Play Developer Console, if you select your app and go into the **Manage releases** option in the sidebar, you will be asked to either upload a new APK or add an existing APK from the library. In this scenario, I chose **Add APK from library**, since I had already uploaded the `Friends APK` file previously.

Then I was asked to select from my list of existing APKs:

Afterwards, give the app a **Release Name** and a **Description** regarding what is new with this release, before pressing the **Review** button in the bottom-right corner.

In the next step, you will be asked to review the details of your release before you roll it out to the public. Once you have confirmed the details are correct, press the **Start rollout to production** button in the bottom-right corner. You will be prompted for confirmation.

Once you have confirmed, the app will begin rolling out to the Google Play Store!

Alpha and beta testing Android apps

In the **Manage releases** page, you may have noticed there are buttons to manage alpha and beta releases of your app.

Functionality-wise, there are currently no differences between an alpha and beta test. However, you can test two different versions of your app at the same time by running an alpha test for one version and a beta test for the other.

Each test can be run against one of three different testing methods, available to each track:

- **Open:** This lets anyone with an opt-in link subscribe to it
- **Closed**: This is where you have to specifically invite people to the test with their e-mail address
- **Testing using Google Groups or Google+ Communities**: This is where only users in the groups or communities you specify will be allowed to join the test

You will also need to create an app release for each test track, which goes through the same workflow as rolling out an app to production.

Once you have created a release for your test, a link will be generated for you to distribute among your testers, so they can install the app on their devices.

Summary

That's it for this chapter! You've just taken your first step into publishing the apps you build with React Native for both iOS and Android devices.

In this chapter, we learned about the requirements and costs of signing up for developer accounts to publish our apps to the Apple App Store and Google Play Store. Then we looked at the requirements for submitting an app to those marketplaces, including app icons and screenshots.

We also built and uploaded app files for both platforms, generated a signed APK for our Android app, and then submitted the apps for distribution. Finally, we discovered how to make our apps available for prerelease testing with TestFlight for iOS and the Google Developer Console for Android.

In the final chapter, we're going to look at parts of the React Native SDK that we couldn't fit into our three existing projects, and discover how to use them.

9
Additional React Native Components

Throughout the book, we touched on a lot of React Native SDKs. However, there were some components where their additions didn't fit with the apps we built.

In this chapter, we will cover some of them so that you will gain some extended practice with the React Native framework. You will learn to do the following things:

- Write a playground application where we will add components and parts of the React Native API that we did not get to work with in the prior projects
- Use the Fetch API to make network calls to a third-party resource
- Utilize the Vibration API to physically vibrate the user's phone
- Make use of the Linking API have your app open a third-party app with a registered link
- Build a slider that can slide around to set a value between a defined minimum and maximum number
- Learn how to use the Action sheet and Share sheet in iOS to share details from your app
- Obtain a user's location data with the Geolocation polyfill

Additionally, the end of this chapter includes a tutorial on how we would build Expenses in Chapter 4, *Advanced Functionality with the Expenses App* for Android.

Setting up a boilerplate project

Using the React Native command-line tools, I created a project titled
AdditionalComponents. In it, the structure is a lot more simplified than our previous
projects.

In each platform-specific index file at the root of the project, it imports an App component
from our app folder and registers it to AppRegistry:

```
// AdditionalComponents/index.ios.js

import App from './app';
import { AppRegistry } from 'react-native';
AppRegistry.registerComponent('AdditionalComponents', () => App);
```

We will be using the index.js file found in the app folder to contain the code for the
examples that we'll be building.

At the end of this step, we have an index.js file:

```
// AdditionalComponents/app/index.js

import React, { Component } from 'react';
import {
  Text,
  View
} from 'react-native';
import styles from './styles';
export default class App extends Component {
  render () {
    return (
      <View style={ styles.container }>
        <Text style={ styles.text }>
          Hello from React Native!
        </Text>
      </View>
    )
  }
}
```

Also, we have a file that holds our styling:

```
// AdditionalComponents/app/styles.js

import { StyleSheet } from 'react-native';
export const styles = StyleSheet.create({
  container: {
```

Chapter 9

```
      flex: 1,
      backgroundColor: '#fafafa'
    },
    text: {
      alignSelf: 'center',
      color: '#365899',
      marginTop: 50
    }
});
export default styles;
```

Making Fetch happen

The first thing we will do is make a request to a third-party API during the `componentDidMount` life cycle. Our intention is to grab a set of JSON data from that API and use it to populate the `Picker` component that we'll be creating in the next section.

The third-party API that I will be using is a nifty one that produces JSON placeholder data--`https://jsonplaceholder.typicode.com`.

To grab data from this third-party API, we'll be using the `fetch` API. `fetch` is a JavaScript API that does not need to be specifically imported into our file. It returns a promise that contains a response. If we want to use promises, we can call `fetch` like this:

```
fetch(endpoint, object)
  .then((response) => {
    return response.json();
  })
  .then((result) => {
    return result;
  })
```

We can also call `fetch` using the `async/await` keywords:

```
async fetchAndReturnData (endpoint, object) {
  const response = await fetch(endpoint, object);
  const data = await response.json();
  return data;
}
```

[347]

The first argument that `fetch` accepts is the API `endpoint`. The second is an optional `object`. By default, `fetch` assumes that you are making a `GET` request. In order to make a `POST`, you will have to pass in this object with the `POST` property as a string to a key titled `method`. This object can also accept any headers you wish to include along with all other parameters to be sent in your request.

For example, an object can look like this:

```
const obj = {
  method: 'POST',
  headers: {
    'Accept': 'application/json',
    'Content-Type': 'application/json',
    'Origin': '',
    'Host': 'api.test.com'
  },
  body: JSON.stringify({
    'client_id': apiKey,
    'client_secret': apiSecret,
    'grant_type': grantType
  })
}
```

In your `App` component, let's create a `componentDidMount` life cycle event to fetch data from our `JSONPlaceholder` API using the following `endpoint`:

```
https://jsonplaceholder.typicode.com/json
```

When data is fetched, go ahead and save it to your component's `state` and log it in the `console` to show that it's been populated. The code you write may end up looking like the following:

```
// AdditionalComponents/app/index.js

...
export default class App extends Component {
  constructor (props) {
    super (props);
    this.state = {
      data: []
    }
  }
  async componentDidMount () {
    const endpoint = 'https://jsonplaceholder.typicode.com/users';
    const response = await fetch(endpoint);
    const data = await response.json();
```

```
    this.setState({
      data
    });
  console.log(this.state.data);
    }
    ...
}
```

This is all you need to do to make a GET request from an endpoint using fetch in your React Native apps! Next up, we will use the Vibration API to send a vibration to the user's device whenever our fetch function successfully resolves.

Vibration

The Vibration API allows us to tap into the vibration motor for our user's mobile devices and send a vibration to it.

This demo will require the use of actual hardware to test, but it is worth the setup if you have one to play with. On devices that don't support vibration, including the simulator, there will be no effect.

There are a couple of caveats to using the Vibration API that you should be aware of.

From a user experience standpoint, the use of vibration in your apps should be as a feedback mechanism to let your users know that some sort of interaction has occurred.

Additionally, extended use of the vibration motor on a user's phone will lead to larger stress on their device's battery performance.

It's very easy to abuse this API and include vibrations on all aspects of your app, but I would heavily recommend that this feature is reserved to acknowledge key interactions that a user may have with your app.

It also has access to two methods:

- The first method is Vibration.vibrate(), which accepts two arguments:
    - The first is either a number or an array of numbers. The number (or numbers) is considered the pattern for which vibrations occur.

- If a number is passed, an Android device will behave by vibrating for that number of milliseconds. On iOS, it will always result in a 1 vibration.
- If an array of numbers is passed to this function, the vibration motor will follow a different pattern. An Android device will wait the number of milliseconds equal to the first index, and then vibrate a number of milliseconds equal to the second index. This pattern where the vibration motor switches between wait and vibrate continues for the length of the array.
- For example, an array of [100, 200, 300, 400] means that the Android device will wait for 100 milliseconds, then vibrate for 200 milliseconds, followed by waiting 300 milliseconds before finally vibrating for 400 milliseconds.
- The vibration motor's behavior on iOS is different. Rather than alternating between waiting and vibrating based on each index, the iOS functionality will always vibrate for a fixed one-second interval and wait between vibrations based on the next number in the array. Additionally, iOS ignores the first index of the array if it is set to zero.
- For example, an array of [0, 100, 200, 300] means that the iOS device will skip that first index and vibrate for 1 second, then wait 100 milliseconds before vibrating for another second. After that, it waits 200 milliseconds and then vibrates for 1 second again. Finally, it waits 300 milliseconds after that vibration and then vibrates one final time for 1 second.
- The second argument that `Vibration.vibrate()` accepts is a Boolean that tells the motor whether to restart the vibration pattern once it completes (indefinitely) or to stop after one iteration.

- The second method is `Vibration.cancel()`, which cancels the vibration that is currently in place. This is important to build in if you're setting the repeat Boolean to `true` in your `vibrate` method.

Additionally, for Android devices, you will need to add the following line to your `AndroidManifest.xml` file:

```
<uses-permission android:name="android.permission.VIBRATE"/>
```

In this section, let's create a callback that is fired when data becomes available for the `Picker` to access and vibrates the device a few times. This is the code that I came up with; yours may be similar:

```
// AdditionalComponents/app/index.js

...
import {
  ...
  Vibration
} from 'react-native';
...
export default class App extends Component {
  ...
  async componentDidMount () {
    const endpoint = 'https://jsonplaceholder.typicode.com/users';
    const response = await fetch(endpoint);
    const data = await response.json();

    this.setState({
      data
    });

    this._onDataAvailable();
    }
  ...
  _onDataAvailable () {
    Vibration.vibrate([1000, 2000, 1000, 2000], false);
  }
}
```

It is simple and straightforward! In the next section, we will look at how to open a link to another installed app on the device.

Linking apps with a button

Deep linking allows us to interact with incoming and outgoing links to and from other apps. By creating a deep link for your app, you can enable other apps to talk to it directly and pass arguments to it, if desired.

You can also access other apps' deep links, opening them with custom arguments. In this chapter, we will learn how to access other apps using their deep links.

We will create a Button component that, on press, finds out whether Facebook is installed on the user's device and if it is, launches the app and tells it to open the Notifications page. If Facebook is not installed, it will open the React Native documentation on the device's default browser.

It's important to note that you can call Linking as part of any callback you wish. It does not have to be tied to the `Button` component at all!

Here are the two methods that we will use with `Linking`:

- `canOpenURL`: This is a function that accepts a URL as an argument. It returns a promise containing a Boolean as its result, stating whether or not the URL you provided can be opened. This URL can either be a deep link to another application or a web-based URL to open a web page.
- `openURL`: This is a method that also accepts a URL as an argument and attempts to open it with an installed app. This method fails if your user's device does not know how to open the URL passed, which is why it's best to use `canOpenURL` to first check for the ability to open it.

On iOS devices, we need to tweak the Xcode project file a bit to allow `Linking` to open custom URL schemes. First, we need to link the React Native `Linking` binary with our project. Open your project in Xcode and then, in the left-hand navigator, expand the `Libraries` folder, then `RCTLinking.xcodeproj` within it, followed by the `Products` folder within that:

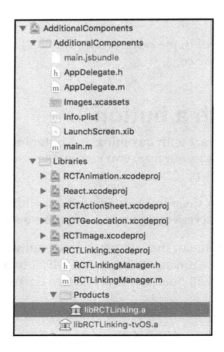

Go back to the root project file for `AdditionalComponents`, into **Build Phases**, and drag the **libRCTLinking.a** file under **Link Binary With Libraries**:

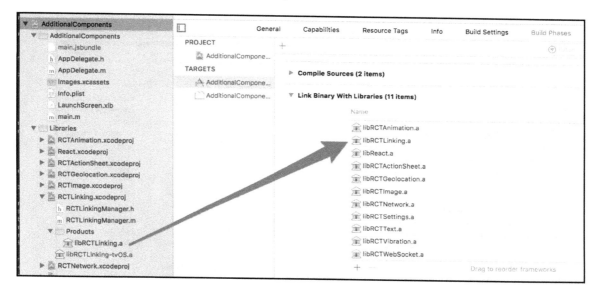

Afterward, head over to the **Build Settings** tab and add an entry to the **Header Search Paths** array pointing to the `Linking` library. For this specific project, the path is `$(SRCROOT)/../node_modules/react-native/Linking`.

You can keep the search non-recursive:

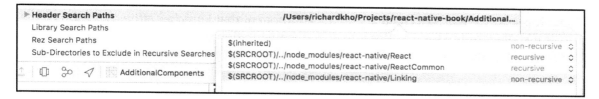

There's one last step to perform. As of iOS 9, we have to register our intent to access Facebook's URL scheme within the app.

Open up the `Info.plist` file in the sidebar and create an array entry called `LSApplicationQueriesSchemes`. Add a string to this array with the value of the URL scheme you wish to access. Facebook's URL scheme is simply `fb`:

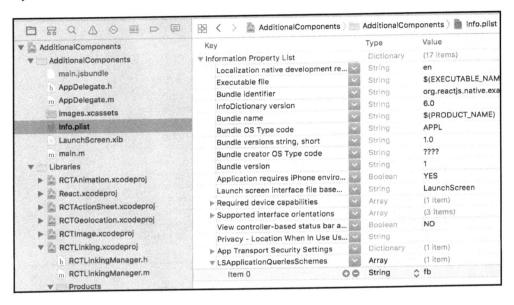

Once you have completed this, your app should be linked to iOS!

On Android, no further action is necessary; you should already have access to other URL schemes by default.

Using this knowledge, let's create a `Button` component that launches either the Facebook app, if installed, or links to the React Native documentation on the user's device, if it isn't. Here's how I wrote it:

```
// AdditionalComponents/app/index.js

...
import {
  Button,
  Linking,
  ...
} from 'react-native';
...
export default class App extends Component {
  ...
  render () {
    return (
```

```
      <View style={ styles.container }>
        ...
        <Button
          color={ '#365899' }
          onPress={ () => this._onButtonPress() }
          title={ 'Open Link' }
        />
      </View>
    )
  }

  async _onButtonPress () {
    const facebookURL = 'fb://notifications';
    const canOpenLink = await Linking.canOpenURL(facebookURL);

    if (canOpenLink) {
      Linking.openURL(facebookURL);
      return;
    }

    Linking.openURL('https://facebook.github.io/react-native');
  }
  ...
}
```

The `Button` component in our `render` method fires the `_onButtonPress` callback when pressed. It checks the `Linking` API to check whether the Facebook app can be opened on the device, and if so, opens it. If not, it will open a link to the React Native documentation website in the device's default browser.

Slider

Sliders are common UI components found on the Web. In this section, you will see how easy it is to create one in your React Native applications.

While `Slider` has access to at least nine different props, we will use just the following:

- `maximumValue`: This is a number that sets the starting maximum value of the `Slider`. It defaults to `1`.
- `minimumValue`: This is a number that sets the starting minimum value of the `Slider`. It defaults to `0`.
- `onSlidingComplete`: This is a callback that is fired when the user finishes interacting with the `Slider`.

- onValueChange: This is a callback that is fired continuously as the user is dragging the Slider.
- step: This is a number that sets the step value of the slider. Each tick of the Slider moves it by this number of steps. It defaults to 0 and ranges between 0 and the difference between the maximum value and minimum value.

Take a moment to create a Slider component. Give it any minimum and maximum values you like, any step count, and create some text that shows the current value of the slider whenever either movement happens or interaction stops. This is how I implemented it:

```
// AdditionalComponents/app/index.js

...
import {
  ...
  Slider,
} from 'react-native';
...
export default class App extends Component {
  ...
  constructor (props) {
    ...
    this.state = {
      ...
      sliderValue: undefined
    }
  }
  ...
  render () {
    return (
      <View style={ styles.container }>
        ...
        <Text style={ styles.sliderSelectionText } >
          Your Slider Value is: { this.state.sliderValue }
        </Text>
        <Slider
          maximumValue={ 100 }
          minimumValue={ 0 }
          onSlidingComplete={ (value) =>
          this._onSliderValueChange(value) }
          onValueChange={ (value) => this._onSliderValueChange(value) }
          step={ 3 }
        />
      </View>
    )
  }
```

This renders a new `Slider` component on the page with a value range from 0 to 100. It changes the value of the `Slider` whenever the user is either in the process of dragging the slider or has completed the dragging action. Each movement of the slider increases the value by 3.

This callback handles setting the `sliderValue` property in state. The code for the `sliderValue` property is as follows:

```
  ...
  _onSliderValueChange (sliderValue) {
    this.setState({
      sliderValue
    });
  }
}

// AdditionalComponents/app/styles.js

...
const styles = StyleSheet.create({
  sliderSelectionText: {
    alignSelf: 'center',
    color: '#365899',
    marginTop: 20
  },
  ...
});
...
```

Using ActionSheetIOS

The `ActionSheetIOS` API lets us display either an action sheet or share sheet for the user to interact with.

The action sheet is an overlay of options that the user can interact with in the app.

The Share sheet allows the user to share almost anything, anywhere, using the built-in sharing system. This could mean sending content in the form of a text message, e-mail, or to a third-party app.

Creating an action sheet

The two methods that ActionSheetIOS makes available are showActionSheetWithOptions and showShareActionSheetWithOptions.

The first method, showActionSheetWithOptions, accepts two arguments: an options object and a callback function.

The options object must contain at least one of the following properties. We use all five in this example:

- options: This is an array of strings that map to the multiple options that appear in the overlay.
- cancelButtonIndex: This is a number that points to the index where the **Cancel** button, if it exists, is located in the options array. This sends the **Cancel** button to the very bottom of the overlay.
- destructiveButtonIndex: This is a number that points to the index where a destructive button, if it exists, is located in the options array. This turns the color of the destructive option's text to red.
- title: This is a string that shows above the action sheet.
- message: This is a string that shows right below the title.

The callback that showActionSheetWithOptions takes in will have one argument passed to it, which is the index of the option that is selected by the user when the action sheet is interacted with. If the user taps outside the action sheet in order to hide it, it has the exact same effect as if the **Cancel** button's index were selected:

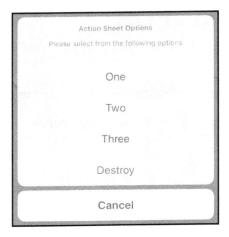

Try creating an action sheet of your own. Have some sort of interaction to toggle it, followed by any sort of interaction you can think of when an index is selected. Make sure to give your action sheet a `title`, `message`, some `options`, a `cancel` index, and a `destructive` index.

This is the code I came up with. Call a function to render the `ActionSheetIOS` and `ShareSheetIOS` components. I added the reference to `ShareSheetIOS` in the function name in anticipation of the next section:

```
// AdditionalComponents/app/index.js

...
import {
  ActionSheetIOS,
  ...
} from 'react-native';
...
export default class App extends Component {
  ...
  render () {
    return (
      <View style={ styles.container }>
        ...
        { this._renderActionAndShareSheets() }
      </View>
    )
  }
}
```

Alert the selected index of the `ActionSheetIOS` component to the user:

```
_onActionSheetOptionSelected (index) {
  alert('The index you selected is: ' + index)
}
```

Open `ActionSheetIOS` and add the following code:

```
...
_openActionSheet () {
  const options = ['One', 'Two', 'Three', 'Cancel', 'Destroy'];
  ActionSheetIOS.showActionSheetWithOptions({
    options: options,
    cancelButtonIndex: 3,
    destructiveButtonIndex: 4,
    title: 'Action Sheet Options',
    message: 'Please select from the following options'
  }, (index) => this._onActionSheetOptionSelected(index))
}
```

Don't render anything if the user is on an Android device, since these components are iOS-exclusive:

```
_renderActionAndShareSheets () {
  if (Platform.OS === 'android') {
    return;
  }
```

Return a `Button` that calls `_openActionSheet` when pressed:

```
  return (
    <View>
      <Button
        color={ '#365899' }
        onPress={ () => this._openActionSheet() }
        title={ 'Open Action Sheet' }
      />
    </View>
  )
  }
}
```

Sharing content with ShareSheetIOS

The share sheet, on the other hand, is a different type of interaction. As I mentioned earlier, the Share sheet lets our app share content with it. To open it, we call `showShareActionSheetWithOptions`. It accepts three arguments: an `options` object, a `failureCallback` function, and a `successCallback` function.

The Share sheet's `options` object is different from the one that the action sheet accepted. It can contain the following properties:

- `url`: This is a stringified URL to share. The `url` property is required if the message property is not available. The url can point to a local file or base-64 encoded `url`; it can share images, videos, PDFs, and other types of files this way.
- `message`: This is a string that contains a message for the user to share. The message property is required if the `url` property is not available.
- `subject`: This is a string that contains a subject for the message.

The `failureCallback` is fired when a Share sheet action fails or is canceled by the user, while the `successCallback` is fired when a Share sheet action is successfully carried through by the user.

Let's modify the index file to do the following:

- Modify `_renderActionAndShareSheets` to return a second button, directly underneath the first, that will open the ShareSheet when tapped on
- Create a function, called `_openShareSheet`, to handle the opening of that Share sheet

This is how my version came about. Call the `showShareActionSheetWithOptions` method of `ActionSheetIOS`, giving it a link to open and a message to share, along with a `subject` and `error/success` callbacks:

```
// AdditionalComponents/app/index.js

...
export default class App extends Component {
  ...
  _openShareSheet () {
    ActionSheetIOS.showShareActionSheetWithOptions({
      url: 'https://facebook.github.io/react-native',
      message: 'Check out the React Native documentation here,
      it's really helpful!',
      subject: 'Link to React Native docs'
    }, (error) => alert(error),
    (success) => {
      alert(success);
    })
  }
```

Take a look at the following code:

```
_renderActionAndShareSheets () {
  ...
  return (
    <View>
      ...
      <Button
        color={ '#365899' }
        onPress={ () => this._openShareSheet() }
        title={ 'Open Share Sheet' }
      />
    </View>
  )
  }
}
```

Grabbing user geolocation data

The `Geolocation` API for React Native is an extension of the `Web Geolocation` API. It's available by calling `navigator.geolocation` and does not need to be imported.

 Location data is a very important part of the mobile experience and as a best practice, this data should not be requested from your users until there is an explicit benefit for the user to provide the said information.

As location data is private until the user consents to share it with you, treat the sharing of this information as a bond of trust between the user and your app.

Always make the assumption that your users will select **No** when asked to share their location, and devise a strategy for how to handle that rejection when it inevitably happens.

On iOS, if you created your project using React Native in it, Geolocation will be enabled by default. If not, you will need to go to your `Info.plist` file and add the `NSLocationWhenInUsageDescription` key to it.

On Android devices, you will need to add the following line to the `AndroidManifest.xml` file:

```
<uses-permission android:name=
"android.permission.ACCESS_FINE_LOCATION" />
```

The `Geolocation` API has access to four different methods. These are the three we will be covering in our example:

- `getCurrentPosition`: This is a function that gets the current location of the device. It accepts up to three arguments:
  - The first, a `success` callback, is mandatory and is called with the current location information.
  - The second, an `error` callback, is optional.
  - The third is an optional options array that can contain the following supported options: `timeout` (in milliseconds), `maximumAge` (in milliseconds), and `enableHighAccuracy` (a Boolean).

- `watchPosition`: This is a function that watches the device's location and returns a watch ID number. It accepts up to three arguments:
  - The first is a mandatory `success` callback that is fired whenever the location changes.
  - The second is an optional callback to handle errors.
  - The third is another optional options object that can contain the `timeout`, `maximumAge`, and `enableHighAccuracy` properties with the same types as the options object of `getCurrentPosition` as well as a `distanceFilter` property that accepts a number in meters.

- `clearWatch`: This is a function that accepts a watch ID number and stops watching that position.

Here is a sample of the current location object that the `Geolocation` API returns:

```
{
  coords: {
    accuracy: 5,
    altitude: 0,
    altitudeAccuracy: -1,
    heading: -1,
    latitude: 37.785834,
    longitude: -122.406417,
    speed: -1
  },
  timestamp: 1483251248689.033
}
```

Using the `Geolocation` API, let's modify the index file so that we can do the following things:

- Grab the user's location during the `componentDidMount` life cycle
- Show their latitude and longitude on the screen
- Additionally, create a button that watches the device's location and updates it whenever it changes on press
- Then, create a button that clears it

Here is the code that I wrote for this section. Make a call to the `getCurrentPosition` method of the `Geolocation` API during the `componentDidMount` life cycle, saving the location to state:

```
// AdditionalComponents/app/index.js

...
export default class App extends Component {
  ...
  async componentDidMount () {
    ...
    navigator.geolocation.getCurrentPosition((location) => {
      this.setState({
        location
      });
    });
  }
```

Render the latitude and longitude of the user in `Text` components:

```
render () {
  return (
    <View style={ styles.container }>
      ...
      <Text style={ styles.latLongText }>
        Your Latitude is: { this.state.location ?
        this.state.location.coords.latitude : 'undefiend' }
      </Text>
      <Text style={ styles.latLongText }>
        Your Longitude is: { this.state.location ?
        this.state.location.coords.longitude : 'undefined' }
      </Text>
```

Render one button to start and another to stop the watch process:

```
<Button
  color={ '#80B546' }
```

```
        onPress={ () => this._onBeginWatchPositionButtonPress () }
        title={ 'Start Watching Position' }
      />
      <Button
        color={ '#80B546' }
        disabled={ this.state.watchID !== undefined ? false : true }
        onPress={ () => this._onCancelWatchPositionButtonPress () }
        title={ 'Cancel Watching Position' }
      />
    </View>
  )
}
```

Set the location of the user when they begin watching their position:

```
  ...
  _onBeginWatchPositionButtonPress () {
    const watchID = navigator.geolocation.watchPosition((watchSuccess)
    => {
      this.setState({
        location: watchSuccess
      });
    });
```

Save the ID of the `watchPosition` call to state:

```
    this.setState({
      watchID
    });
  }
```

Call `clearWatch` when the user presses the **Cancel Watching Position** button and erase the `watchID` in state:

```
  _onCancelWatchPositionButtonPress () {
    navigator.geolocation.clearWatch(this.state.watchID);

    this.setState({
      watchID: undefined
    });
  }
  ...
}
```

Great job! You finished the playground section of this chapter. In the next section, we will switch gears and revisit the `Expenses` app from `Chapter 4`, *Advanced Functionality with the Expenses App*.

Expenses for Android

In *Chapter 4*, *Advanced Functionality with the Expenses App*, we completed building the iOS version of Expenses, our budget tracking application. Due to the page count of the chapter, I thought it would be best to place the Android portion at the end of this chapter instead.

This section picks up immediately from where we left off at the end of *Chapter 4*, *Advanced Functionality with the Expenses App*.

 An example code for the Android version of Expenses can still be found in the code repository for *Chapter 4*, *Advanced Functionality with the Expenses App*.

Android modifications

For Android support, we want to do the following things to our code base:

- Import the `react-native-vector-icons` library via Gradle
- Swap out the `TabBarIOS` component for an Android-based solution using the `DrawerLayoutAndroid` and `ToolbarAndroid` components to create a navigation bar that contains a drawer that slides out to toggle between the current and previous months' expenses
- Replace any `NavigatorIOS` instances with `Navigator`
- Remove `ProgressViewIOS`
- Remove the `ExpandableCell` components in `AddExpensesModal` and replace `DatePickerIOS` with `DatePickerAndroid`
- Add any Android-specific files to components that require them

Installing the vector icon library

You should not need to do anything extra to have the `react-native-vector-icons` library installed for Android since React Native link should have taken care of the entire process for you.

However, if you decided to link the library manually for iOS, the readme file for `react-native-vector-icons` has the latest, up-to-date instructions for importing the library manually for Android devices. As these instructions can change with newer releases to the library, I heavily recommend you follow them directly from the `README` file.

If you already have the package installed in your project's `node_modules` folder, you can read the instructions from there without requiring further Internet access.

The instructions on importing with Gradle are very straightforward. You will also want to follow the instructions for integrating the library for `getImageSource` and `ToolbarAndroid` support.

ToolbarAndroid

On Android, the preferred way to navigate the UI is through its top-placement toolbar. This differs from the iOS experience because rather than having all the available tabs at the bottom of the screen, navigation is hidden inside a drawer that the user taps to expose.

`ToolbarAndroid` is a React Native, Android-specific component that wraps around the Android SDK's native toolbar widget. Like `TabBarIOS`, we have access to a `react-native-vector-icons`-specific version of the component that we render by calling `<Icon.ToolbarAndroid />`. We will be using the following props when using `Icon.ToolbarAndroid` in our app:

- `title`: This is a string that is displayed at the top of the toolbar showing the name of the app
- `titleColor`: This sets the color of the `title` string
- `navIconName`: This is a string that sets the icon of the navigation menu in the toolbar
- `height`: This is a number to set the height of the toolbar
- `backgroundColor`: This sets the background color of the toolbar
- `onIconClicked`: This is a callback that is executed when the navigation icon is tapped on by the user

However, you may have noted that there's no room for the actual `Navigation` drawer that this Navigation icon traditionally opens. That's because we will use `Icon.ToolbarAndroid` in conjunction with `DrawerLayoutAndroid`, the component that handles the actual navigation drawer.

DrawerLayoutAndroid

This component is typically used for navigation. Think of this as the place where the tabs in TabBarIOS will be made available.

The `DrawerLayoutAndroid` component has access to the `openDrawer` and `closeDrawer` methods responsible for its visibility. To use it, pass a ref to the component and use it to call either method.

While this component has many props available to it, we will be using just the following:

- `drawerLockMode`: This is one of the three strings that determine whether the drawer responds to touch gestures, such as sliding the drawer open/closed. This does not disable the toolbar's navigation icon from opening and closing the drawer:
    - `unlocked`: the drawer responds to touch gestures
    - `locked-closed`: the drawer stays closed and does not respond to touch gestures
    - `locked-open`: the drawer stays open and does not respond to touch gestures
- `ref`: This is a reference string to pass to the drawer. This is so that we can reference the drawer within its child components, which will be necessary to open and close it.
- `renderNavigationView`: This is a function responsible for the rendering of your drawer.

Connecting ToolbarAndroid and DrawerLayoutAndroid

The way we connect these two components together is to start by writing an `Icon.ToolbarAndroid` component:

```
<Icon.ToolbarAndroid
  title={ 'Expense' }
  titleColor={ '#7D878D' }
  navIconName={ 'menu' }
  height={ 56 }
  backgroundColor={ '#4E92B5' }
  onIconClicked={ () => this._openDrawer(); }
/>
```

Then, create a `DrawerLayoutAndroid` component and wrap it around two children: the `Icon.ToolbarAndroid` component you just created along with the `Navigator` following it:

```
<DrawerLayoutAndroid
  drawerLockMode={ 'unlocked' }
  ref={ 'drawer' }
  renderNavigationView={ () => this._renderDrawerLayout() }
>
  // Insert Toolbar here
  <Navigator
  initialRoute={{ index: 0 }}
  ref={ 'navigator' }
  renderScene={ (routes, navigator) => this._renderScene(routes, navigator)
}
  />
</DrawerLayoutAndroid>
```

When integrating the three components, we want to ensure that the following is always true:

- `DrawerLayoutAndroid` is always positioned above everything else so that the drawer doesn't get tucked underneath `Icon.ToolbarAndroid`
- When using the options of `DrawerLayoutAndroid` to navigate from one view to another, the same instance of `Icon.ToolbarAndroid` should be present so that we are not rendering a whole new `Icon.ToolbarAndroid` component every single time, nor will it contain an animation of the said toolbar ever *leaving* the screen to be replaced by *another*

What we'll do here is nest `Icon.ToolbarAndroid` and `Navigator` within `DrawerLayoutAndroid`, and set a `ref` for `Navigator` so that we can use that `Navigator` to push new scenes into the app, as needed within our root file.

Once you have implemented both the `Icon.ToolbarAndroid` and
`DrawerLayoutAndroid` components, you will be able to have in-app navigation that looks
like this:

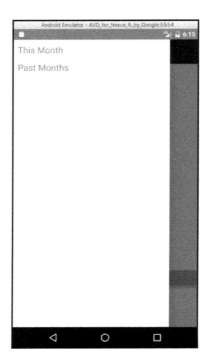

Here is how the big picture looks:

```
// Expenses/index.android.js

import React, { Component } from 'react';
import {
  AppRegistry,
  DrawerLayoutAndroid,
  Navigator,
  StyleSheet,
  View
} from 'react-native';

import App from './app/App';
import CurrentMonthExpenses from './app/components/CurrentMonthExpenses';
import Drawer from './app/components/Drawer';
import EnterBudget from './app/components/EnterBudget';
import PreviousMonthsList from './app/components/PreviousMonthsList';
```

These are the four components that this index file will work with. The App, EnterBudget, and PreviousMonthsList components will be part of our navigation routes. The Drawer component is used to render the navigation view for DrawerLayoutAndroid.

As Android software has a different design language from iOS apps, I imported the MaterialIcons pack instead of FontAwesome since it's built with Google's Material Design guidelines in mind:

```
import Icon from 'react-native-vector-icons/MaterialIcons';
```

A property titled expenses is set to be undefined. This is to pass over to PreviousMonthsList since it expects the list of expenses as a prop.

Visible routes are passed to the Drawer component. I purposefully omit the route that handles entering a budget for the month because it isn't one that the user should be able to manually navigate to.

In the WillMount component life cycle, I call the _updateExpenses method to set the expenses key in state to the expenses object. Check out the code for the explanation given here:

```
class Expense extends Component {
  constructor (props) {
    super (props);
    this.state = {
      expenses: undefined,
      visibleRoutes: [
        { title: 'This Month', index: 0 },
        { title: 'Past Months', index: 2 }
      ]
    }
  }

  componentWillMount () {
    this._updateExpenses();
  }

  render() {
    const routes = [
      { title: 'Expense', index: 0 },
      { title: 'Enter Your Budget', index: 1 },
      { title: 'Previous Month List', index: 2 },
      { title: 'Past Expenses', index: 3}
    ];
    return (
      <View style={ styles.container }>
```

```
        <DrawerLayoutAndroid
          drawerLockMode={ 'unlocked' }
          ref={ 'drawer' }
          renderNavigationView={ () => this._renderDrawerLayout ()
            }
        >
```

Within the `DrawerLayoutAndroid` component, I am nesting both `Icon.ToolbarAndroid` and `Navigator`. Like I mentioned earlier, this is to physically place the drawer on a layer above the rest of the app. Check out the following code:

```
        <Icon.ToolbarAndroid
          titleColor="white"
          navIconName="menu"
          height={ 56 }
          backgroundColor="blue"
          onIconClicked={ () => this._openDrawer () }
        />
        <Navigator
          initialRoute={{ index: 0 }}
          ref={ 'navigator' }
          renderScene={ (routes, navigator) =>
            this._renderScene (routes, navigator) }
        />
      </DrawerLayoutAndroid>
    </View>
  );
}

_openDrawer () {
  this.refs['drawer'].openDrawer ();
}
```

Having given `DrawerLayoutAndroid` a ref of `drawer` earlier, I can use it to open the drawer when the navigation icon is tapped on by the user. I also gave `Navigator` a ref of `navigator` so that I can push to it at the root `index.android.js` level.

The `DrawerLayoutAndroid` component's `render` method returns this `Drawer` component that I import from a custom component I wrote. I pass it a callback under the prop name of `navigateTo`, whose function pushes the index of the `navigator` and closes `DrawerLayoutAndroid`:

```
_navigateTo (index) {
  this.refs['navigator'].push ({
    index: index
  });
  this.refs['drawer'].closeDrawer ();
```

```
}

_renderDrawerLayout () {
  return (
    <Drawer
      navigateTo={ (index) => this._navigateTo(index) }
      routes={ this.state.visibleRoutes }
    />
  )
}
```

The rendering of `PreviousMonthsList` with `_renderScene` is configured to pass in the expenses object and `updateExpenses` function.

```
_renderScene (route, navigator) {
  if (route.index === 0) {
    return (
      <App
        title={ route.title }
        navigator={ navigator }
      />
    )
  }

  if (route.index === 1) {
    return (
      <EnterBudget
        title={ route.title }
        navigator={ navigator }
        { ...route.passProps }
      />
    )
  }

  if (route.index === 2) {
    return (
      <PreviousMonthsList
        title={ route.title }
        navigator={ navigator }
        expenses={ this.state.expenses }
        updateExpenses={ () => this._updateExpenses() }
      />
    )
  }
  if (route.index === 3) {
    return (
```

```
            <CurrentMonthExpenses
              title={ route.title }
              navigator={ navigator }
              { ...route.passProps }
            />
          )
        }
      }
```

The _updateExpenses function passed into PreviousMonthsList as the prop titled updateExpenses is a modified version of the _updateExpenses function found in the App component. We only care about the expenses object in this component, so we will not bother setting any other data:

```
      async _updateExpenses () {

        let response = await storageMethods.getAsyncStorage();

        if (response) {
          this.setState({
            expenses: response
          });
        }
      }
    }

    const styles = StyleSheet.create({
      container: {
        flex: 1
      }
    })

    AppRegistry.registerComponent('Expense', () => Expense);
```

Then, I built the Drawer component:

```
    // Expenses/app/components/Drawer/index.android.js

    import React, { Component, PropTypes } from 'react';

    import {
      ListView,
      Text,
      TouchableHighlight,
      View
    } from 'react-native';

    import DrawerRow from '../DrawerRow';
```

```
import styles from './styles';
```

The DrawerRow component that Drawer imports is responsible for rendering individual
rows of data for the ListView component of Drawer.

```
export default class Drawer extends Component {
  static propTypes = {
    navigateTo: PropTypes.func.isRequired,
    routes: PropTypes.array.isRequired
  }

  constructor (props) {
    super (props);
    this.state = {
      ds: new ListView.DataSource({
        rowHasChanged: (r1, r2) => r1 !== r2
      })
    }
  }

  render () {
    const dataSource = this.state.ds.cloneWithRows(this.props.routes);

    return (
      <View style={ styles.container }>
        <ListView
          automaticallyAdjustContentInsets={ false }
          dataSource={ dataSource }
          enableEmptySections={ true }
          renderRow={ (rowData, sectionID, rowID) =>
          this._renderDrawerRow(rowData, sectionID, rowID) }
          renderSeparator={ (sectionID, rowID) =>
            <View
              key={ rowID }
              style={ styles.separator }
            />
          }
        />
      </View>
    )
  }
```

The `render` method of `Drawer` returns a simple `ListView` that uses the routes array passed to it as a prop to generate each row of data.

```
_renderDrawerRow (rowData, sectionID, rowID) {
    return (
      <View>
        <TouchableHighlight
          style={ styles.row }
          onPress={ () => this.props.navigateTo(rowData.index) }
        >
          <DrawerRow routeName={ rowData.title } />
          </TouchableHighlight>
      </View>
    )
  }
}
```

Then, I created a basic `StyleSheet` for this component:

```
// Expenses/App/components/Drawer/styles.js

import { StyleSheet } from 'react-native';

const styles = StyleSheet.create({
  container: {
    flex: 1
  },
  separator: {
    height: StyleSheet.hairlineWidth,
    marginLeft: 10,
    marginRight: 10,
    backgroundColor: '#E5F2FD'
  }
});

export default styles;
```

After that, I wrote the `DrawerRow` component:

```
// Expenses/app/components/DrawerRow/index.android.js

import React, { Component } from 'react';

import {
  Text,
  View
} from 'react-native';
```

```
import styles from './styles';

export default class DrawerRow extends Component {

  setNativeProps (props) {
    this._root.setNativeProps(props)
  }
```

Since `DrawerRow` is a custom component and the `TouchableHighlight` component that wraps around it from the `_renderDrawerRow` method of the `Drawer` component does not call `setNativeProps` for user-created components automatically, I manually called it:

```
  render () {
    return (
      <View
        style={ styles.container }
        ref={ component => this._root = component }
        { ...this.props }
      >
        <Text style={ styles.rowTitle }>
          { this.props.routeName }
        </Text>
      </View>
    )
  }
}
```

The `DrawerRow` component also has its own `StyleSheet`:

```
// Expenses/app/components/DrawerRow/styles.js

import { StyleSheet } from 'react-native';

const styles = StyleSheet.create({
  container: {
    flex: 1,
    height: 40,
    padding: 10
  },
  rowTitle: {
    fontSize: 20,
    textAlign: 'left'
  }
});

export default styles;
```

Android-specific app component

Next, I created an Android-specific version of App.js, renaming the original App.ios.js. Only two components are imported to App.android.js because any components being navigated to are handled in the root index.android.js file:

```
// Expenses/app/App.android.js

import React, { Component } from 'react';

import {
  Text,
  View
} from 'react-native';

import styles from './styles';

import * as dateMethods from './utils/dateMethods';
import * as storageMethods from './utils/storageMethods';

import AddExpenses from './components/AddExpenses';
import CurrentMonthExpenses from './components/CurrentMonthExpenses';
```

The state of the App component does not need a selectedTab property since we are not using tabbed navigation on Android:

```
export default class App extends Component {
  constructor (props) {
    super();

    this.state = {
      budget: '',
      expenses: {},
    }
  }
}
```

There are no changes to componentWillMount from its iOS counterpart:

```
componentWillMount () {
  ...
}
```

As a result of removing tabbed navigation, the render method of this component has been simplified to just render the CurrentMonthExpenses and AddExpenses components:

```
render () {
  return (
```

```
    <View style={ styles.androidContainer }>
      { this._renderCurrentMonthExpenses() }
    </View>
  )
}
```

Like `componentWillMount`, `_renderCurrentMonthExpenses` has retained the exact same logic from the iOS version of the `App` component:

```
_renderCurrentMonthExpenses () {
  return (
    <View style={ styles.androidContainer }>
      <CurrentMonthExpenses
        ...
      />
      <AddExpenses
        ...
      />
    </View>
  )
}
```

The `_renderEditBudgetComponent` method has been changed to account for how `Navigator` handles its `push` method differently from the `push` method of `NavigatorIOS` as mentioned in the following code:

```
_renderEnterBudgetComponent () {
  this.props.navigator.push({
    index: 1,
    passProps: {
      monthString: dateMethods.getMonthString(this.state.month),
      saveAndUpdateBudget: (budget) => this._saveAndUpdateBudget(budget),
      updateExpenses: () => this._updateExpenses()
    }
  });
}
```

While the iOS App component's `_renderPreviousMonthsList` method has been removed on Android, the logic for `_saveAndUpdateBudget`, `_updateBudget`, and `_updateExpenses` remains the same, as mentioned in the following code:

```
async _saveAndUpdateBudget (budget) {
  ...
}

async _updateBudget () {
  ...
```

```
    }

  async _updateExpenses () {
    ...
  }
}
```

Finally, I added a simple `flex` container style for the `App` component:

```
// Expenses/app/styles.js

...
const styles = StyleSheet.create({
  androidContainer: {
    flex: 1
  },
  ...
});

export default styles;
```

EnterBudget styling changes

Since Android text fields normally do not contain a border, I used some conditional logic with the `Platform` API to remove it:

```
// Expenses/app/components/EnterBudget/index.js

...
import {
  Platform,
  ...
} from 'react-native';
...
export default class EnterBudget extends Component {
  ...
  render () {
    ...
    return (
      <View style={ styles.enterBudgetContainer }>
        ...
        <TextInput
          style={ Platform.OS === 'ios' ? styles.textInput :
          styles.androidTextInput }
          ...
        />
```

```
      ...
      </View>
    )
  }
  ...
}
```

The styling for the `TextInput` component in the `render` method of `EnterBudget` now checks to see whether the user's operating system is iOS or Android. If it is iOS, it keeps the original `textInput` style from before; if it is Android, it sets it to a new `androidTextInput` style.

```
// Expenses/app/components/EnterBudget/styles.js

...
const styles = StyleSheet.create({
  androidTextInput: {
    color: '#3D4A53',
    margin: 10,
    padding: 10,
    textAlign: 'center'
  },
  ...
});

export default styles;
```

Next up, we will make some changes to `CurrentMonthExpenses`.

CurrentMonthExpenses for Android

In the `CurrentMonthExpenses` component, I am rendering a `ProgressViewIOS` component that visually tracks the amount spent by the user using a colored, horizontal bar.

The React Native SDK for Android has a similar component, `ProgressBarAndroid`, and we will swap out `ProgressViewIOS` for it.

Additionally, we want to add a back button event listener for this component that is only fired when the user navigates to `CurrentMonthExpenses` by way of `PreviousMonthsList` with `BackAndroid`.

The `ProgressBarAndroid` component is similar to `ProgressViewIOS`. I'm using the following props in mine:

- `color`: This determines the color of `ProgressBarAndroid`.
- `indeterminate`: This is a Boolean that, when set to true, keeps the progress bar animated indefinitely.
- `progress`: Just like `ProgressViewIOS`, this determines how far along the progress bar should move.
- `styleAttr`: This is a string to tell how `ProgressBarAndroid` should be rendered. For mine, I used `horizontal`.

The `render` method for `CurrentMonthExpenses` now calls a `_renderProgressIndicator` method to determine which progress indicator to render: `ProgressViewIOS` is to be rendered for iOS devices, and `ProgressBarAndroid` for Android ones.

The `ListView` is now wrapped around a `View` to give it some separation from the progress indicator:

```
// Expenses/app/components/CurrentMonthExpenses/index.js

...
import {
  ...
  BackAndroid,
  Platform,
  ...
} from 'react-native';
...
export default class CurrentMonthExpenses extends Component {
  ...
  componentWillMount () {
    BackAndroid.addEventListener('hardwareButtonPress', () =>
    this._backButtonPress());
  }

  componentWillUnmount () {
    BackAndroid.removeEventListener('hardwareButtonPress', () =>
    this._backButtonPress())
  }

  render () {
    ...
    return (
      <View style={ ... }>
```

```
      <View style={ styles.currentMonthExpensesHeader }>
        ...
        { this._renderProgressIndicator() }
      </View>
      <View style={ styles.listViewContainer }>
        <ListView
        ...
        />
      </View>
    </View>
  )
}
```

I am only calling pop on the navigator if it is a previous month's data the user is looking at. Otherwise, they will run into an error when attempting to call pop without any other routes visited:

```
_backButtonPress () {
  if (this.props.isPreviousMonth) {
    this.props.navigator.pop();
    return true;
  }
}
```

There have been no changes to the iOS progress indicator logic:

```
...
_renderProgressIndicator () {
  if (Platform.OS === 'ios') {
    return (
      <ProgressViewIOS
        progress={ this._getProgressViewAmount() }
        progressTintColor={ '#A3E75A' }
        style={ styles.progressView }
      />
    )
  }
```

The Android progress indicator is returned at the end of the function. I am reusing the _getProgressViewAmount method here:

```
  return (
    <View style={ styles.progressView }>
      <ProgressBarAndroid
        color={ '#A3E75A' }
        indeterminate={ false }
        progress={ this._getProgressViewAmount() }
        styleAttr={ 'Horizontal' }
```

```
        />
      </View>
    )
  }
  ...
};
```

No other code for this component was changed, and its Android-specific version was not necessary because of the minimal changes.

The styling for `CurrentMonthExpenses` has been changed to add the `listViewContainer` property:

```
// Expenses/app/components/CurrentMonthExpenses/styles.js

...
const styles = StyleSheet.create({
  ...
  listViewContainer: {
    flex: 1,
    marginTop: 20
  },
  ...
});

export default styles;
```

Removing ExpandableCell from AddExpensesModal

As the `DatePickerAndroid` and `Picker` components render as a modal on an Android device, I made some modifications to the `AddExpensesModal` component to remove the instances of `ExpandableCell`.

This resulted in a new Android-specific file because of the large number of changes. I removed the `categoryPickerExpanded` and `datePickerExpanded` properties in state, as well as the importing of `DatePickerIOS` and `ExpandableCell`:

```
// .../app/components/AddExpensesModal/index.android.js

...
import {
  DatePickerAndroid,
  ...
```

```
} from 'react-native';
...
export default class AddExpensesModal extends Component {
  ...
  constructor (props) {
    super (props);

    this.state = {
      amount: '',
      category: undefined,
      date: new Date(),
      description: '',
    }
  }
```

These two constants previously started with the prefix of expandableCell, but that prefix has been removed since the ExpandableCell component is not being used in the Android version of this component:

```
render () {
  const datePickerButtonTitle = ...
  const categoryPickerButtonTitle = ...
```

The onRequestClose callback is a required prop for Modal components on Android. The callback is executed when the user presses the back button on an Android device while the modal is open. In this case, I perform the same action as if the user pressed the **Cancel** button:

```
return (
  <Modal
    ...
    onRequestClose={ () => this._clearFieldsAndCloseModal() }
  >
```

Android-specific styles for the two TextInput components were made to accommodate stylistic differences between Android and iOS applications:

```
<ScrollView style={ styles.modalContainer }>
  <View style={ styles.amountRow }>
    ...
    <TextInput
      ...
      style={ styles.androidAmountInput }
    />
  </View>
  <Text style={ styles.descriptionText }>
    ...
```

```
    </Text>
```

The `View` that was previously styled to `expandableCellContainer` have been changed to `androidPickerContainers`. The preceding `Button` component calls `_renderDatePicker` when pressed, which handles the rendering of `DatePickerAndroid`:

```
<TextInput
  ...
  style={ styles.androidDescriptionInput }
/>
<View style={ styles.androidPickerContainers }>
  <Button
    color={ '#86B2CA' }
    onPress={ () => this._renderDatePicker() }
    title={ datePickerButtonTitle }
  />
</View>
```

Since the regular `Picker` component is not opened with an asynchronous function like `DatePickerAndroid`, I kept its logic intact:

```
<View style={ styles.androidPickerContainers }>
  <View style={ styles.categoryIcon }>
    { this.state.category &&
    iconMethods.getIconComponent(this.state.category) }
  </View>
    <Picker
      ...
      prompt={ categoryPickerButtonTitle }
    >
    { this._renderCategoryPicker() }
  </Picker>
</View>
  ...
</ScrollView>
    </Modal>
  )
}
```

The `_clearFieldsAndCloseModal` method was modified to remove the setting of the now-removed `ExpandableCell`-specific properties in state:

```
...
_clearFieldsAndCloseModal () {
    this.setState({
      amount: '',
      category: undefined,
```

```
      date: new Date(),
      description: ''
    });

    this.props.toggleModal()
  }
  ...
```

Finally, _renderDatePicker was created to handle the asynchronous nature of the
DatePickerAndroid component.

In the Android version of the AddExpensesModal component, none of the iOS version's
methods were removed:

```
async _renderDatePicker () {
  const options = {
    date: this.state.date
  };

  const { action, year, month, day } = await
  DatePickerAndroid.open(options);

  if (action === DatePickerAndroid.dismissedAction) {
    return;
  }

  this.setState({
    day,
    month,
    year
  });

  this._onDateChange();
}
...
}
```

Modifying Navigation for PreviousMonthsList

The next thing to do is modify the push method of navigator for Android:

```
// Expenses/app/components/PreviousMonthsList/index.js

...
import {
  Platform,
```

```
  . . .
} from 'react-native';
  . . .
export default class PreviousMonthsList extends Component {
  . . .
  render () {
    <View style={ Platform.OS === 'ios' ? styles.previousMonthsListContainer
: {}       }>
  . . .
    </View>
  }
  . . .
```

I made a styling adjustment for the View container that wraps around the rest of PreviousMonthsList for Android devices to keep the ListView just below the navigation bar on Android.

There have been no changes to the original rendering method if on iOS:

```
_renderSelectedMonth (rowData, sectionID, rowID) {
  if (Platform.OS === 'ios') {
    . . .
  }
```

The Android method pushes to an index instead of a component, and the props passed to it are the exact same ones:

```
  if (Platform.OS === 'android') {
    this.props.navigator.push({
      index: 3,
      passProps: {
        . . .
      }
    });
  }
  }
}
```

After this section, we have successfully converted Expenses into an Android app that looks, feels, and behaves just like one!

Summary

Congratulations! You've finished the final chapter of *React Native by Example*. In this chapter, you learned to use more of the React Native library by working on components and APIs that we did not fit into previous apps in the book.

Specifically, you built a playground app where you learned how to use the `fetch` API to make requests to external resources for data and gained control of the `Vibration` API to control the vibration motor of a user's device.

Afterward, you used the `Linking` API to open third-party applications on both iOS and Android, which allowed your app to talk to others. Then, you built a `Slider` component that lets users select a value between two predetermined ones.

Finishing the playground app, you created `Buttons` to open an `ActionSheetIOS` overlay that presents options for your users to interact with and allowed your users to share content from your app using the Share sheet. As a finishing touch, you made use of the `Geolocation` API to grab your user's location data.

In the last section, we converted the app to Android. We started by ensuring that the vector icon library was imported via Gradle, swapped out the iOS-specific tabbed navigation for Android's drawer and toolbar combination, replaced `NavigatorIOS`-specific logic with `Navigator`, replaced the progress indicator with an Android-specific one, and then tweaked the rest of our components to have the look and feel of an Android app.

Index

X

Xcode

www.ingramcontent.com/pod-product-compliance
Lightning Source LLC
Chambersburg PA
CBHW060922060326
40690CB00041B/2918